Interventions

Series editors: Anna Barton, Andrew Smith

Editorial board: David Amigoni, Isobel Armstrong, Philip Holden, Jerome McGann, Joanne Wilkes, Julia M. Wright

Interventions: Rethinking the Nineteenth Century seeks to make a significant intervention into the critical narratives that dominate conventional and established understandings of nineteenth-century literature. Informed by the latest developments in criticism and theory, the series provides a focus for how texts from the long nineteenth century, and more recent adaptations of them, revitalise our knowledge of and engagement with the period. It explores the radical possibilities offered by new methods, unexplored contexts and neglected authors and texts to re-map the literary-cultural landscape of the period and rigorously re-imagine its geographical and historical parameters. The series includes monographs, edited collections, and scholarly sourcebooks.

Already published

Charlotte Brontë: Legacies and afterlives	Amber K. Regis and Deborah Wynne (eds)
The Great Exhibition, 1851: A sourcebook	Jonathon Shears (ed.)

Interventions
Rethinking the nineteenth century

Edited by Andrew Smith
and Anna Barton

Manchester University Press

Copyright © Manchester University Press 2017

While copyright in the volume as a whole is vested in Manchester University Press, copyright in individual chapters belongs to their respective authors, and no chapter may be reproduced wholly or in part without the express permission in writing of both author and publisher.

Published by Manchester University Press
Altrincham Street, Manchester M1 7JA, UK
www.manchesteruniversitypress.co.uk

British Library Cataloguing-in-Publication Data is available

ISBN 978 1 7849 9510 2 *hardback*
ISBN 978 1 5261 0870 8 *paperback*

First published by Manchester University Press in hardback 2017

This edition first published 2019

The publisher has no responsibility for the persistence or accuracy of URLs for any external or third-party internet websites referred to in this book, and does not guarantee that any content on such websites is, or will remain, accurate or appropriate.

For William Hughes, AS.
For Gladys Giltrap, AB.

Contents

Notes on contributors ix
Acknowledgements xii

Introduction 1
Andrew Smith and Anna Barton

Part I: Critical reflections 13

1 On measuring the nineteenth century 15
  John Schad

2 Literature and science 33
  David Amigoni

3 Locke in pentameters: Victorian poetry after (or before) posthumousness 53
  Anna Barton

4 Reading the Gothic and Gothic readers 72
  Andrew Smith

Part II: Rethinking national contexts and exchanges 89

5 The global circulation of Victorian actants and ideas: liberalism and liberalisation in the niche of nature, culture, and technology 91
  Regenia Gagnier

6 Literary folk: writing popular culture in colonial Punjab, 1885–1905 111
  Churnjeet Mahn

Contents

7 'Across the waters of this disputed ocean': the material production of American literature in nineteenth-century Britain 129
Katie McGettigan

8 Gruesome models: European displays of natural history and anatomy and nineteenth-century literature 149
Laurence Talairach-Vielmas

Part III: Afterlives **167**

9 Adaptive/appropriative reuse in neo-Victorian fiction: having one's cake and eating it too 169
Marie-Luise Kohlke

10 Populism and ideology: nineteenth-century fiction and the cinema 188
Richard J. Hand

11 True histories of the Elephant Man: storytelling and theatricality in adaptations of the life of Joseph Merrick 207
Benjamin Poore

Index 225

Contributors

David Amigoni is Professor of Victorian Literature at Keele University where he is also Pro Vice-Chancellor for Research and Enterprise. He is the author of numerous publications on Victorian literature and science, including *Colonies, Cults and Evolution: Literature, Science and Culture in Nineteenth-Century Writing* (2007). He is presently writing a book about ideas of biological and cultural inheritance in the scientific and literary writings of the Darwin, Huxley and Bateson families, across three generations. He is part of a team planning a digital edition of a complete edition of the notebooks of Samuel Butler. He has edited the *Journal of Victorian Culture* and, more recently, *Literature Compass*.

Anna Barton is Senior Lecturer in Victorian Literature at the University of Sheffield where she also co-directs the Centre for Nineteenth-Century Studies. Her work on nineteenth-century poetry includes *Tennyson's Name: Identity and Responsibility in the Poetry of Alfred, Lord Tennyson* (2008) and *In Memoriam: A Reading Guide* (2012) as well as articles and chapters on Blake, Clough, Edward Lear, Swinburne and Barrett Browning. Her most recent monograph, *Nineteenth-Century Poetry and Liberal Thought: Forms of Freedom* is forthcoming with Palgrave. With Andrew Smith she edits this series 'Interventions: Rethinking the Nineteenth Century' for Manchester University Press. She also co-edits the Victorian Literature section of *Literature Compass*.

Regenia Gagnier is Professor of English at the University of Exeter, Editor of *Literature Compass*'s Global Circulation Project, and Senior Research Fellow in Egenis, the Centre for the Study of Life Sciences. Her single-authored books include *Idylls of the Marketplace: Oscar Wilde and the Victorian Public* (1986); *Subjectivities: A History of Self-Representation in Britain* (1991); *The Insatiability of Human Wants: Economics and*

Notes on contributors

Aesthetics in Market Society (2000); and *Individualism, Decadence and Globalization: on the Relationship of Part to Whole 1859–1920* (2010). From 2009 to 2012 she was President of the British Association for Victorian Studies. Her current research is on the global literatures of liberalisation.

Richard J. Hand is Professor and Head of Media, Film and Television at the University of East Anglia. He is the founding co-editor of the international peer-reviewed *Journal of Adaptation in Film and Performance* and his interests include adaptation, translation and interdisciplinarity in performance media (with a particular interest in historical forms of popular culture especially horror) using critical and practical research methodologies. He is the author of books on Grand-Guignol theatre, radio drama, Joseph Conrad and Graham Greene.

Marie-Luise Kohlke lectures in English Literature at Swansea University, with main research foci in neo-Victorianism, trauma narrative and theory, and gender and sexuality. She is the Founding Editor of the e-journal *Neo-Victorian Studies* (http://neovictorianstudies.com) and Series co-editor (with Christian Gutleben) of Brill/Rodopi Neo-Victorian Series, including *Neo-Victorian Trauma* (2010), *Neo-Victorian Families* (2011), *Neo-Victorian Gothic* (2012), and *Neo-Victorian Cities* (2015). She has also published journal articles and chapter contributions on the novels of Margaret Atwood, Liana Badr, Pat Barker, Barbara Chase-Riboud, Michael Ondaatje, and Sarah Waters, among others.

Churnjeet Mahn is a Senior Lecturer in English Literature at the University of Strathclyde. Her primary area of interest is the relationship between travel writing and discourses of nationality and sexuality. Her first monograph, *British Women's Travel to Greece, 1840–1914: Travels in the Palimpsest* (2012), analysed the representation of Greece as semi-Oriental space in British Victorian women's travel writing. Since then she has worked as an Arts and Humanities Research Council (AHRC) UnBox Fellow and led an AHRC research project on remembering and memorialising Eastern Punjab's Islamic heritage.

Katie McGettigan is a Lecturer in American Literature at Royal Holloway, University of London. Her current research explores how the publication and circulation of antebellum American Literature in Britain shaped the development of a national American literary tradition. Her first book, *Herman Melville: Modernity and the Material Text* is forthcoming from the University Press of New England, and her research is funded by a Leverhulme Trust Early Career Fellowship.

Notes on contributors

Benjamin Poore is Lecturer in Theatre in the Department of Theatre, Film and Television at the University of York. His books include *Heritage, Nostalgia and Modern British Theatre: Staging the Victorians* (2011) and *Theatre & Empire* (2016). He has published widely on stage and screen adaptations of Victorian fiction. His other interests include George Bernard Shaw, and historical drama. Benjamin has just completed work on an edited collection, *Neo-Victorian Villains*, and on a monograph on recent stage adaptations of Sherlock Holmes, both to be published in 2017.

John Schad is Professor of Modern Literature at the University of Lancaster. His monographs include *Victorians in Theory* (1999), *Queer Fish: Darwin to Derrida* (2004), *Someone Called Derrida* (2007) and *The Late Walter Benjamin* (2012). He has also had two retrospectives published: *Hostage of the Word, 1993–2013* (2013) and *John Schad in Conversation* (2015); he has read his work on BBC Radio 3, and written for the stage with productions at The Oxford Playhouse, Watford Palace Theatre and the Sheldonian Theatre Oxford.

Andrew Smith is Professor of Nineteenth-Century English Literature at the University of Sheffield where he co-directs the Centre for the History of the Gothic. His 20 published books include *Gothic Death 1740–1914: A Literary History* (2016), *The Ghost Story 1840–1920: A Cultural History* (2010), *Gothic Literature* (2007, revised 2013), *Victorian Demons: Medicine, Masculinity and the Gothic at the fin de siècle* (2004) and *Gothic Radicalism: Literature, Philosophy and Psychoanalysis in the Nineteenth Century* (2000). He is a past President of the International Gothic Association.

Laurence Talairach-Vielmas is Professor of English at the University of Toulouse Jean Jaurès, and Associate Researcher at the Alexandre Koyré Centre for the History of Science and Technology. Her research specialises on the interrelations between Victorian literature, medicine and science. She is the author of *Fairy Tales, Natural History and Victorian Culture* (2014), *Wilkie Collins, Medicine and the Gothic* (2009) and *Moulding the Female Body in Victorian Fairy Tales and Sensation Novels* (2007). She has also edited several collections of articles on the popularisation of science, as well as two novels by Mary Elizabeth Braddon: *Thou Art the Man* [1894] (Valancourt Books, 2008) and *Dead Love Has Chains* [1907] (Valancourt Books, 2014).

Acknowledgements

This book takes its place as the inaugural publication in the series 'Rethinking the Nineteenth Century'. We would like to thank Matthew Frost at Manchester University Press for his support of our editorship of the series and his enthusiasm for this and other volumes that currently constitute the series.

Andrew Smith contributed to this book during a period of research leave from the University of Sheffield in the Spring term of 2015 and acknowledges the support provided by colleagues on the School of English's Research Strategy Committee. He would also like to thank Mark Faulkner, Anna Barton, and Valerie Hobbs who took over his administrative duties at this time. Anna Barton undertook research towards her chapter at the Browning Library, Baylor University, Texas and acknowledges the support provided by the library's fellowship programme. She would like to thank Rita Patterson and her colleagues at the library for the hospitality, knowledge and support they provided during her time at Baylor. She would also like to thank Madeleine Callaghan who read an early draft of the chapter and provided invaluable feedback.

Andrew Smith would like to thank his wife, Joanne Benson, for her love and tolerance throughout the editing of this book and other projects completed during the period of research leave. Anna Barton would like to thank Iain Vaughan for his care and encouragement.

Introduction

Andrew Smith and Anna Barton

> Those that of late have fleeted far and fast
> To touch all shores, now leaving to the skill
> Of others their old craft seaworthy still,
> Have charter'd this;
>
> Alfred Tennyson, Prefatory Sonnet to *The Nineteenth Century* (1877)

> The history of the Victorian Age will never be written: we know too much about it
>
> Lytton Strachey, Preface to *Eminent Victorians* (1918)

This book addresses a number of concerns that have emerged in recent scholarship on the nineteenth century. By exploring these concerns it aims to contribute to, and move beyond, existing dialogues that consider how the nineteenth century can be thought about and critically rethought through literature and other kinds of textual production. This kind of critical rethinking is nothing new. Intellectual and literary reflection about the nineteenth century famously began twenty-three years before it drew to a close when, in March 1877, James Knowles published the first number of his new monthly periodical, *The Nineteenth Century*. Knowles's letters record that the bold title of the periodical, the subject of some deliberation before its publication and some derision after, was first suggested by Knowles's friend, Alfred Tennyson, who also supplied a prefatory sonnet for the opening number. The sonnet, which pictures the journal's contributors as sailors 'putting forth' in their new craft 'to rove the world about', revisits Tennyson's much earlier poem, 'Ulysses'; but, whereas the shared 'will' to 'seek' is called into question in the earlier poem by the ironic rhetoric of the dramatic monologue, in this sonnet Tennyson speaks directly and sincerely, apparently forgetful of the hubris that he once associated with this kind of heroic quest. The intellectual adventurers may set sail for 'seas of death and sunless gulfs of Doubt', but no such doubt is expressed concerning the voyage itself, which is described in good faith. The sonnet strikes the keynote for the journal; its contents pages list titles that address topics metaphysical, political, religious, scientific and literary, reflecting its ambition to capture the spirit of the age within its pages.

Knowles's liberal confidence did not long survive the century itself and by 1918 Lytton Strachey was asserting that it was exactly the kind of compendious knowledge that was the project of *The Nineteenth Century* which meant that the history of what he chose to call 'the Victorian Age' would never be written. Close to a century on, Strachey's high modernist scepticism concerning both knowledge and writing remains more recognisable than the intellectual optimism of Knowles and Tennyson. Arguably, we know even more than Strachey did. It is certainly the case that developments in information technologies in recent decades means that our access to that knowledge and the nature of our encounters with it have changed significantly. We also have to contend with our knowledge about Strachey's own century, the century that now separates us from the Victorians. To know the nineteenth century it becomes necessary first to know the twentieth century as the century that gave the Victorians to us, coloured and shaped by its own modern and post-modern preoccupations. While this collection does not claim to provide answers to questions about how and whether it is possible to know and to write about the nineteenth century at the beginning of the twenty-first century, it aims to reflect and continue debates about the nineteenth century and its literatures that are, in part, the product of this particular historical moment, debates that have been taking place within various nineteenth-century academic associations, discussion groups, journals, and book series in recent years. It draws out some of these innovative strands of enquiry, explores how the critical map of the nineteenth century is being redrawn, and suggests ways in which the critical field can be advanced. Before reflecting on the ambitions of this volume it is therefore helpful to take stock of the various academic associations and the publishing outlets that have shaped and supported the direction of research into the period.

A key area, which defines the area of nineteenth-century studies, relates to its international range and one measure by which we might gauge the global reach of period-defined scholarship is through the growth of national associations dedicated to its academic support. On that measure, the nineteenth century fares well. The two largest of these are The British Association for Victorian Studies (BAVS, established in

Introduction

2000) and the North American Victorian Studies Association (NAVSA, established in 2002). NAVSA postdates a number of regional Victorian studies associations in America such as the Northeast Victorian Studies Association (founded in 1975) and the Midwest Victorian Studies Association (founded in 1977). Other organisations such as the Victorian Interdisciplinary Studies Association of the Western United States (VISAWUS, founded in 1995) have pursued a more narrow definition of the period with their constitution stating that 'The purpose of the organization shall be to promote in an interdisciplinary way the study of the Victorian period as defined by Britain and its empire between 1837 and 1901'.[1] Other organisations include the interdisciplinary Victorian Studies Association of Ontario (VSAO, founded in 1967) and the Victorian Studies Association of Western Canada (VSWAC, founded in 1972). The Australasian Victorian Studies Association, founded in 1972, has provided a forum for scholars working in Australia, New Zealand, Hong Kong, Japan and Singapore. The presence of these longstanding regional associations, and comparatively more recent national associations, indicates just how much worldwide interest there is in the period. The fact that a number of shared conference themes have been developed across these national associations indicates just how critically reflexive the field has become as it responds to contemporary issues and seeks to demonstrate how relevant the Victorians are to our own social, economic, and environmental concerns.

The growth and diversity in Victorian studies is also indicated by the academic journals dedicated to research on the period. *Victorian Studies* was first published in 1956 and has been, beyond its historical remit, a pioneering journal of interdisciplinary research into the humanities. The four issues published each year do not just carry articles, but also provide important review forums as well as copious book reviews.[2] The journal is linked to NAVSA and one issue a year is devoted to the annual conference, which ensures that the conference theme is fed into the wider research culture. *The Journal of Victorian Culture* has been published since 1996 and also produces four copies a year under the Taylor & Francis imprint. The aims of the journal are to publish research centred on 'the long nineteenth century, its legacies, and echoes in the present day, the journal encourages articles which interrogate periodisation, historiography and critical traditions' and it is explicitly inter- and multi-disciplinary. An important feature of the journal is the round-table discussions that bring together a number of key critical voices to debate the pressing topics of the time. The journal also carries lengthy book reviews (up to 2,000 words). *The Victorian Review: An Interdisciplinary Journal of Victorian Studies* has been published since 1972 and is international in its range of scholarship and also features a regular forum for debate. *The Victorian Institute Journal* has been published since 1972 and is closely affiliated to the Victorian Institute that brings together scholars working in the mid-Atlantic region of the USA. Other Victorian associations such as Interdisciplinary Nineteenth-Century Studies and The Australasian Victorian Studies Association also publish journals. The Wiley supported online venture, *Literature Compass* also includes an innovative Victorian section (from 2004), which because of the flexible nature of online delivery easily permits occasional features such as 'cluster' discussion groups.[3] This is, of course, to mention but just a few publications but again it is to acknowledge that as Victorian scholars we have been notably well served by the activities of academic associations and their often related journal publications.

The support of research into the period has also been augmented by resources that have supported the teaching of the Victorians. The first of these is The Victorian Web, established by Brown University in 1988 to support access to contextual materials for students studying modules on the Victorians.[4] The web provides a rich overview of a number of contexts which serve as a useful guide to students as well as incorporating links to other important sources. More recently, the Networked Infrastructure for Nineteenth-Century Scholarship (NINES) has been developed as a peer-reviewed platform to support the digitisation of nineteenth-century archival materials and scholarship.[5]

Research into the nineteenth century has also been supported by a number of book series including those published by university presses such as Cambridge, Chicago, Virginia, Ohio State and the State University of New York. Other notable series include those published by Palgrave Macmillan and Ashgate. This current volume takes its place within a new series, also titled 'Interventions: Rethinking the Nineteenth Century', published by Manchester University Press. This series (also edited by us) aims to provide a space in which scholars can reflect on the nature, scope, and direction of nineteenth-century studies. Whilst wishing to support ongoing research into the period it also aims to foster unorthodox approaches to the nineteenth century which challenge and problematise conventional models of the Victorians and to that end it engages with a notion of the long nineteenth century which extends from 1780–1914, and supports research which is interdisciplinary and multidisciplinary, and international in its focus. In other words it is a series

Introduction

that reflects the concerns about temporality, globalisation and forms of political history, which have become a feature of both recent significant conferences and journal publications. This book also takes its place within this remit and aims to outline a number of areas of critical enquiry that provide spaces in which we can start to rethink how we approach the nineteenth century.

A question raised by the names of these various associations, publications and resources is one of nomenclature: how, and should we, differentiate between the Victorian period and a more broadly, although perhaps more vaguely, defined version of the long nineteenth century? The 2015 BAVS conference, held at Leeds Trinity University on the theme of 'Victorian Age(s)' explicitly addressed these issues of periodicity by emphasising the importance of examining how the Victorians could be related to the Romantics, the Edwardians, and Modernists. This attempt to discuss and conceptualise what we mean by the long nineteenth century illustrates just how difficult it can be to contain the Victorians within any simplified model based on the reign of a monarch. Likewise, the 2016 conference, at Cardiff, included a series of panels devoted to the topic of 'Victorian afterlives', a phrase that reminds us of the period's tendency to outstrip itself, encroaching into the early twentieth and, by way of neo-Victorian literature and culture, the twenty-first centuries. At the same time, individual paper titles such as 'The past as news: Seeing and hearing Vesuvius in London 1820–1845' and 'Performing tourism in 1850s London: Albert Smith's *Ascent of Mont Blanc*' reflect a countervailing critical inclination to do away with the idea of a monolithic Victorian-ness and to better understand it decade by decade. Reflecting these different trends and the fact that both 'nineteenth century' and 'Victorian' are still current within and vital to debates about the definition of the period, the essays within this volume employ both terms. The title of this volume, and the series of which it is a part, follows Knowles and Tennyson rather than Strachey in order to create a broad and diverse field of enquiry both in terms of history and of geography.

The disciplinary, or pre-disciplinary, range of Knowles's journal illustrates a second and perhaps more methodologically significant challenge for scholars of the nineteenth century working within and between the disciplinary boundaries that were just emerging by the century's end. *The Nineteenth Century* was one of the first journals to recognise literary criticism, and especially writing on the novel, as a topic of discussion that could sit alongside political and scientific debate. The programmes for recent BAVS and NAVSA conferences attest to the multi- and

Interventions: rethinking the nineteenth century

inter-disciplinary vibrancy of the field and to the fact that the disciplinary scope of nineteenth-century studies continues to expand. The history of art and science, the study of anthropology and folklore, as well as music and archaeology are now well-established areas of interest. This collection and the series differ slightly from the work of nineteenth-century studies associations in that, largely as a result of the disciplinary specialism of its editors, it takes literary scholarship and criticism as its starting point. Nevertheless, 'literary' is understood in the broadest terms to include all kinds and aspects of textual production and dissemination, from the close formal analysis of individual works to the cultural and material economics of book production and circulation to the visual and performed texts of theatre and cinema. Although we share Strachey's scepticism regarding the possibility of writing the history of the Victorian period, that scepticism is, perhaps, tempered by a Tennysonian doubtful faith in the ability of the writing of the nineteenth century, be that literary, scientific, anthropological, historical or political, to reveal something of its history.

The book is structured into three sections. The first section on 'Critical reflections' explores a number of ways in which an engagement with recent scholastic developments in English can be applied to the nineteenth century. A critical reflection suggests the importance of creating a space where we can look at the period in a new, self-reflexive, way. Each of the four chapters in the section adopts a particular stance towards how we can read the nineteenth century and advance critical claims that enable us to rethink issues such as temporality, science, the Gothic, and the relationship between poetics and philosophy.

John Schad in 'On measuring the nineteenth century' offers a theoretical consideration of the concept of the nineteenth century, paying particular attention to how it might be measured (if it is not to be defined in simple calendrical terms). The essay takes as its primary text Walter Benjamin's famous work *The Arcades Project* (1927–40), with its myriad insights into the nineteenth century, not least its claim that Paris is 'the capital of the nineteenth century'. Particularly important both to Benjamin and to the essay are the voices of such major nineteenth-century thinkers as Baudelaire, Proudhon, Bakunin, Michelet, Marx and Nietzsche. Schad sets these continental figures alongside various contemporaneous British figures, such as Arnold, Carlyle and Wilde to explore a number of defining themes of the century – in particular: revolution, democracy, realism, bureaucracy, the university, the death of God, the arcade, the exhibition and the fear of hell. The chapter concludes by bringing together a number of these themes in an exploration of Poe's seminal story, 'The Man of the Crowd' (1840), which, following Benjamin, is read as an allegory of the nineteenth century, seeing in its central figure not only what Baudelaire calls 'the man of the century' but also its very face.

In 'Literature and science' David Amigoni focuses on a 'long nineteenth-century viewpoint' delivered from an unusual source: the novelist Arnold Bennett in an essay entitled 'The Rising Storm of Life' written for the popular magazine *T.P.'s Weekly* in 1907. While there has emerged a canon of Victorian literature and science writers, shaped substantially by the work of Gillian Beer and George Levine and their focus on Darwin (in which Eliot and Hardy figure strongly), a focus on Bennett's essay permits a concentration on the retrospective and prospective moods that structured the self-conscious end-of-century transition. Bennett's essay enables a reconsideration of science's contribution to the experience of modernity through technological development and the harnessing of energy sciences (the work of Crosbie Smith on 'North British' science is also considered). The relative impacts of evolutionary thinkers is also explored, and Bennett's sense of the importance of Herbert Spencer's evolutionism provides an opportunity to discuss some of the revisionist work that has appeared on Spencer (from Thomas Dixon and Chris Renwick), to balance against the dominance of Darwin. Finally, Bennett's use of the popular essay/popular magazine format provides an opportunity to review some of the most important developments in the 'history of the book', and contributions to Victorian literature and science studies, from the work of James Secord to the work of Gowan Dawson.

Anna Barton in 'Locke in pentameters: Victorian poetry after (or before) posthumousness' reassesses the critical commonplace that Victorian poetry can be considered a belated form that is defined by its post-Romantic concerns. Whilst valuing the work of Isobel Armstrong in her seminal *Victorian Poetry: Poetry, Poetics, Politics* (1994), where Armstrong asserted a post-Kantian context for a reading of Victorian poetics, Barton revisits the idea that Victorian poetry's cultivation of aesthetic factors should be confined to the post-Kantian. The essay argues that the philosophical engagements of poetry from the period do not reflect an easy transition from British empiricism to German idealism. Rather the British empiricist tradition plays an important role in shaping nineteenth-century poetry and this is clear from an examination of how John Locke's account of metaphysics retains a defining presence within the nineteenth century. To that end Victorian poetry is not a belated or posthumous form, but rather one that is indebted to an older British philosophical tradition. Such an approach indicates how reading poetry through philosophical contexts generates a new way of rethinking the construction of poetics during the period.

In 'Reading the Gothic and Gothic readers', Andrew Smith outlines how recent developments in Gothic studies have provided new ways of critically reflecting upon the nineteenth century. Smith then proceeds to explore how readers and reading, as images of self-reflection, are represented in the fin de siècle Gothic. The self-reflexive nature of the late nineteenth-century Gothic demonstrates a level of political and cultural scepticism at work in the period which, Smith argues, can be applied to recent developments in animal studies as a hitherto largely overlooked critical paradigm that can be applied to the Gothic. To that end this chapter examines representations of reading, readers and implied readers in Arthur Machen's *The Great God Pan* (1894), Bram Stoker's *Dracula* (1897) and Arthur Conan Doyle's *The Hound of the Baskervilles* (1902), focusing on how these representations explore the relationship between the human and the non-human. An extended account of *Dracula* identifies ways in which these images of self-reflection relate to the presence of the inner animal and, more widely, the chapter argues for a way of rethinking the period within the context of animal studies via these ostensibly Gothic constructions of human and animal identities.

The second section of the book focuses on 'Rethinking national contexts and exchanges'. As the above overview of conference activity has noted, there has been considerable recent interest in exploring the nineteenth century within a global context. It is by examining these links and exchanges that a much broader picture of the period emerges and the chapters in this section explore how various national contexts, including China, America, India, and mainland Europe support different versions of the relationships that were central to the long nineteenth century.

Regenia Gagnier in 'The global circulation of Victorian actants and ideas: liberalism and liberalisation in the niche of nature, culture, and technology' considers the implications for Victorian Studies suggested by recent developments in the fields of world literatures and globalisation. The chapter draws attention to the global scope of Victorian literature as an actant in world affairs, as in processes of liberalisation, democratisation, and trade, but also to the specificity of each local environment and moment of transculturation, as witnessed by the example of Asia. Gagnier also makes a methodological intervention on behalf of interdisciplinary and intercultural studies by providing a framework to address

Introduction

two current problems. First, how may we, in language and literature studies, best study global processes of modernisation, democratisation, and liberalisation without losing the specificity of the local? Second, how may we best study the uniqueness of distinct locales where the forces of tradition and modernisation meet? The actants discussed include Victorian geopolitical ideologies such as individualism, collectivism, nationalism, internationalism, and cosmopolitanism.

In 'Literary folk: writing popular culture in colonial Punjab, 1885–1905' Churnjeet Mahn explores the exchanges which took place between Indian and British cultures by exploring how writings from Punjab, which came out of complex and diverse cultural and religious contexts, were (mis)interpreted by a process of British cultural curation which erroneously formed these texts into a monolithic cannon of Punjabi folkculture. By looking at the role played in this process by those associated with the colonial administration, Mahn illustrates how acts of colonial appropriation were, in part, driven by an inability to understand the unique cultural forms of the Punjab. This chapter thus explores the ways in which Punjabi literary culture became filtered in British writing and provides a clear example of the issue of cultural exchange in the period and the factors that scholars need to take into account when examining these relationships.

Katie McGettigan in '"Across the waters of this disputed ocean": the material production of American literature in nineteenth-century Britain' argues that attending to the fashioning of American texts by British publishers enables us to rethink the emergence of American literature as a material as well as an imaginative phenomenon, and one which was fashioned outside of, as much as within, America itself. This, in turn, produces new insights into the development of American national literary identity and transatlantic print culture, revealing a neglected history of transatlantic material exchange in the production of nineteenth-century American literature. Again, as in Mahn's chapter, it is by paying attention to the specificity of exchange that the precise dimensions of the cultural exchanges become clear. This is an issue addressed in this section's final chapter, which addresses exchanges within a European literary tradition.

In 'Gruesome models: European displays of natural history and anatomy and nineteenth-century literature' Laurence Talairach-Vielmas explores the process in which from the second half of the eighteenth century to the end of the nineteenth century, medical museums opened their doors throughout Europe and anatomical models circulated between Italy, Germany, France and England, serving to educate professional medical audiences and thrilling lay audiences keen on freaks and fairs. The chapter argues that the popularisation of anatomy and the circulation of anatomical models and modellers, exhibitions and anatomists throughout Europe was reflected in nineteenth-century literature, from Gothic novels to realistic narratives and even children's fiction. Looking at the impact of the material culture of medicine upon the literary field, Talairach-Vielmas examines the relationship between literature and the European anatomical culture by exploring nineteenth-century narratives from Mary Shelley's *Frankenstein* (1818) in the first decades of the nineteenth-century to Charles Dickens's fiction in the 1860s, analysing novels alongside travel guides and journal articles which demonstrate how the specific example of anatomy influenced the literary culture.

The final section of this volume explores the issue of 'Afterlives'. As we nave noted in the overview of recent conferences; papers and panels on the neo-Victorian have proved to be popular. How the Victorians are creatively re-imagined by later writers, and on film, and in the theatre, provides us with a way of accounting for the enduring popularity of the Victorians. How these texts also reconfigure late twentieth- and early twenty-first-century anxieties into Victorian narratives also indicates that to rewrite is a political as well as an aesthetic process.

The online *Journal of Neo-Victorian Studies* has been published since 2008 and is edited by Marie-Luise Kohlke who with Christian Gutleben edits the neo-Victorian book series for Rodopi.[6] Her chapter on 'Adaptive/appropriate reuse in neo-Victorian fiction: having one's cake and eating it too' opens this section and argues that historical fiction writers' persistent fascination with the long nineteenth century enacts a simultaneous drawing near to and distancing from the period, the lives of its inhabitants and its cultural icons, aesthetic discourses and canonical works. Always constituting, at least in part, as a fantasy construction of 'the Victorian' for present-day purposes, the process of re-imagining involves not just a quasi resurrection (of nineteenth-century historical persons, fictional characters, traumas, aesthetics, values and ideologies) but also a relational *transformation* – a change in nature, a conversion into something other, namely what we *want* 'the Victorian' to signify rather than what it was. Hence adaptive practice in the neo-Victorian novel, applied both to Victorian literary precursors and the period more generally, may be better described as adaptive reuse (to borrow a term from urban planning's approach to historic conservation) or, perhaps, *appropriative reuse*. Drawing on a range of neo-Victorian novels Kohlke explores the prevalent perspectival frames and generic forms employed in

Introduction

neo-Victorian appropriative reuse and their divergent effects on present-day conceptions of Victorian culture.

Richard J. Hand in 'Populism and ideology: nineteenth-century fiction and the cinema' explores the adaptation of nineteenth-century fiction into film. The focus of the chapter is on the cinematic adaptation of four extremely different yet continuingly popular texts at opposite ends of the nineteenth century: Jane Austen's *Pride and Prejudice* (1813), Mary Shelley's *Frankenstein* (1816), Henry James's *The Turn of the Screw* (1898) and Joseph Conrad's *Heart of Darkness* (1899). After outlining the legacy of the selected examples of fiction on film, Hand explores the critical issues and the ideological ramifications that surface through these adaptive processes. The dramatisation of each text brings out diverse issues relating to popularisation and ideology. This is particularly pertinent with the processes of both inter-cultural adoption and inter-generic transposition, such as the relocating of Austen within a contemporary Indian context, the redeployment of Conrad's narrative within the Vietnam War and the appropriation of Shelley and James into the populist contexts of the horror genre.

In 'True histories of the Elephant Man: storytelling and theatricality in adaptations of the life of Joseph Merrick' Benjamin Poore takes the example of 'The Elephant Man' as a test case for how Victorian narratives have been developed in a neo-Victorian theatrical context. After outlining the way that a neo-Victorian stage culture has been developed Poore argues that Bernard Pomerance's play *The Elephant Man* (1977) and David Lynch's 1980 film *The Elephant Man* can be regarded as twin foundational texts in the modern-day repurposing of the story of Joseph Merrick. The film, originally adapted in part from the surgeon Frederick Treves's *The Elephant Man and Other Reminiscences* (1923) was subsequently adapted back into a film novelisation by Christine Sparks. Since the early 1980s, Merrick's story in its various iterations has become a popular way to view nineteenth-century mores and to speculate on how far 'we' have come. However, Poore argues that there is a series of tensions between the lip-service paid to the condemnation of Victorian freak shows and the increasingly diverse uses, from comedy sketches to comic books, to which Merrick's image and story are put. This chapter then considers the wider implications of the case of Merrick for nineteenth-century studies and the neo-Victorian.

This volume thus seeks to demonstrate a number of ways in which we can rethink the nineteenth century, both in terms of the categories which structure this book, and through the specific examples which are elaborated within each section. This volume proposes a number of ways in which we might begin a critical conversation that is mapped in the diversity of contexts and approaches that are developed here and in some ways it suggests a range of approaches which are not that dissimilar from Strachey's suggestion that in order to fathom the Victorians we need to rethink our approaches because, as he puts in his outmoded gendered idiom:

> It is not by the direct method of a scrupulous narration that the explorer of the past can hope to depict that singular epoch. If he is wise, he will adopt a subtler strategy. He will attack his subject in unexpected places; he will fall upon the flank, or the rear; he will shoot a sudden, revealing searchlight into obscure recesses, hither-to undivined. (Strachey, 1918)

This is a process of critical rethinking to which this book, and its connected series are dedicated.

Notes

1 Please see the Association's website at www.visawus.org/.
2 For an example of a recent book review forum see the discussion of Frederic Jameson in *Victorian Studies* Vol. 57, Issue 1 Autumn 2014, pp. 89–112.
3 The website can be found here: http://literature-compass.com/victorian/.
4 The website can be found here: www.victorianweb.org/index.html.
5 The website can be found here: www.nines.org/.
6 The website for *Neo-Victorian Studies* is www.neovictorianstudies.com/.

References

Strachey, Lytton (1918). Preface to *Eminent Victorians*. New York: G. P. Putnam's Sons.
Tennyson, Alfred (1987). *Poems of Tennyson in Three Volumes*. Ed. Christopher Ricks. Harlow: Longman.

Part I

Critical reflections

1

On measuring the nineteenth century

John Schad

> Surrealism…'wave of dreams'…new art of flânerie. New nineteenth-century past – Paris its classic locale. Here [is] fashion…[And here] the clerk, death, tall and loutish, measures the century by the yard, serves as mannequin himself to save costs, and directs personally the 'liquidation' that in French is called 'revolution.'…We look on…empty offices…
>
> Walter Benjamin, *The Arcades Project*[1]

The nineteenth century. I have been assigned the task of considering what might be meant by the nineteenth century, the long one, the one longer than a century. But how much longer? I must, it seems, somehow determine that. I must, that is, contrive to measure the century, not unlike Walter Benjamin's most peculiar clerk. Indeed, this makes some sense in that, as a scholar, I am a kind of clerk, being one who dwells in an office making notes, copying out, setting things down. I am, though, mindful of another scholar, albeit not of the nineteenth century – namely, Jacques Derrida, who writes that 'the time is out of joint…the world is going badly' and, thus, 'we lack the measure of the measure' (Derrida, 1994: 77). If so, and the world *does* appear to be going badly, then why on earth try to measure a century? As the Dadaists declare, in 1918, only 'idiots brood over the century' (Motherwell, 1989: 85). I shall, however, do as asked, instructed, just as a dutiful clerk might do.

I can perhaps encourage myself by imagining that I am seeking not merely to measure the nineteenth century but, in the words of Karl Marx, to 'solve the riddle [*Rätsel*] of the century' (Marx, 1973a: 318), to decipher, as if an heroic Oedipus, what it means, what it hides, what is its secret. 'The proletariat,' adds Marx, 'is the secret [*Geheimnis*] of the

Critical reflections

nineteenth century' (Marx, 1973b: 299), but a scholar, or even a clerk, however 'loutish', can hardly be called proletarian, and thus may never be privy to the secret. I shall, therefore, examine not only the words of Marx but also those of others, in particular those collated within *The Arcades Project*, a work of monumental quasi-clerical endeavour on which Benjamin, its 'author' (if that is the word), spent thirteen years, 1927–40. Over these years, he copies out and classifies thousands of quotations from hundreds of sources, each one concerning nineteenth-century Paris, and all dedicated to the dream that Paris is, to quote the Arcadist himself, 'the capital of the nineteenth century' (Benjamin, 1999: 3).

Some there are who might protest at this, citing W. H. Auden's 'Our time has no favourite suburb, no local features,' (Auden, 1966: 101) but by '*our* time' Auden means the 1930s. For us, here, in this essay, 'our time' is, of course, the nineteenth century. And so, as I work through the Arcadist's book, I too come to dream that the nineteenth century can be measured by the Parisian yard – by Paris fashions, Paris people, Paris revolutions and, above all, Paris streets:

> Paris is…swarming with blind alleys, cul-de-sacs…mysterious passages [and] labyrinths…[all of which] lead you to the devil [*diable*]. (Benjamin, 1999: 524)

To the devil? I had not expected to encounter such as him. 'Charlatans… rubber-jointed men, clowns making a comeback…[and] jugglers,' all of whom are also mentioned, are familiar enough to a scholar of the nineteenth century, but not the devil. After all, did not Hegel argue that 'history is the unfolding of God'? (Dudley, 1999: 217). It is true that this unfolding is to be a dialectical affair, rubber-jointed as it were, with each term or moment pregnant with its contrary; but here, in the Arcadist's Paris, it is not God but the devil who seems to wait at the end of the nineteenth-century street. Note how the Arcadist carefully copies out a claim, from 1864, that 'Baudelaire incarcerated…the man of the nineteenth century…in the prison of hell' (Benjamin, 1999: 304).

So, query: Is the nineteenth century to be considered an infernal century? One is tempted to answer 'yes', if only because so very many of its millions believe in hell – Satan, pain, forever, etc. This is difficult for scholars, of course, since we are not supposed to believe in hell any more than in, say, ghosts: 'A traditional scholar does not believe in ghosts' – Derrida (Derrida, 1994: 11). Or indeed, for that matter, any more than we really believe in centuries: 'What exactly is the difference from one century to the next?' – Derrida again (Derrida, 1994: 39).

On measuring the nineteenth century

But perhaps hell *is* the difference between the nineteenth and the twentieth centuries. Hence my query: *Could* the nineteenth century be, in some sense, a season of hell? I think immediately of Theodor Adorno, who will write that 'the determination of the nineteenth century as hell became untenable with the rise of the Third Reich' (Adorno, 1981: 238). Adorno here comments specifically on the Arcadist, his friend and fellow German Jew, and is doubtless mindful that the Arcadist does not escape the hell that is the Third Reich. Unless, of course, suicide is escape. As you may know, in 1940, in a hotel room in occupied France, the Arcadist, for fear of capture by the Nazis, will kill himself. In contrast, Adorno, a scholar, finds refuge in the American academy: a quiet room, a safe office. But I have digressed – in the words of Oscar Wilde, 'I forgot I was…in the nineteenth century' (Wilde, 1949: 87). To return to Adorno's commentary, the Arcadist encounters, in his lifetime, an era so terrible as to make if not a heaven of the nineteenth century then at least a purgatory.

It is a vision that is, in a sense, shared by Marx: 'The revolution', he writes in 1852, 'is still on its way through purgatory' [*Fegefeuer*] (Marx, 1973b: 236). Marx appears confident that, in this instance, purgatory will not last long, that the revolution will soon complete its almighty progress; but, even now, some there are – Marxists, Anarchists, Utopians – still awaiting revolution. For them, the nineteenth century is not finished, its revolutionary work not completed. For them, the century is still a soul on its way through purgatory.

According to Catholic tradition it is, of course, the duty of the living to pray for those in purgatory, which begs a most unlikely question – namely: Should we pray for the nineteenth century? An unlikely question, as I say; however, the nineteenth century does itself cry aloud in prayer. In 1888, Michelet groans, 'Holy, holy Revolution, how slowly dost thou come!' (Michelet, 1967: 79); in 1851, Proudhon pleads, 'The Revolution in the nineteenth century will be the work of fate. Fate! have pity on us!' (Proudhon, 1969: 184). Hearing these groans and pleas, should we not at least consider adding *our* voices, *our* prayers? Note that the Arcadist, born in 1892, writes this of the phantom hunchback that haunts his infant years, his own nineteenth-century years:

> His voice…whispers to me over the threshold of the century: 'Dear child, I beg of you, / *Pray* for the little hunch-back'. (Benjamin, 2006: 122)

It is, I admit, one thing for a *child* to pray for those who might call to us from the nineteenth century but another for a *scholar* to do so. Søren Kierkegaard knows this: 'How as a scholar,' he asks, 'does he [the scholar] understand himself as someone [also] praying?' (Kierkegaard, 1996: 207). How indeed. An office, you might say, is not a church. And yet, as Derrida recalls, there was a time (he is thinking of the beginning of *Hamlet*) when a scholar was precisely the one expected to address spirits, to speak to the ghost: 'Thou art a Scholler – speake to it Horatio.' And that is exactly what Horatio does.

Kierkegaard, in contrast, appears constrained by a nineteenth-century understanding of scholarship as secular, disinterested, and rational – a kind of higher clerkdom, if you will. We should not forget that Kierkegaard's examiners at the University of Copenhagen considered his doctoral thesis, *On the Concept of Irony*, to be too informal, too humorous – too ironic. Kierkegaard is, as they say of Baudelaire, 'out of place [*dépaysé*] in the stupid nineteenth century' (Benjamin, 1999: 245). In short, he seems to have come too early; for, you see, one defining characteristic of the twentieth century is its declaration that the era of the scholar, or at least of the sober and orderly scholar, is or should be over. In short, the scholar-clerk should, by now, be gone; we should, by now, like the Arcadist, be 'look[ing] on...empty offices'. I think, here, of Marinetti and the Futurists, those self-appointed gravediggers of the nineteenth century, who in 1909 declare not only that 'We stand on the promontory of the centuries!' but also that 'We will destroy...academies of every kind' (Marinetti, 1971: 42). This, though, has been coming, this threat. Nietzsche, who numbers himself among the 'first-born of the twentieth century' (Nietzsche, 1973: 147), is forever ridiculing scholarship: 'A scholar I?' he writes, 'I've no such skill' (Nietzsche, 2001: 19).

It is no surprise that our Arcadist, for all his learning, will also never be a scholar as such; or at least not a salaried, university scholar. He too has no such skill, no such luck, no such security. His work, like Kierkegaard's, is considered out-of-place in the academy – the stupid academy, as it were. And it is never more out-of-place than in *The Arcades Project*, which is all but a parody of the academy in that it takes to an absurd, even surrealist, extreme the scholarly habit of quotation. You see, this book, if book it be, is very nearly nothing but quotations without any connecting discussion, argument or narrative. Indeed, it was the Arcadist's ambition that the book would have included no words of his own, none at all, that he would himself exit the book, get the hell out of it, as it were. But he does not complete his escape; his book, the book of the nineteenth century, was never finished. Suicide came first, of course; when he was, finally, cornered, trapped. And the

On measuring the nineteenth century

Arcadist would not have been surprised, for he knew his nineteenth century, knew his Marx, he who writes of the 1848 revolutions that, 'Whilst the professors made the *theory* of history, history itself went on its own stormy [*stürmischen*] way and worried very little about...the professors' (Benjamin, 1999: 185).

Stormy indeed. For scholars of the nineteenth century are often caught in a storm and not just in a metaphorical storm. Consider Ruskin (*Professor* Ruskin, of course) and his 1884 lecture 'The Storm-Cloud of the Nineteenth Century.' It is true that this title suggests he has in mind some kind of political or historical weather, but Ruskin's interest here really is in actual clouds. Oscar Wilde once wrote that 'Whenever people talk...about the weather, I always feel they mean something else' (Wilde, 1996: 431), but, as Ruskin insists, he himself has 'no *arrière pensée*' (Ruskin, 1912 Vol. 34: 1). In short, his lecture really *is* no more, and no less, than a lecture on nineteenth-century rain. Professor Ruskin is measuring the century by the inch, inch of rain. And he is not alone. There is also Matthew Arnold, he who keeps a rain diary: 'New Year's Day 1882. We have had a pleasant week, not one rainy day; but today it has just begun to rain – thermometer [indicates] 47' (Arnold, 2001 Vol. 5: 237).

It might be said that a century cannot be meaningfully measured by rainfall or, indeed, Fahrenheit; but weather, to some extent, *is* history. This they know well in France where *le temps* means, of course, not only time but weather; and then there is Waterloo – about which Victor Hugo writes, 'Had it not rained in the night of 17–18 June 1815, the future of Europe would have been different' (Hugo, 1982: 285). Indeed, had it not rained on 10 April 1848, the future of our particular corner of Europe might have been different, if only a little. Arnold hints at this; of the mass-gathering held on this day, in London, by the Chartists, he remarks: 'the crowd dispersed...then came, ½ an hour after, the hard rain – there may be a little row in the evening...but nothing much, I think' (Arnold, 1996 Vol. 1: 200). The rain will see to that.

And the rain affects, or shapes, not only our century's politics but also its architecture. Witness, of course, the new Parisian arcade: 'During sudden rain showers, the arcades are a place of refuge' (Benjamin, 1999: 31). 'Weather', adds the Arcadist in a terse, one-word commentary. 'Mackintosh', he remarks elsewhere, as another one-word coda, this time to a citation that reads 'Diminishing magic of the power of rain' (Benjamin, 1999: 839). There is, though, precious little rain in the

Arcadist's *own* nineteenth century, his *childhood* nineteenth century, which seems to be an indoor, closeted season:

> Like a mollusk in its shell, [as a child] I had my abode in the nineteenth century, which now lies hollow before me like an empty shell. I hold it to my ear. What do I hear? Not the noise of field artillery...[but] the anthracite as it falls from the coal scuttle...the dull pop of the flame as it ignites the gas-mantle, and the clinking of the lampshade on its brass ring when a vehicle passes by. (Benjamin, 2006: 98)

This indoor nineteenth century is one with which we office-bound flâneurs have, perhaps, an affinity – as the Arcadist observes, 'the flâneur [can] go...for a walk in his own room' (Benjamin, 1999: 421). Nevertheless, it is, I suspect, something of a wished-for nineteenth century. After all, the Arcadist, though a child of the nineteenth century is a man of the twentieth, and thus knows that the weather outside has got worse, much worse. Note how three of the most fabled moments at which the nineteenth century is said to have ended are emblematised by famously terrible weather: the famous cold that, in 1910, freezes forever both Captain Scott and the nineteenth-century hero; the famous ice that, in 1912, sinks both the Titanic and nineteenth-century engineering; the famous rain that, in 1914, turns to mud both the trenches and nineteenth-century civilisation. Weather. Weather. And, again, weather; weather in which even the mackintosh, that greatest of nineteenth-century fabrics, is quite useless. It is enough to make one think that human life is, in the twentieth century, overly exposed to the elements, to the world without; or rather, that, in the nineteenth century there is only ever an inside to the world. The Arcadist writes this:

> The nineteenth century, like no other century, was addicted to dwelling.... What didn't the nineteenth century invent some sort of casing for? Pocket watches...egg cups, thermometers...The twentieth century with its porosity and transparency, its tendency toward the well-lit and airy, has put an end to the world of the shell – *for the living, through hotel rooms; for the dead, through crematoria.* (Benjamin, 1999: 221)

Here we must pause to recall that it is, of course, within a hotel room that the Arcadist will commit suicide, and will do so to escape the crematoria of the Nazi liquidation camps. It is, then, as if death is, for the Arcadist, a kind of shelter, or lean-to, providing him with something of the interiority of the nineteenth century. Or should we say his *childhood* nineteenth

On measuring the nineteenth century

century, his *Berlin* nineteenth century; for in arcadian Paris the century feels very different. After all, what space could be more airy, lighter, more transparent than a glassy arcade? The Arcadist writes, 'As we travel through the arcades...doors give way and walls yield' (Benjamin, 1999: 40).

Doors and walls also give way, yield, and even disappear within the vast, glass *exhibition* spaces of the century; to quote the Arcadist, or rather a quotation of his: 'Each epoch would appear to be engaged in unfolding a specific architectural problem...and for the nineteenth century...[it is the] exhibition' (Benjamin, 1999: 407) – the place of pure visibility, the very opposite of the shell, or case, or office. Witness, not only our very own Great Exhibition (1851) but also the Vienna Exposition (1873), the Philadelphia Exposition (1876), the Chicago Exposition (1893), and indeed the Paris Expositions of 1878, 1889, and 1900. There is, clearly, much to see of the nineteenth century; many monumental moments in which the century is on display. Indeed, as well as the great exhibitions there are, notes the Arcadist, 'panoramas, dioramas, cosmoramas, navaloramas, pleoramas...' and, of course, the scholar's favourite, 'picturesque journeys in a room' (Benjamin, 1999: 527).

If we are, then, to consider the nineteenth century, to take its measure, we must, it seems, endeavour somehow to *see* it, to *look* at it. As the Arcadist writes, 'an effort must be made to secure a foothold...from which to cast a form-and-distance-creating glance on the nineteenth century' (Benjamin, 1999: 407). The difficulty, though, as the Arcadist's own life so vividly demonstrates, is to *find* a foothold, a position that is sufficiently secure to mean one does not slip, slide, or even 'Decline and Fall Off.' I think here of the one-legged Silas Wegg, he who in Dickens's *Our Mutual Friend* is hired to read aloud a book that he keeps mistakenly calling 'The Decline and Fall off the Rooshan Empire' (Dickens, 1997: 65). I am sorry, again I digress – fall off, as it were; however, when it comes to measuring history, is a secure foothold really to be desired? Consider Nietzsche, who mocks anyone who dreams of a vantage point, of viewing from a distance: 'Is a race of eunuchs needed', he asks, 'to watch over the great historical world-harem?' (Nietzsche, 1983: 84). Perhaps not. And not even a scholar would want to be called a eunuch. After all, a race of eunuchs is, presumably, condemned to extinction. But, then, would the world miss its eunuch-scholars? No, says Nietzsche, who accuses scholars of 'stand[ing] guard over history [only in order] to see that nothing comes...of it' (Nietzsche, 1983: 84).

Nietzsche may, I suppose, have a point; perhaps we who seek to examine the centuries do so in order to police them. Consider, please, yet another citation filed away by the Arcadist, this time the remarkable insistence that 'Wherever the nineteenth century feels itself to be unobserved, it grows bold' (Benjamin, 1999: 154). The Arcadist here cites Siegfried Giedion, of Harvard, writing in 1928. To observe the nineteenth century, hints Professor Giedion, is to ensure it does *not* grow bold, does *not* get out of hand. Cue Proudhon the anarchist who, in 1851, declares that: 'to be governed is to be kept in sight, inspected, spied upon...registered... measured' (Proudhon, 1969: 295).

I am now, more than ever, uneasy about examining the nineteenth century. Again I feel as if it is a kind of clerical work, that as a scholar my view of the nineteenth century is, necessarily, the view from the office, Whitehall in fact. However, at least one almighty moment within the long nineteenth century *can*, perhaps, be glimpsed from Whitehall. Consider a letter written in April 1855 by the poet Clough, at the time a civil servant working in Downing Street:

> Here we sit at 5pm waiting to see from our Office windows the French Emperor and Empress pass on their way... – They should have been here before this, but I suppose it is not on account of some refugee's pistol! (Clough, 1957 Vol. 2: 499)

Clough is right; the emperor and his wife are merely late for their train. There is, though, to be, on 28 July 1914, in Sarajevo, another imperial couple who *are* held up on account of a desperate man's pistol: Archduke Franz Ferdinand and wife, in their car, shot dead by Gavrilo Princip. It is, many argue, the event that really marks the end of our century. In this respect, the office window, or at least Clough's office window, affords a grandstand view of the nineteenth century, the long one. Here, the clerk almost sees it all, even the bullets that might divide one century from another.

We scholars do tend to measure centuries by the bullet – the nineteenth century, we often say, not only ends with the bullets of 1914 but begins with the bullets of 1789. However, there are those within the nineteenth century who deploy the bullet not just to stop one century and start another but to stop one *calendar* and begin another. Again, the Arcadist:

> In the July revolution [of 1830]...on the first evening of fighting it turned out that the clocks in towers were being fired on simultaneously and independently from several places in Paris. (Benjamin, 1968: 253)

The Parisians are hoping to do as they did in the Great Revolution, and to begin the world again, to announce that the year is not, say, 1789 or

On measuring the nineteenth century

1830 but 'Year 1' of a whole new calendar, thus leaving the scholar without a nineteenth century at all. In this sense, in 1830, the Parisians are shooting not only at clocks but scholars. In short, the office is not safe, not safe anywhere; as is remarked in 1832, 'Every bullet of the workers of Paris is on its way round the world' (Benjamin, 1999: 735). And, over the years, the bullets aimed at the clocks of Paris *continue* to make their way round the world, or at least Europe: in 1919, in Germany, the Dadaists announce the 'founding of [a] new calendar' (Huelsenbeck, 1993: 139); in 1888, in Switzerland, Nietzsche writes, 'One calculates time from the...*first* day of Christianity! *Why not rather from its last? From today?*' (Nietzsche, 1968: 197).

Nietzsche by no means exaggerates the dependence of the nineteenth-century calendar upon Christianity. Note, for example, that on Saturday 7 April 1838, Clough enters in his diary: 'On this day, as it were, – 1800 Years ago – our Lord was in Bethany, just arrived; – this His last Sabbath day' (Clough, 1990: 38). Another victim of the bullets aimed at the clocks is, then, 'our Lord.' And the nineteenth-century Christ is, indeed, there to be shot at – if only because he takes the outward form of what Alphonse de Lamartine, in 1845, calls 'the industrial Christ' (Benjamin, 1999: 123). As such, he is also the *revolutionary* Christ: to quote yet another Arcadian quotation, '"Jesus is a great man of 48"' (Benjamin, 1999: 814) – 1848, of course, the year of several revolutions; all temporary, all eventually shot-down.[2] According to the Arcadist, 'Lamartine's industrial Christ re-appears at the end of the century' (Benjamin, 1999: 363), a clown, if you will, making a comeback; but he does so only once again to be shot: in 1890 Wilde writes of 'These Christs that die at the barricades' (Wilde, 1997: 126).

The bullets of the nineteenth century, aimed as they often are at the clocks, may well make it difficult to measure the century by the year; however, with the bullets hitting so many a Christ one might just measure the century by the Christ, the dead Christ. After all, this is the century in which God most famously dies – as Nietzsche's madman declares, in 1882, 'God is dead!...And we have killed him!' (Nietzsche, 2001: 120). If, then, the nineteenth century *is* any particular kind of century, it might well be the 'Atheistic Century' – to quote Diogenes Teufelsdrockh, Thomas Carlyle's imagined Professor of Things in General (Carlyle, 1987: 140). This, though, only makes the nineteenth century still harder to measure. Consider, if you will, Professor Teufelsdrockh's claim that 'Our Wilderness is the wide World in an Atheistic Century [and] our Forty Days are long years of suffering' – a claim that confounds, I suggest, any simple sense of duration. For whilst the Professor here speaks of a century that is as short as 'Forty Days' (the length of Christ's withdrawal to the desert), his reference to 'Wilderness' is suggestive of the Exodus, a season of forty years – longer but still substantially less than a usual century. The Atheistic Century is, then, as here described, indeterminately short. To complicate things still more, its years are, for Professor Teufelsdrockh, '*long* years of suffering,' thus suggesting a century that is as long as is pain. And how long is that? On this point the Professor is unclear; he does, though, assure us that 'to these [years] comes an end' (Carlyle, 1987: 140), that there will be an end to the pain which is the Atheistic Century. But that is all he is prepared to say. And rightly so, for pain cannot be measured in terms of time nor vice versa. It is true that Nietzsche remarks, of previous centuries, that 'perhaps in those days pain did not hurt as much as it does today' (Nietzsche, 1996: 49); but he jests, is clowning. Alas.

To summarise, then: the Atheistic Century is no place for the clock-watching scholar. And Nietzsche's madman warns us of this; when we murdered God, he declares, 'we [thereby] unchained the earth from its sun' and have no idea as to where it 'is moving to now – backwards, sidewards, forwards...in all directions' (Nietzsche, 2001: 120). No sun, no orientation, no measure to measure time.

In 1840, Professor Teufelsdrockh claims that 'the...deep-thinking German...stand[ing] peace[fully] on his scientific watchtower... [can] tell the Universe...what o'clock it really is' (Carlyle, 1987: 4). As we have seen, though, Nietzsche seems to be a very different kind of deep-thinking German; or, to put it another way, by the 1880s even the deep-thinking Germans cannot tell what o'clock it really is. And things will only get worse once that deep-thinking German, Albert Einstein, announces in 1905 that time is relative to space, and, therefore, that there is no universal clock. As the Futurists put it in 1909, 'Time...died yesterday' (Marinetti, 1971: 41).

It would be tempting to say that this death of time marks the beginning of the twentieth century,[3] but if time *has* died, how would we know it was yesterday that it died? By what clock do we measure the time since the death of time? Indeed, if there is now no measure for measuring time then I cannot speak of the nineteenth century at all; or, at least not without becoming one of those disreputable familiars of its Parisian capital: the juggler, the rubber-jointed, the charlatan, the clown making a comeback. Only such – the dextrous, the double, or untimely – could even begin to do justice to unmeasurable time. I think now of Carlyle, inventor of the clown Teufelsdrockh and himself a kind of juggler: 'Time', he writes, 'is infinitely divisible'. Carlyle adds, by way of explanation, that there is no unit of time that cannot be divided again and again – for example, 'an hour, with its emotions, events, etc, might be diffused', he says, 'to such expansion as should cover the whole field of memory' (Carlyle, 2010 Vol. 28: 172). This insight is telling; and it is, I think, no surprise that it comes from a thinker who never held a university post and who here appeals to the disorderly, un-administered, and out-of-office realm of lived, or experienced time.

There is, as it happens, another who offers us an almost identical insight – namely, Gerard Manley Hopkins; in 1885, on a stray half-sheet of paper, he writes this: 'But where I say / Hours I mean years, mean life' (Hopkins, 1970: 101). Hopkins is, I admit, a scholar – indeed, he is at the time Professor of Greek and Latin at University College, Dublin; these words, though, are no disinterested scholarly observation, but rather a whisper from a dying and desperate man in a poem that begins 'I wake and feel the fell of dark.' Part of the 'fell' that Hopkins feels is, I suggest, its unspoken rhyming twin: hell. Hopkins, as devout Catholic, here not only thinks of the damned but believes he already shares their fate: 'I see the lost are like this.' Where, then, he says 'life' he means death, eternal death, pain that goes on and on. In another poem of 1885 he writes, 'No worst there is none' (Hopkins, 1970: 100) – that is to say, there is no ultimate bad, no worst, instead only and always worse, and it *is* getting worse, now and forever. This too is no mere anticipation of hell.

The nineteenth-century fear of hell is, I think, so terrible as to be itself an experience of hell; if so, it is a fearfully acute apprehension of the infinite distance housed within seemingly finite time. It is true that other famously nineteenth-century experiences effect something similar – most obviously, the Romantic sublime or a Wordsworthian 'spot of time'; but such are, for the most part, *blissful* openings up of finite time, openings up to that which is eternal not merely in terms of duration but also in terms of character, nature, quality. In contrast, the fear of hell, in foreseeing eternal pain, apprehends an eternity in which duration, length, sheer going on and on and on, is all there is. Hell, then, is not just a terrible hole in nineteenth-century time but a hole of such depth, or length as to suggest a century that is infinitely long. There can be no talk, no measuring, of the length of the nineteenth century without reference to hell, and the fear thereof.

I will return to hell anon. For now, we must stay with the infinite divisibility of time, to which the Arcadist, as it happens, gives the very twentieth-century name of nuclear fission. Note how he describes his attempt to 'liberate the enormous energies of history bound up in classical historiography' as 'comparable in method to the process of splitting the atom' (Benjamin, 1999: 463). The Arcadist's account of the nineteenth century explodes, goes bang, goes off; and thus goes in so many directions that it defeats all attempts to measure it. I think now of Joseph Conrad's *The Secret Agent* (1907) with its memory of the anarchist Martin Bourdin who, in 1894, sets out to blow up the Greenwich Observatory – *the* office, of course, for the measuring of time. Bourdin famously fails, succeeding only in blowing himself to pieces; but Bourdin's fate might just make us wary of the Arcadist and his splitting of the atom of nineteenth-century time, wary of the 'enormous energies of history' that the Arcadist 'liberates'. We should perhaps stand back, well clear.

After all, observing from a safe distance and with due scholarly detachment is the way, or dream of nineteenth-century scholarship; as the Arcadist says, 'history that showed things "as they really were" was the strongest narcotic of the century' (Benjamin, 1999: 463). The Arcadist, however, so 'liberates the energies' of the century that it cannot be mistaken for something that is simply to be viewed, but instead is revealed as something that has an active, intentional existence with respect to those who seek to view it. If the Arcadist's nineteenth century has agency enough to 'grow bold' when '*un*observed' then it has agency enough to return our gaze when it *is* observed, or at least to know it is being observed.

Consider Nietzsche's passing reference to 'the historical sense [of]... the nineteenth century' as 'its *sixth* sense' (Nietzsche, 1973: 152), as almost a telepathic faculty; and one discernible, I think, in the way that the nineteenth century is, variously: astonished by us ('each century [is]...amazed by the century following it' – Dickens [Dickens, 1958: 132]), makes raids on us ('the social revolution of the nineteenth century draw[s] its poetry from the future' – Marx [Marx, 1973b: 149]), and has its eye on us: 'the hunchback,' he who whispers over the threshold of the century, 'always saw me [first]' – the Arcadist (Benjamin, 2006: 122). The nineteenth century, you might say, sees us coming. Or, as Derrida remarks of all the ghosts in Marx: they are 'waiting for us...so many...heads that look at us' (Derrida, 1994: 107).

In one particular novel of the late twentieth century, the question is asked, 'What are we faced with in the nineteenth century?' The answer, I think, is: a face, of sorts. Ask Adorno, he who sees in the work of his Arcadist friend nothing less than the 'physiognomic traits of the nineteenth century' (Adorno, 1981: 237). These traits might, though, prove alarming since they are, warns Adorno, 'extreme'. Ours, of course, is the century that, through Darwin, sees in the human face and its expressions a resemblance to the extreme physiognomic traits of animals. The face of the nineteenth century is, to that extent, a bestial face. Cue Bakunin the anarchist, writing in 1873, with respect to that infamous apparatchik of the German nation-state, the army officer:

> Just take a look at this civilised brute, this lackey by nature and executioner by calling. If he is young, you will be surprised to see not a monster but a blond youth, fresh-faced and downy-cheeked....He knows...Goethe by heart, and all the humanistic literature of the great eighteenth century has passed through his head, [but has done so] without leaving a single humane thought in his heart. (Bakunin, 1990: 79)

This particular face of the nineteenth century anticipates, of course, one of the most terrible faces of the twentieth – that of the blond, civilised Nazi brute. As is often remarked, some of Hitler's most determined death-camp executioners were extremely well read; and, as George Steiner writes,

> Let us not [try and] take the easy way out and say 'the man who did these things in a concentration camp just *said* he was reading Rilke [or] was not reading him well.' I am afraid that is an evasion. He may have been reading him very well indeed. (Steiner, 1979: 83)

So, yes, I do recognise the face of Bakunin's civilised brute; and, in doing so, am like the historian of whom Nietzsche writes, 'To him who knows history it must seem more and more as though he were recognizing old familiar features in a face' (Nietzsche, 1983: 208).

Familiar, very familiar; in fact the more I examine the face of the civilised brute, the more I recognise it as my own, or at least as that of the Arcadist's curious clerk for, as you may just have noticed, he, the clerk, is a killer: 'The clerk, *death*...measures the century...and directs personally the *"liquidation"*' (Benjamin, 1999: 833).

It is discomforting to find one's clerkly face reflected, however dimly, in that of Bakunin's civilised brute, the erudite killing-face of the nineteenth century. Self-recognition is, though, in a sense, only what a scholar of the nineteenth century might expect, given that Hegel – the century's scholar of scholars – famously argues that history culminates at the point in which, with the perfection of European civilisation, the World-Spirit finally and absolutely re-presents Itself to Itself; in short, achieves 'pure self-recognition' (Hegel, 1977: 14). According to Hegel, this moment of self-recognition is to be a glorious apotheosis; however, for the scholar of the nineteenth century, it would appear to be utterly *in*glorious.

I am reminded of Baudelaire's peculiar anecdote concerning 'a frightful man' who looks at himself in a mirror but does so with displeasure; when asked why, he explains: 'Sir, according to the immortal principles of the '89, all men are equal in rights; therefore I possess the right to see my image; with pleasure or displeasure' (Baudelaire, 2010: 93). The principles of 1789 are, of course, invariably taken to be the founding principles of the nineteenth century – in particular, that of popular sovereignty with its dream that each and every citizen will have political representation, will see their own reflection in the face of government. It is, then, something of a surprise to find that Baudelaire's 'frightful man' does not necessarily enjoy what he sees in the mirror, particularly given the nineteenth century's supposed love of realism. There is, however, Wilde's famous declaration that 'the nineteenth-century dislike of realism is the rage of Caliban seeing his own face in a glass' (Wilde, 1949: 5). Wilde does add that the 'nineteenth-century dislike of Romanticism is the rage of Caliban *not* seeing his own face in a glass' – and Wilde, as ever, is right; there is only one thing as bad as seeing one's reflection in the face of the nineteenth century, and that is not seeing it.

This is, I suggest, the strange lesson of Edgar Allan Poe's 'The Man of the Crowd' (1840), the short story seized upon by the Arcadist as, in effect, an allegory of the nineteenth century, the *century* of the crowd. The story is told by a man in London and tells of how, one day, whilst seated in a café, he becomes obsessed with a stranger he glimpses in the passing crowd; the narrator then pursues the stranger for a day, a night and another day, before finally, in 'the street of the D– Hotel,' even as the narrator grows 'wearied unto death', he finally re-encounters the stranger and, 'stopping fully in front of the wanderer, gazed at him steadfastly in the face' only to find that 'He noticed me not' (Poe, 1980: 104). Here, at the last, the narrator, the student of the crowd, might as well be without a face; he too, if you will, becomes a man of the crowd. But such is the way of the century:

> Before the appearance of omnibuses, railroads, and streetcars in the nineteenth century, men were not in a situation where, for minutes or hours at a time, they could or must look at one another without talking to one another. (Benjamin, 1999: 433)

So, face to face, and yet *not* – for there is no talking. In the crowded nineteenth century the face is only partially known. As the Arcadist writes, whilst 'every date from the sixteenth century trails purple after it...those of the nineteenth century are only now receiving [*erhalten*] their physiognomy' (Benjamin, 1999: 546). For the Arcadist, even in the 1930s, the face of the nineteenth century is a face in the making.

The face of the twentieth century would seem, however, to be more nearly completed, more decidable. Consider Virginia Woolf's *Mrs Dalloway* (1924) and the face in the motor-car that is chauffeur-driven through the streets of central London. The precise identity of the face is, at first, in doubt: 'Was it the *Prince of Wales's, the Queen's, the Prime Minister's?...*Nobody knew' (Woolf, 1992: 15); but it *is* an important face, that much is decided, and more will be: 'The face in the motor car,' we read, '*will*...be known' – the world-historical face (Prince, Queen, Prime Minister) *will* be known (Woolf, 1992: 18). And so it is. Witness one particular tiny face in that famous photograph of the vast crowd of faces in Munich's Odeonplatz on 2 August 1914, a crowd gathered to celebrate Germany's declaration of war on Russia; at that moment, the face is *un*known but, in a decade or two, the face will be known – known, of course, as the face of Adolf Hitler. Here, at the very point at which many say the nineteenth century ends, many also say they see the face of the man who 'directs personally' [*leitet personlich*] the twentieth century. If Poe's man of the crowd is the man of the nineteenth century, this man of the crowd is the man of the twentieth century, and his face will indeed be known. No man will, in fact, be better known.

The contrast with Poe's man of the crowd could not be greater. His face is barely described, and he remains throughout 'the stranger' – we never know his name. And it is precisely this anonymity that makes him the man of the *nineteenth* century. If, then, we are ever really to know or grasp the century, we must, finally, seek out a real-life avatar of Poe's anonymous stranger, the man last seen in 'the street of the D– Hotel.' And this avatar is, I think, to be detected, or chanced upon, within a single, passing but haunting remark in Arnold's *Culture and Anarchy* (1869):

> The newspapers a short time ago contained an account of the suicide of a Mr Smith, secretary to some insurance company, who, it was said, 'laboured under the apprehension that...he was eternally lost'. (Arnold, 1932: 157)

What makes Mr Smith so anonymous, so much a man of the crowd, is that both his Christian name and the name of the company for which he works are unknown or omitted, by the newspaper and/or Arnold. And then there is the surname, 'Smith', quite possibly a pale anonymising invention – even if not, it is the most common English surname of all. Here, then (though blink and you will miss him) is the man of the nineteenth century; moreover, here is the man who, by committing suicide for fear of hell, is also, I think, the man of the *long* nineteenth century, indeed the longest nineteenth century, for Mr Smith knew as well as anyone ever could the terrible point at which finite time is quite emptied of meaning and all that exists, or seems to exist, is endless damnation.

To return to where we began, Mr Smith is the clerk who really measures the century, the long one, the one so long as to be infinite. By killing himself he measures the century with his life, his death, his eternity. Indeed, bearing in mind that the Arcadist's peculiar clerk is a fashion-house clerk, we might say that Mr Smith dares to try on, or model the infinite nineteenth century for himself. To quote the Arcadist, 'the clerk...serves as mannequin'. As the Arcadist adds, 'We look [now] on empty offices', or at least *one* empty office, the empty office of Mr Smith, the clerk that is no more. Gone, departed, the office is empty. And there we locate the really long nineteenth century, the one that only the suicide knows. Ask the Arcadist, last seen in his own D– Hotel. *His* office is empty. I am still in mine. Still. As a mannequin.

Notes

1 Benjamin, 1999: 833 and Benjamin, 1972–1989: 5: 1000. Where Eiland and McLaughlin's translation reads 'manages single-handedly' I have 'directs personally,' preferring that as a translation of *leitet persönlich.*
2 See Evans and von Strandmann, 2000.
3 See Lukacs, 1968: 275–95.

References

Adorno, Theodor (1981). *Prisms*, tr. Samuel and Shierry Weber. Cambridge, MA: MIT Press.
Arnold, Matthew (1932). *Culture and Anarchy*, ed. J. Dover Wilson. Cambridge: Cambridge University Press.
––––––– (1996). *The Letters of Matthew Arnold*, Vol. 1, ed. Cecil Y. Lang. Charlottesville: University Press of Virginia.
––––––– (2001). *The Letters of Matthew Arnold*, Vol. 5, ed. Cecil Y. Lang. Charlottesville: University Press of Virginia.
Auden, W. H. (1966). *Collected Shorter Poems*. London: Faber.
Bakunin, Mikhail (1990). *Statism and Anarchy*, ed. Marshall Shatz. Cambridge: Cambridge University Press.

Baudelaire, Charles (2010). *The Flowers of Evil and Paris Spleen*, tr. Wallace Fowlie. New York: Dover.
Benjamin, Walter (1968). *Illuminations*, ed. Hannah Arendt. London: Fontana.
—— (1972–89). *Gesammelte Schriften*, 7 vols, ed. Rolf Tiedmann and Hermann Schweppenhäuser. Frankfurt am Main: Suhrkamp.
—— (1999). *The Arcades Project*, tr. Howard Eiland and Kevin McLaughlin. Cambridge, MA: Belknap Press.
—— (2006). *Berlin Childhood around 1900*, tr. Howard Eiland. Cambridge, MA: Belknap Press.
Carlyle, Thomas (1987). *Sartor Resartus*, ed. Kerry McSweeney and Peter Sabor. Oxford: Oxford University Press.
—— (2010). *The Works of Thomas Carlyle*, Vol. 28. Cambridge: Cambridge University Press.
Clough, Arthur Hugh (1957). *The Correspondence of Arthur Hugh Clough*, 2 vols, ed. F. L. Mulhauser. Oxford: Oxford University Press.
—— (1990). *The Oxford Diaries of Arthur Hugh Clough*, ed. Anthony Kenny. Oxford: Clarendon Press.
Derrida, Jacques (1994). *Specters of Marx*, tr. Peggy Kamuf. London: Routledge.
Dickens, Charles (1958). *The Uncommercial Traveller*. Oxford: Oxford University Press.
—— (1997). *Our Mutual Friend*, ed. Adrian Poole. Harmondsworth: Penguin.
Dudley, Will (1999). Ed., *Hegel and History*. New York: SUNY Press.
Evans, Robert and Pogge von Strandmann (2000). *The Revolutions in Europe, 1848–1849*. Oxford: Oxford University Press.
Hegel, G. W. F. (1977). *Phenomenology of Spirit*, tr. A. V. Miller. Oxford: Oxford University Press.
Hopkins, Gerard Manley (1970). *The Poems of Gerard Manley Hopkins*, ed. W. H. Gardner and N. H. MacKenzie. Oxford: Oxford University Press.
Huelsenbeck, Richard (1993). Ed., *The Dada Almanac*. London: Atlas Press.
Hugo, Victor (1982). *Les Misérables*. Harmondsworth: Penguin.
Kierkegaard, Søren (1996). *Papers and Journals*, tr. Alastair Hannay. Harmondsworth: Penguin.
Lukacs, John (1968). *Historical Consciousness: The Remembered Past*. London: Transaction.
Marinetti F. T. (1971). *Selected Writings*, ed. R. W. Flint. New York: Farrar, Strauss and Giroux.
Marx, Karl (1973a). *The Revolutions of 1848*, ed. David Fernbach. Harmondsworth: Penguin.
—— (1973b). *Surveys from Exile*, ed. David Fernbach. Harmondsworth: Penguin.
Michelet, Jules (1967). *History of the French Revolution*, tr. George Cocks. London: Chicago University Press.

Motherwell, Robert (1989). Ed., *The Dada Painters and Poets*. Cambridge, MA: Harvard University Press.
Nietzsche, Friedrich (1968). *Twilight of the Idols / The Anti-Christ*, tr. R. J. Hollingdale. Harmondsworth: Penguin.
——— (1973). *Beyond Good and Evil*, tr. R. J. Hollingdale. Harmondsworth: Penguin.
——— (1983). *Untimely Meditations*, tr. R. J. Hollingdale. Cambridge: Cambridge University Press.
——— (1996). *On the Genealogy of Morals*, tr. Douglas Smith. Oxford: Oxford University Press.
——— (2001). *The Gay Science*, tr. Josefine Nauckhoff. Cambridge: Cambridge University Press.
Poe, Edgar Allan (1980). *Selected Tales*. Oxford: Oxford University Press.
Proudhon, P. J. (1969). *General Idea of the Revolution in the Nineteenth Century*, tr. John Robinson. New York: Haskell House.
Ruskin, John (1912). *The Library Edition of John Ruskin*, Vol. 34, ed. E. T. Cook and Alexander Wedderburn. London: George Allen.
Steiner, George (1979). *Language and Silence*. Harmondsworth: Penguin.
Wilde, Oscar (1949). *The Picture of Dorian Gray*. Harmondsworth: Penguin.
——— (1997). *Complete Poetry*, ed. Isobel Murray. Harmondsworth: Penguin.
——— (1996). *Plays, Prose Writings and Poems*, ed. Anthony Fothergill. London: Everyman.
Woolf, Virginia (1992). *Mrs Dalloway*, ed. Stella McNicholl. Oxford: Oxford University Press.

2

Literature and science

David Amigoni

'The conveyance of thought' in the wonderful century of science

In this chapter, I critically reflect on the interface between literature and science in the long nineteenth century. I map trends in the field suggesting that, methodologically, literature and science paradigms are quite fundamental to the understanding of interdisciplinary nineteenth-century studies: in so far as the literature-science field has been characteristically concerned with the transmission of thought and its conveyance by the material channels of technological media. I consider the case of a 'transitional' literary writer who has not been seen, hitherto, as a contributor to the field: that writer is Arnold Bennett. In making the case for including Bennett I examine aspects of his novel-writing practice that speak of his subtle engagement with Victorian ideas about science and technology in everyday life that have not, to date, been so prominent given the field's (understandable) preoccupation with Darwin and the question of evolution. I also explore Bennett's essay 'The Rising Storm of Life' (1907) as a magazine publication which provides a context for reflecting on more direct exchanges between popular writing and scientific ideas; and which, thereby, acknowledges the important role played by book and print history at the literature and science interface across the long nineteenth century.

I begin in 1899, on the cusp of the new century, when Alfred Russel Wallace published *The Wonderful Century*, a fin de siècle review of the remarkable progress of science during the nineteenth century as that century shaded into the twentieth. Wallace had a reputation as both scientist

Critical reflections

and social radical (Wallace, 1913) who had experienced poverty through an underprivileged childhood (Wallace, 1908). In 1899, he was still best known for his role in the articulation of the theory of evolution by natural selection, alongside the more prominent, prestigious and socially privileged Charles Darwin in 1858. Evolution was evinced in the 'wonderful' selections and adaptations of species that Darwin and Wallace commonly observed through their independently realised theorisations of Thomas Malthus's population principle (Wallace, 1899: 139). Wallace refers to evolution as 'the great scientific work of the nineteenth century' (p. 134), noting also that the philosopher of evolution, Herbert Spencer, wrote with 'skill and logical powers' that did much to prepare the minds of 'unprejudiced readers' (p. 138). Significantly, Wallace's 'wonderful century' cast its net wider to reflect on the revolution in everyday life delivered by science and technology, beginning with the railway revolution: the origins of which Wallace recalled autobiographically, travelling (1837–38) in third-class supreme discomfort from Leighton Buzzard to Watford (1899: 4).

Wallace also recorded the effects of labour-saving machinery on everyday life: the domestic sewing machine for making clothes (1899: 12); and the typewriter for producing, with great mechanical ingenuity, a 'clear impression' of thought on paper. Wallace was struck by the sheer variety of typewriters available, all of which appear to have reached a high standard of efficiency (p. 13). It was perhaps this sense of the abundance of the means of productivity that led to Oliver Herford's caricature of the late Victorian and Edwardian writer Arnold Bennett who became known for his prolific capacity for writing (Figure 2.1).

In Figure 2.1, Bennett is presented as taking full advantage of the productive capacity of the four typewriters he has at his disposal. Hands and feet are fully engaged: Bennett becomes a kind of human extension of the machines as his twenty digits (fingers and toes) rattle out impressions of thought on the swirling mass of papers. I will return to Bennett in due course.

Wallace's *Wonderful Century* marks the extent to which 'The Conveyance of Thought' – the title of his third chapter, reflecting on the way in which thought might be passed from one consciousness to another – had itself been revolutionised in the nineteenth century. Though Wallace enacts science's indebtedness to literature by peppering his chapters with poetical epigrams from sources that reflect on science (Shelley, Tennyson, Sir Lewis Morris), Wallace was most concerned with what we might call the infrastructures supporting thought conveyance: in

Literature and science

2.1 Oliver Herford, 'Arnold Bennett' (Charles Scribner and Sons, New York, 1917)

a progressive account of developments he identifies the postal services; followed by the electric telegraph, which had achieved worldwide coverage by the final third of the century (Wallace, 1899: 19–20); and finally the telephone, 'a marvellous and unexpected discovery', which organised and conveyed vocal vibrations through an electronic signal to reproduce voice from metallic discs (pp. 21–2). Though Wallace was concerned to explain the science, Steven Connor points to the link between ideas of disembodied voice and the spiritual in the nineteenth century which 'coil so closely together with…work of the scientific imagining and understanding' (Connor, 2000: 363). Indeed, Wallace was himself a convinced spiritualist and wrote a chapter defending psychical research and hypnotism (Wallace, 1899: 194–212). He was also attuned to the darker sides of scientific advance: the subtitle of Wallace's book was *Its Successes and Failures* and, for Wallace, the terrible failures of nineteenth-century science included military technology, which Wallace condemned as 'the Curse of Civilisation' (pp. 324–41). Thus in 1899, Wallace told a highly complex story about nineteenth-century science and the variety of evolutions and transports, including transports of radical, material, spiritual and genocidal thought, that it had licensed.

Darwin and beyond: literature and science, methods and stories

I begin deliberately at the end of the century because of the way in which writers were addressing the question of their 'present' and where, in all uncertainty, it might lead: the end of the century was simultaneously the closure of one episode, the deeply uneasy opening of another. The field of Victorian literature and science studies has in its own illustrious past arguably been dominated by the heavyweights of literature and evolutionary science in the canonical mid-Victorian period, c.1850–80: George Eliot, the early Thomas Hardy, Charles Darwin and Thomas Henry Huxley. Eliot and Hardy were writers who were self-consciously literate *consumers* of Victorian scientific writing and Gillian Beer, in *Darwin's Plots* (1983), has been the most authoritative and innovative expositor of the way in which these canonical writers self-consciously wove advanced scientific thought into their fictional writings. Beer's method was innovative because it went beyond a unidirectional model of 'influence', which had been widely used prior to Beer's arrival (as early, in fact, as Edward Dowden's essay on 'The Scientific Movement in English Literature' of 1877). Beer was most interested in the complex ways in which ideas 'travelled', often far from directly or indeed under the direct supervision of consciousness. Her 'two-way traffic' metaphor, which looked not only at the way in which scientific 'reference' was adapted into literature, but also the way in which scientific ideas were themselves shaped by literary discourse, narrative and other genres, has been highly influential (Beer, 2009: 5).

Beer's work played a role in shaping George Levine's later *Darwin and the Novelists* (1988) because Levine was precisely interested in a wider, and earlier, range of nineteenth-century writers, including Jane Austen. Consequently, Levine's writers were not always avid, attentive readers of advanced scientific writing. While Levine's study could, on the one hand, show the extent to which Dickens's journalism and fiction was in dialogue with contemporary scientific ideas, Levine was also interested in the way in which the writings of Dickens and Darwin were commonly, and more or less unconsciously exploring narrative 'patterns' or 'thematic' projections of, for example, ecological connectedness (Levine, 1991: 131).

In his awareness of the broader Victorian historical and cultural context, Levine also generated ways of thinking about Beer's metaphor of 'traffic' in ways that were both conceptual and material. Scientific ideas, for Levine, were embedded in cultural practices and, early in his book, he acknowledged the way in which science also revolutionised the technologies that structured Victorian culture, including the systems of transportation that moved people and ideas between, say, a lecture on 'Evenings at a Microscope' and the home (Levine, 1991: 3–4). Alan Rauch's *Useful Knowledge* (2001) was another important contribution to the perception of early nineteenth-century science as information: useful and valuable knowledge that could be imparted through books and magazines as well as exhibitions and museums (Rauch, 2001: 3). The full methodological effects for the literature-science interface of this kind of research would be realised in the later work of, most notably, James Secord in his study of Robert Chambers's pre-Darwinian (1844) evolutionary 'sensation', *Vestiges of the Natural History of Creation* (Secord, 2000). Secord's masterful study drew out the way in which scientific ideas were materialised through the technologies of print, magazine and book production, to be consumed, debated and further disseminated through particular 'geographies' or networks of reading and social interaction. Secord and Jonathan R. Topham developed versions of the history of the book, and magazine and periodical culture, that have come to be highly important to the history of science through the work of Sally Shuttleworth's 'SciPer' project (see Cantor et al., 2004, *Science in the Nineteenth-Century Periodical*); and in particular to research at the literature–science interface.

Secord's work, foregrounding as it does the mid-century battle over natural history and the evolution question, is capacious in its grasp of the full range of sciences that contributed to pre-Darwinian evolution controversy, including for example astronomy and Laplace's Nebular Hypothesis (Secord, 2000: 90–1). Yet it still only tells part of the story about the Victorian science and literature relation. In turn, it needs to be seen in relation to the work of Crosbie Smith's narrative about the importance of the 'science of energy' in the later Victorian period. Smith's narrative reminds us of the importance of other scientific authorities and the phenomena they theorised and introduced to public attention: Lord Kelvin on the laws of thermodynamics, James Clerk Maxwell and Sir Oliver Lodge on electro-magnetic waves. To explore Victorian science and literature from the perspective of 'energy science' introduces different forces, temporalities (the later Victorian period) and other geographies of knowledge formation and dissemination. Crosbie Smith's focus on what he characterised as 'North British' sciences of energy and electricity moves the narrative away from clerical Oxbridge and its theologically driven arguments over human distinctiveness and design that produced the 'science and religion' conflict; and towards a 'North British' science that was more imbricated into the fabric of industrial Britain and its emergence as a mass consumer culture (Smith, 1998). Smith's work on energy science needs also to be seen in the light of Laura Otis's research (2001) on the nineteenth-century railway and telegraph systems as modes for understanding, analogically, nervous embodiment, connectivity and the very idea of the circulatory or informational networks. If Beer read Eliot's 'web' metaphors in *Middlemarch* in the context of Darwinian evolutionary ecologies and theories of sexual selection, Otis read the novel in the light of communication networks. Otis's work connects Smith's late Victorian concerns with energy to the electronic sources of the telegraph revolution that were developed much earlier in the Victorian period, following the Romantic period experimentation of Galvani.

The lives of pioneer scientists who developed ground-breaking forms of electrical experimentation traversed these overlapping temporalities as the workings of these forces became clearer. Sir Oliver Lodge was himself a major public figure during the late nineteenth and early twentieth centuries; though now somewhat forgotten. The first person to transmit a wireless signal, he was born (1851) and educated in the industrial heartlands of the Victorian Potteries. Lodge pursued higher education through the University of London: he recorded in his autobiography *Past Years* (1931) how John Tyndall's tenure as lecturer at the Royal Institution during the 1870s, following in the footsteps of Michael Faraday, inspired Lodge's early scientific education (Lodge, 2012: 78). Once established, Lodge pioneered higher educational opportunities in industrial cities: he was founding professor of Physics at Liverpool University, and the first Principal of Birmingham University. Lodge's research on electricity, energy science and the idea of ether – a theoretical, perhaps even mysterious, space-filling medium for transmission of light and electro-magnetic waves – developed at Liverpool, was recast into popular lectures and publications and widely read and acclaimed. Lodge's theoretical work also translated into technological innovation: his experimental work on spark ignition, for example, would revolutionise the internal combustion engine through the development of the spark plug by two of his sons. Lodge was also a committed spiritualist: and, through writing about communication with the deceased son he lost in the Great War, a public advocate of spiritualism. Lodge, a socialist educated in the tradition of John Ruskin (Lodge, 2012: 267), brings us back to Alfred Russel Wallace's own diverse formation, his complex make-up and the complex story he told about Victorian science and progress in 1899. But Lodge's birthplace – the mid-Victorian Potteries – also points us towards the writer Arnold Bennett.

Arnold Bennett between the Victorians and moderns: literature, science, technology and 'life'

Arnold Bennett is a persistently under-valued writer who was not, seemingly, engaged with science, despite a long friendship with the writer H. G. Wells, the 'father' of the scientific romance. Bennett merits attention here precisely because of the way in which he existed across multiple temporalities given that he began his writing career as a late Victorian. He operated, moreover, in a complex field of middlebrow and popular genres during the 1890s and 1900s: for example, his fashionable 'fantasia novel' *The Ghost* (1907) was a story about high bourgeois romance in the operatic worlds of London and Paris which is built around the plot of a deeply malevolent haunting from the spirit world; a haunting so malevolent that the ghost of the title can seemingly prompt both a terrible storm and a train crash, both of which are described by the narrator in great detail. Bennett's sensational popular fiction could thus trade on the catastrophic possibilities that might lurk behind the apparently smooth-running Victorian technologies of *transportation*, in both material and metaphorical senses of the word.

Bennett has attracted most regard for his quality 'Edwardian' fiction which reflected on the provincial Victorian past. Virginia Woolf almost succeeded in subsequently killing his reputation through her disdain for what she perceived as the non-artistic accumulation of material detail characterising Edwardian fiction. Though prolific – witness again the caricature of Bennett and his typewriter mania – Bennett was always a more subtle and self-aware novelist than Woolf could acknowledge, even, or perhaps especially, in the fictional 'Five Towns' novels, based on the Potteries where he was born in 1867: a younger but no less intellectually ambitious contemporary of Sir Oliver Lodge. Bennett negotiated, as I shall show, a variety of magazine and popular publishing contexts that can be seen as intertexts for his working through of concerns about life, science, technology, progress and culture. This volume considers, among other topics, questions of adaptation and the construction of neo-Victorian literatures. Bennett's contribution to the literature and science interface adds, I suggest, to this construction of a complex 'Victorian' periodicity.

Overarching his reconstruction of the Victorian period, Bennett's writing project was committed to an exploration of the complex meanings associated with the term 'life': the fourth book of his 1908 novel, *The Old Wives' Tale* (Bennett, 1996), traversing life in the Potteries and Paris between the 1860s and 1907, was gnomically entitled 'What Life Is'. In every sense, Bennett's project was representational and he used the aesthetic paradigms of nineteenth-century realism – but also the science and nascent sociology that had been woven into the fabric from the legacy of the French novelist Balzac – both to guide and extend the exploratory power of his project (Amigoni, 2015). Bennett's conception of human 'life' was consequently also grounded in discourses of science and technology: again, Bennett drew attention to this in another book that he published in 1908: a kind of self-help guide tellingly entitled *The Human Machine*, where the help required was precisely one of recognition: 'considering that we have to spend the whole of our lives in this human machine, considering that it is our sole means of contact and compromise with the rest of the world, we really do devote to it very little attention' (Bennett, 1908a: 14). The nature of the fleshly decline of the body may be unrecognisable to oneself: but others can recognise it as a malfunctioning machine, as Bennett acknowledges in a metaphor of an emerging automobile technology that Sir Oliver Lodge's science was beginning to revolutionise: 'Anyone can see the sparking apparatus is wrong' (Bennett, 1908a: 13).

In his fictions, Bennett subtly drew attention to the transforming presence of science and technology in everyday life: his first novel, *A Man from the North* (1898) placed as a backdrop to consciousness the technology that could connect an aspiring young northern man to the dream of London: yet, while the heat of the steam engine could be felt from the platform from which Richard Larch observes its embarking passengers, prompting deep envy of the stoker (Lord Kelvin's laws of thermodynamics in everyday life and longing, one might say), the passengers' powers of conveyance to the pavements of Piccadilly Circus and the Strand remain somehow magical, a source of wonder (Bennett, 1908b: 1).

Bennett's later 'Five Towns' novel, *The Price of Love* (1914) immerses the reader in the transforming early twentieth-century world of comic-romantic domestic intrigue (marriage and the suspected theft of money); again, Bennett's setting for the novel illuminates the transition from a Victorian gas-lit, to an electronically dazzling, world. The heroine, Rachel Fleckring, begins the novel as the youthful housekeeper to the widowed, ageing Victorian matriarch Mrs Maldon. At the opening of the novel, Bennett's narrator takes the trouble to describe for his readers the precise task that Rachel performs in lighting the drawing room gas mantle: from collecting the metal pipe (imitation brass) full of tapers; lighting it at the open fire; and standing on a stool to reach the gas-fitting, 'which is a flexible pipe, resembling a thick black cord, and swinging at the end of it a specimen of that wonderful and blessed contrivance, the inverted incandescent mantle within a porcelain globe' (Bennett, 2006: 2). While this could be seen as damning evidence fuelling the Woolf campaign against superfluous detail, Bennett introduces subtle perspectival shifts that comment on the experience of technological innovation. Though coal gas as a source of power had been harnessed and stored in urban gasometers as early as 1824 in Leeds, and the first electric power station opened in Deptford in 1889, for many, gas power was a still a novel arrival into late Victorian domestic life. For Mrs Maldon, as a pillar of Five Towns respectability, gas lighting had only recently been adopted 'as the dangerous final word of modern invention' – the danger underlined by the 'mild, disconcerting explosion, followed by a few moments' uncertainty as to whether or not the gas had "lighted properly"' (2006: 2). It is as though technology places everyday domestic life precipitously on the edge of catastrophe.

The yet more advanced energy of electricity could prompt other potential crises: the youthful perspective of Rachel registers the seductive powers of electronically conveyed 'pleasures' in the form of the new cinema in the Potteries town of Bursley: as Rachel settles into this new environment 'she was in bliss. She surrendered herself to the joy of life, as to a new sensation. She was intoxicated, ravished, bewildered…The screen glowed again.' (2006: 145–6) Bennett reminds his readers of the multiplicity of temporalities through which science and its technological offspring could be experienced, in the realms both of the real and fantasy.

These complex temporalities were also evident in the more widely known and indeed acclaimed novel *Clayhanger* of 1910 ('a very great novel' according to the, *North American Review*: Hepburn, 1981: 264). The novel is a bildungsroman, the history of young Edwin Clayhanger's development of self as he does battle with his poverty-hardened father, the self-made printer Darius. In Chapter 12, entitled simply 'Machinery', Bennett rendered the presence of a technological object that is at once mechanical *and* animal. The old printing press in Darius Clayhanger's Victorian printing works is a good example of Bennett's 'weaving' of a complex of discourses from Victorian scientific naturalism along a cultural binary (animal/machine): the printing press is an object that conveys something of the complex cultural evolution that it has helped to shape, creating a sense of time and being that disrupts simple binaries:

> Then there was what was called in the office the 'old machine,' a relic of Clayhanger's predecessor, and at least eighty years old. It was one of those machines whose worn physiognomies, full of character, show at once that they have a history. In construction it carried solidity to an absurd degree. Its pillars were like the piles of a pier. Once, in a historic rat-catching, a rat had got up one of them, and a piece of smouldering brown paper had done what a terrier could not do. The machine at one period of its career had been enlarged, and the neat seaming of the metal was an ecstasy to the eye of a good workman. Long ago, it was known, this machine had printed a Reform newspaper at Stockport. Now, after thus participating in the violent politics of an age heroic and unhappy, it had been put to printing small posters of auctions and tea-meetings. Its movement was double: first that of a handle to bring the bed under the platen, and second, a lever pulled over to make contact between the type and the paper. It still worked perfectly. It was so solid, and it had been so honestly made, that it could never get out of order nor wear away. And, indeed, the conscientiousness and skill of artificers in the eighteenth century are still, through that resistless machine, producing their effect in the twentieth. But it needed a strong hand to bestir its smooth plum-coloured limbs of metal, and a speed of a hundred an hour meant gentle perspiration. The machine was loved like an animal. (Bennett, 1910: 100–1)

The machine communicates a 'life force' through physiognomy, signified by limb-like protuberances and the suggestion of character features. 'Loved like an animal', the machine has dispatched pests in the manner of a faithful pet which is however not subject to the same laws of decay: the product of eighteenth-century 'artificers', it is also itself the maker and conveyer of meanings that have shaped cultural history, from the founding mission to print a radical newspaper in the late eighteenth century, to its present occupation printing posters supporting respectable middle-class life (auctions and tea meetings).

Though Bennett does not 'declare' his sources there are, it seems to me, sources of nineteenth-century scientific writing with which Bennett (as we shall see) was familiar that permeate this portrait of the machine. Herbert Spencer, as a Lamarckian philosopher of evolution, devised a theory which probed the fine dividing line between organic and inorganic, the animal and the machine with which Bennett plays. His founding text of evolutionary philosophy, *First Principles* (1862) theorised a universal process of movement and particle organisation that represented the triumph of the complex heterogeneous over the simple homogenous. Moving from the organisation of animal bodily structure to the organisation of the complex social organism and its attendant artistic and industrial 'machinery' of modernity, *First Principles* theorised precisely the way in which levers and axles could themselves develop in complexity and confederacy to become an organised, productive, cooperative evolutionary force (Spencer, 1946: 290). Notably, the printing press in the Clayhanger office is worked by a simple handle and lever; but, it has been added to, improved, integrating additional parts to make it into a more heterogeneous whole, which has contributed to *both* the history of radical struggle and its consolidation in peaceable respectability.

The detail that Bennett employs here is indicative of what might be seen as an investment in Spencer's radical Victorian scientific philosophy, which has been somewhat overlooked in work on Victorian literature and science, given Darwin's prominence. Indeed, recent revisionist work on Spencer's philosophy draws out Spencer's radical reputation. Spencer is now best known for his phrase 'the survival of the fittest', which has led to his being viewed as a crude apologist for power and, in the context of late Victorian imperialism, racial supremacy and empire. Chris Renwick, Thomas Dixon and Naomi Beck are all scholars who have recently recovered Spencer's other reputation as a pacifist and arch critic of imperialism appealing to an audience 'of profoundly left-leaning convictions' (Renwick, 2012: 75. See also Beck, 2003; Dixon, 2003). Bennett, we need to remember, was a figure of the liberal left.

I shall turn now, finally, to Bennett's explicit reference to Spencer's *First Principles* for it is included in one of Bennett's few direct and indeed radical discussions of scientific writing, published in 1907; but it also illustrates the way in which the continuation of a tradition of popular magazine publication could act as a nexus of ideological exchange and social thinking, positioned as it was between the fiction market and Victorian traditions of scientific writing in the long nineteenth century.

Penny magazines, 'rising storms' and the politics of literature and science

Spencer's *First Principles* comes to play a significant role in Bennett's brief essay of 1907, 'The Rising Storm of Life', published in the popular *T. P.'s Weekly* (5 July). For Bennett, *First Principles* was nothing short of revolutionary: 'it turned a universe upside down' (Bennett, 1979a: 108). I shall establish the context for Bennett's discussion of Spencer in a moment, for the philosopher of evolution figures as part of Bennett's reflection on an 'economy' of writerly influence from the fields of science (Spencer, Wallace, Darwin) and literature (Dickens). First, the magazine context: *T. P.'s Weekly* which was a penny magazine, established by the radical Liberal MP T. P. O'Connor in 1902 with a mission to bring literature to the masses. Perhaps its most remarkable achievement in this regard was the serialisation of Joseph Conrad's *Nostromo* in 1904, which Cedric Watts has discussed while also giving a flavour of the lower middle-class, culturally aspiring audience that the magazine sought to captivate – not least through its advertisements for the products of a burgeoning consumer culture (Watts, 2007: 99–100). In doing this, *T. P.'s Weekly* was continuing a mission that had started in the early nineteenth century with 'improving' popular scientific publications such as *The Penny Magazine* (Topham, 2004: 37–9), and which continued with Dickens's *Household Words* (1850) and the great innovation of the shilling monthlies, led by the *Cornhill* from 1859, in which a mission to entertain was blended with the mission to educate. Bennett wrote for *T.P.'s Weekly* in that spirit: chapters from what came to be published as *The Human Machine* were published in the magazine in instalments during 1908 (Hepburn, 1981: 50).

Bennett's essay 'The Rising Storm of Life' appeared in the magazine on 5 July 1907: it sought to entertain through a vividly literary idiom, though its purpose was to urge the recognition of the prescience and power of Spencer's philosophy of science; in so doing, it offered a provocation to conventional thinking. Bennett, who was living in France, records returning to London on a bright windy Sunday in June. 'Everything was moving as fast as the wind' he notes, as he climbs the stairs of a motorised omnibus while seeking to hold on to his hat. The bus is a 'street steamer', one of a number that 'swept past in long rattling curves like ships with their bolts loose'. Indeed, much is 'loose' in London: from Bennett's wind-disturbed hat to 'new blouses and neckties' that seem to be swarming the streets independently of their smiling wearers, so that at 'every corner the earth threw up blouses and neckties as a volcano throws up lava' (Bennett, 1979a: 107). If the nineteenth century was a period when geological and mining sciences revealed the inner secrets of the earth, from rock formations to fossil evidence of extinctions, it is significant that a metaphor from what may be described as the extractive imagination delivers a sense of the newness afoot in London: transportation machines move beneath the ground as though they are insects in burrows: 'I could almost see the electric trains flitting about in their lighted burrows under the sewers.' The tactic of defamiliarisation is central to the question that Bennett poses to reflect the profound shock that this experience of intense movement offers the observer in a post-Victorian world. 'Is this London, and Sunday?' (1979a: 106). Bennett's imaginative construction of a post-Victorian world increasing in pace and intensity is registered in the shock that this is a Sunday afternoon in 'Spurgeon's city!' C. H. Spurgeon had been the most publicly visible preacher in a London dominated by Sabbatarian orthodoxy when, as Baptist minister of the Metropolitan Tabernacle, he preached to multitudinous crowds: whereas the 'joyous, expectant, pagan, well-dressed crowd' that Bennett sees in Piccadilly seek 'luxury and pleasure' from a popular restaurant that he initially mistakes for a gold and marble palace. By the fin de siècle and early twentieth century, evolutionary science and scientific naturalism figured ambiguously in new meanings that came to be associated with aestheticism and pleasure. As Gowan Dawson has argued in *Darwin, Literature and Victorian Respectability* (2007), this was an association that troubled Huxley and Darwin who sought to promote a public image of respectability. Nonetheless, pleasure and paganism were seen as potentially dangerous cultural by-products of evolutionary scientific arguments in the closing decades of the century: by-products which could range from cartoons forcing an association between the male pleasure in tobacco and a lewd sexual banter licensed by the public discussion of creature congress, to the high cultural revival of paganism pioneered by the man of science John Tyndall and the aesthete Walter Pater (Dawson, 2007, 58 and 82–115).

Bennett seeks to explain this, rehearsing first the thesis of a 'great journalist' who claims that the pleasure-seeking 'pagan' crowds turn to hedonism because 'they are no longer sure of another life' (1979a: 107). Bennett rejects this, not least because religious organisations seem equally invested in a fast-paced and strident mission to attract ('I was...struck by a long, glaring banner which tempted people to God by the offer of precisely similar attractions' (1979a: 108). The London crowds are communally invested in and dependent on the extraction of earthly goods, communication and 'co-operative organisation'. Bennett consequently explains the vigorous windy day and the intense activity of people that he witnesses through the idea of vitalism: a persistent form of nineteenth-century scientific thought which held that there was a 'vital' principle of life that exceeded the material elements of natural history or biology, chemistry and electricity. Bennett sees evidence of 'a general quickening of vitality' (1979a: 108) or 'the revolutionary force of life itself' (1979a: 109). As Robert Mitchell has recently argued in his wide-ranging account of Romantic vitalism *as* science, the idea that life is a '*provocation*', or a complex process that demanded new forms of conceptual and practical experimentation to unlock its meaning, was a way of seeing that had its origins in the late eighteenth and early nineteenth centuries. Crucially, for our context, Mitchell notes the revival of vitalism at the fin de siècle and early twentieth century (Mitchell, 2013: 2). Bennett's sense of a revolutionary life force drew on vital science as a means of minimising the boundaries that were appearing between proliferating fields of scientific expertise and specialisation (for example between the biological and energy sciences). Thus in an earlier essay published in *T. P.'s Weekly* (28 September 1906) entitled 'The Secret of Content', Bennett observed that: 'All Force is the same Force. Science just now has a tendency to call it electricity' (Bennett, 1979c: 103); thus simultaneously adopting Spencer's theories of the limits of symbolic conceptions ('the Unknowable') while capitalising on print culture's fascination with electrical force as a conveyancing power in the later decades of the nineteenth century: 'the electric thrill in the air which is affecting the nerves of civilisation' as W. T. Stead put it in the *Review of Reviews* in 1890, forging a metaphor of atmospheric nervous contagion and *conveyance* (Gooday, 2004: 238). If electricity represented the cutting edge of science for Bennett and many others in the 1890s and 1900s, it was precisely because of its appeal to, as Graeme Gooday has shown, ethereal, almost indeed magical agency: as well as the uncertainty that this engendered (Gooday, 2008).

The telephone, an electronic technology for conveying voice, and Herbert Spencer's philosophy of evolution in *First Principles*, become the means by which the uncertainty about the future as vast, vital storm and impending crisis, are explored rhetorically; in turn they lead to a critique of the different statuses attached to texts and authors in the print cultures in which science and literature were circulated and consumed. In effect, Bennett stages a confrontation between the playful stimulation of simple pleasures, and the rigours of the philosophy of science. His example of the individual man who uses Thomas Edison's invention of the telephone is explicitly contrasted with the deeper effects of Spencer's *First Principles*: this is because:

> The revival of philosophy is infinitely more important than the revival of science, and equally of course its results are less obvious and slower to come. But they are coming. They are coming. And compared with them the results of science are as naught. Herbert Spencer wrote *First Principles* long before Edison hit on the telephone, and not one man in a thousand who uses a telephone has yet read a line of *First Principles*. But *First Principles* laughs at the Edisonian toy and the man who plays with it, for while he is playing with it *First Principles* has turned the universe upside down, and the man absorbed in the telephone has scarce begun to suspect the revolution (Bennett, 1979a: 108).

Sir Oliver Lodge, in his autobiography, described the telephone as 'the fundamental invention of the latter half of the nineteenth century': yet, he also acknowledged that the device had 'become so familiar that one forgets the wonder' that was originally beheld from 'making a spring speak' (Lodge, 2012: 98, 97). Bennett presents Edison's electromagnetic telephone as just a toy: innocent and unaware 'play' with the capacity of the device to convey voice depends on an ethereal agency which is infinitely more powerful, and uncertain in its effects, than the conveyancing technology. By contrast, it is Spencer's *First Principles* which grasps and conveys the philosophical lessons of 'Force', that is equal to the lesson of the 'Rising Storm of Life', and which is in the process of turning the universe 'upside down'. As Bennett seeks to get his reader to understand the scale of the possible changes grasped by Spencer's philosophy of evolution he compares the idea of the blithe unsuspecting man on the telephone with the fortunes of people who have lived through epochal transformation that is, with hindsight, inscribed under labels such as the 'Renaissance', or the 'Reformation'. Bennett compares the historical experience of involuntary, unknowing participation in such epochal transformation by analogy with the experience of a railway accident: the fundamental transportation technology of the Victorian period (1979a: 109). Building on the analogy, Bennett contends:

> In the same way, we are entering now on a mighty change, on a world movement, on a subversive, vitalizing epoch, compared to which, in my

opinion, the Renaissance and Reformation are insignificant...We feel the great storm of life is rising, the clouds gathering, the winds moaning ere they scream. I think that the some of us see that luxury and pleasure are nothing but the 'white horses' flecking the ocean'. (Bennett, 1979a: 109)

Bennett notably changes the register of his essay at this point: if the essay begins as a playful reflection on a vigorous windy day, by this point it enters the prophetic territory formerly cultivated by John Ruskin's lectures delivered at the London Institution in 1884, 'The Storm Cloud of the Nineteenth Century'. Ruskin's lectures, delivered from an institution that had popularised scientific learning throughout the nineteenth century, professed a degenerative connection between relentless industrial production, air pollution and the increasing dominance of terrible storm clouds. Ruskin took as evidence his own observations of the sky (which led him to correspondence with scientific authorities, including Sir Oliver Lodge, on cloud formation); but also visual art and literature. For Bennett, 'luxury and pleasure' become mere epiphenomena, 'white horses' flecking the storm-whipped ocean that threatens to engulf civilisation. Bennett draws upon nautical metaphors to contemplate the best response: those who stand the worst chance of surviving the storm are those who pretend there is no storm, and 'lay up in a cove and drop anchors' (1979a: 109). Tellingly, in employing nautical metaphors to urge courage – 'put out to sea... rejoice openly in the tempest, accepting it, braving it...' – Bennett also looks to literature as a response to the 'rising storm of life'; or, rather, it may be more accurate to say that he looks to reading preferences within print culture.

Bennett interrogates the print culture to which he contributes, which has been shaped by intellectual conservatism; 'no popular magazine...dares to deal with any open question of theology, philosophy or politics' (1979a: 110). It is important to recall that *T. P.'s Weekly* was a penny magazine run by a radical liberal MP; thus, the context of publication licensed Bennett to reflect critically on the culturally cautious legacy inherited from Victorian magazine journalism, exemplified in the *Cornhill*'s eschewal of politics and theology. 'We hate to think', Bennett opines, adding 'We hate those who make us think' (1979a: 109). Critical thought and intellectual courage are associated with 'pioneers of thought', or Herbert Spencer, Alfred Russel Wallace and Charles Darwin, 'creators of the whole fabric of evolution'. However, in focusing on Thomas Malthus as 'the first of the real moderns' through his authorship of *An Essay on the Principle of Population*, Bennett looks to the material production of books to enquire critically into the curation of the 'fabric' of evolutionary thought:

> There is no copyright in *An Essay on the Principle of Population*, a book universally recognised by competent authority as one of the landmarks of human thought. Is it in Everyman's Library? Is it in the Universal Library? Is it in the National Library?
> No. Only one publisher in England to-day dares print it. (Bennett, 1979a: 110)

In making this point, Bennett aligns himself with, and effectively revives, the freethinking controversies of the high Victorian period of the 1870s and 1880s which, politically, go beyond Malthus's status as a 'source' for the argument of Darwin's *Origin*: in particular, the political struggles of Charles Bradlaugh and Annie Besant over Malthus's place in an argument about human birth control into which Darwin was drawn, though much against his will as Gowan Dawson has shown (Dawson, 2007: 116–61). If in 'a competition for esteem Dickens would leave Darwin' and other scientific authorities 'out of sight', Bennett seeks in 'The Rising Storm of Life' to redress that balance of esteem by situating Darwin, again, among a more radical pantheon of scientists, such as Herbert Spencer and Alfred Russel Wallace.

Looking forward, literature and science studies of the long nineteenth century should, I suggest, draw more fully on the complex interconnections between the varied economies of scientific writing, from evolutionary science to energy science, that the wider field has researched in recent years. Given that so much of this is vested in book and print histories, it is important that this work should acknowledge *politically inflected* reading preferences.

Bennett thus makes a contribution to the Victorian, and post-Victorian, fields of literature and science studies, suspended as they were between concerns about evolution and energy, as well as material and spiritual possibilities of explanation *and* fascination. In doing so Bennett also makes a contribution to a febrile sense of catastrophic possibility and foreboding that characterised the fin de siècle and opening years of the twentieth century. If the long nineteenth century had one finite point of termination, then it was between the Great War years of 1914–18. Bennett's 'Rising Storm of Life' and its image of the surging ocean arguably presaged that outcome, in the way that Wallace had glimpsed it, too, in his assessment of the century's failures in *The Wonderful Century*. If

Victorian science was successfully translating its pioneering discoveries into technologies that would revolutionise domestic and social life, there was a double edge to this process. Bennett warned, metaphorically, in 'The Rising Storm of Life' against the dangers of laying up in a cove and dropping anchor; in doing so he was in tune, to a degree, with Sir Oliver Lodge, another radical in science, as he recalled in his autobiography the pleasure of sailing into Cromarty Firth before 1914 only to discover the place 'where the first Dreadnought was at anchor... stowed away there in seclusion'. While Lodge and his party looked at the time upon 'that first Dreadnought as a mere curiosity', with hindsight 'the expensive naval machine' had become, Lodge says in a voice echoing Bennett's friend Joseph Conrad, 'a thing of horror' (Lodge, 2012: 241–2).

References

Amigoni, David (2015). 'Bennett and Realist Aesthetics', in *An Arnold Bennett Companion: A Twenty-First Century Perspective*, ed. John Shapcott. Leek: Churnet Valley Books.

Beck, Naomi (2003). 'The Diffusion of Spencerianism and its Political Interpretations in France and Italy', in *Herbert Spencer: The Intellectual Legacy*, eds. Greta Jones and Robert Peel. London: Galton Institute.

Beer, Gillian (2009 [1983, 2000]). *Darwin's Plots: Evolutionary Narrative in Darwin, George Eliot and Nineteenth-Century Fiction*. Cambridge: Cambridge University Press.

Bennett, Arnold (1907). *The Ghost: A Fantasia on Modern Themes*. London: Chatto and Windus.

—— (1908a). *The Human Machine*. London: New Age Press.

—— (1908b [1898]). *A Man from the North*. New York: Doran and Co.

—— (1910). *Clayhanger*. London: Methuen.

—— (1979a [1907]). 'The Rising Storm of Life', in *Sketches for Autobiography*, ed. James Hepburn. London: George Allen and Unwin.

—— (1979b [1907]). *Sketches for Autobiography*, ed. James Hepburn. London: George Allen and Unwin.

—— (1979c [1906]). 'The Secret of Content', in *Sketches for Autobiography*, ed. James Hepburn. London: George Allen and Unwin.

—— (1996 [1908]). *The Old Wives' Tale*, ed. John Wain. Harmondsworth: Penguin.

—— (2006 [1914]). *The Price of Love*, ed. John Shapcott. Leek: Churnet Valley Books.

Cantor, Geoffrey et al. (2004). *Science in the Nineteenth-Century Periodical*. Cambridge: Cambridge University Press.

Connor, Steven (2000). *Dumbstruck: A Cultural History of Ventriloquism*. Oxford: Oxford University Press.
Dawson, Gowan (2007). *Darwin, Literature and Victorian Respectability*. Cambridge: Cambridge University Press.
Dixon, Thomas (2003). 'Herbert Spencer and Altruism: the Sternness and Kindness of a Victorian Moralist', in *Herbert Spencer: The Intellectual Legacy*, eds. Greta Jones and Robert Peel. London: Galton Institute.
Dowden, E. (1909). 'The Scientific Movement in English Literature', in *Studies in Literature 1780–1877*. London: Kegan Paul, Trench, Trubner & Co.
Gooday, Graeme (2004). 'Profit and Prophecy: Electricity in the Late Victorian Periodical', in *Science in the Nineteenth-Century Periodical*, eds. Geoffrey Cantor et al. Cambridge: Cambridge University Press, pp. 238–54.
────── (2008). *Domesticating Electricity: Technology, Uncertainty and Gender, 1880–1914*. London: Pickering and Chatto.
Hepburn, James (1981). *Arnold Bennett: The Critical Heritage*. London: Routledge and Kegan Paul.
Levine, George (1991 [1988]). *Darwin and the Novelists: Patterns of Science in Victorian Fiction*. Chicago, IL and London: University of Chicago Press.
Lodge, Oliver (2012 [1931]). *Past Years: An Autobiography*. Cambridge Library Collection, Cambridge: Cambridge University Press.
Mitchell, Robert (2013). *Experimental Life: Vitalism in Romantic Science*. Baltimore, MD: Johns Hopkins University Press.
Otis, Laura (2001). *Networking: Communicating with Bodies and Machines in the Nineteenth Century*. Ann Arbor: University of Michigan Press.
Rauch, Alan (2001). *Useful Knowledge; The Victorians, Morality and the March of Intellect*. Durham, NC: Duke University Press.
Renwick, Chris (2012). *British Sociology's Lost Roots: A History of Futures Past*. Basingstoke: Palgrave.
Ruskin, John (1884). 'The Storm Cloud of the Nineteenth Century: Two Lectures Delivered at the London Institution, February 4th and 11th, 1884', in *The Library Edition of the Works of John Ruskin*, ed. E. T. Cook and A. Wedderburn, Vol. XXIV, available at Ruskin Library and Research Centre, Lancaster University. Available at www.lancaster.ac.uk/depts/ruskinlib/stormcloud.
Secord, James (2000). *Victorian Sensation: The Extraordinary Publication, Reception, and Secret Authorship of the* Vestiges of the Natural History of Creation. Chicago, IL and London: Chicago University Press.
Smith, Crosbie (1998). *The Science of Energy: A Cultural History of Energy Physics in the Nineteenth Century*. Chicago, IL and London: Chicago University Press.
Spencer, Herbert (1946 [1862]). *First Principles*, sixth and final edition. The Thinkers Library, London: Watts and Co.
Topham, Jonathan R. (2004). 'The Mirror of Literature, Amusement and Instruction and cheap miscellanies in early nineteenth-century Britain', in *Science in the Nineteenth-Century Periodical*, eds. Geoffrey Cantor et al.

Cambridge: Cambridge University Press, pp. 37–66. Also available at www.sciper.org.

Wallace, Alfred Russel (1899). *The Wonderful Century: Its Successes and Failures*. London: Swan Sonnenschein.

—— (1908 [1905]). *My Life: A Record of Events and Opinions*. London: Chapman and Hall.

—— (1913). *Social Environment and Moral Progress*. London: Cassell.

Watts, Cedric (2007). '*Nostromo* in *T. P.'s Weekly*'. *Yearbook of Conrad Studies*, III, 97–112.

3

Locke in pentameters: Victorian poetry after (or before) posthumousness

Anna Barton

Lastly, the supreme condition of posthumousness, [Victorian poetry] was post-Kantian.

Isobel Armstrong, *Victorian Poetry: Poetry, Poetics, Politics* (1993)

Such are some of the founding doctrines of Kant, who was so sincere in his belief that we may call him twice amidst falsehood and so confirmed in error that amidst scepticism he was dogmatical.

Elizabeth Barrett, 'Kant's Philosophy' (1824)

The belatedness of Victorian poetry has become a critical commonplace. Harold Bloom's reading of the Oedipal struggle between strong Victorian poets and their Romantic father-figures has itself proved to be a strong critical account that has set the agenda for all the most influential readings of individual Victorian poets or of Victorian poetry in general that have come after it (Bloom, 1971). It remains impossible to read Tennyson, or Christina Rossetti, Elizabeth Barrett Browning or Matthew Arnold, without being aware, and aware of their awareness, of the imaginary schism that separates them from the brief, intense decades of Romanticism. This is not to say that Bloomian anxiety has not been successfully challenged by the academy during the nearly half century since it was first diagnosed. Individual poets have been rehabilitated by critics such as Herbert Tucker, who cures Tennyson by repositioning him as the prophet of Romantic doom (Tucker, 1988); while other scholars have found new ways to configure Bloom's bloodlines of influence, either, as Anne K. Mellor and Alison Chapman have done, by proposing networks of influence that challenge the individualist agon of poetic anxiety (Chapman, 2015; Mellor, 1993), or, as Robert Douglas-Fairhurst has done, by providing an historicist account of influence that returns it to its pre-Freudian identity (Douglas-Fairhurst, 2002). Isobel Armstrong's ground-breaking study, *Victorian Poetry: Poetry, Poetics, Politics* (1993), itself now entering its third decade, mounts perhaps the most influential challenge to Bloom with its comprehensive rereading of Victorian poetry that insists on its self-conscious modernity.[1] Armstrong's work has been so important; first, because, under her critical gaze, Victorian poetry's belatedness, or posthumousness, has been transformed into the birth of a new poetics, sceptical, ironic, untrustworthy and 'double', that steals the march on the high modernism of the next century; and second, because she identifies belatedness as the condition, not just of Victorian poetry, but of Victorian culture at large, so that, in articulating its belatedness, Victorian poetry does not confess its own redundancy, but announces itself as part of the zeitgeist, as politically, philosophically charged as its Romantic predecessors.

Although Armstrong's work gets us a long way from Bloom, it nevertheless relies on, indeed broadens and strengthens, a diachronic account of Victorian poetry's development after and out of Romanticism. My aim in this essay is to put pressure on one aspect of Armstrong's account of Victorian poetry's posthumousness: her claim that, after Kant, 'art (and for the Victorians this was almost always poetry) was becoming "pure". Art occupied its own area, a self-sufficing aesthetic realm over and against practical experience' (Armstrong, 1993: 4). There is, of course, no denying that Victorian poetry is post-Kantian. My suggestion, however, is that in terms of nineteenth-century poetry's engagement with British and European philosophy, the succession from British empiricism to German idealism is not straightforward or absolute and that nineteenth-century poetry still frequently configures itself in relation to a British empiricist tradition. In asserting the continuing significance of Lockean metaphysics for nineteenth-century poetry, I aim to provide the basis for a second rereading of a Victorian poetics that is perhaps not quite so modern, nor quite so posthumous as has been previously understood.

A challenge to post-Kantian readings of nineteenth-century poetry and poetics is worth pursuing not only because it might contribute to a reassessment of the relationship between Romanticism and Victorianism, but also because of its implications for methodological divisions between (new) historicist and (new) formalist approaches to the poetry of both periods. This division is described by Marjorie Levinson as the 'dual commitment of materialist critique', taking 'materialist' to mean both 'an intervention practice taking the general form of ideology critique' and 'an attachment to effects that resist re-inscription as social practice' (Levinson, 1998: 258).[2] Levinson answers this disciplinary conundrum by proposing a newly experimental methodological practice, a 'heterology', which resists the critical impulse to solve or resolve the text that it reads and instead carries out 'a hardworking but cumulatively non-productive, non-profit exercise'. Levinson describes this kind of criticism in Kantian terms. She writes of 'aestheticizing critical thought' and compares her critical project to Kant's description of the aesthetic as 'purposiveness without purpose' (Levinson, 1998: 258 and 261). By proposing a post-Kantian methodology as the best response to a post-Kantian literature, Levinson reinscribes Kant's significance for the discipline. In so doing, she also recapitulates the hierarchy of literary value that places Victorian poetry at a disadvantage. Levinson associates her critical practice with Romanticism and the Avant-Garde and markedly ignores the seven decades of literary production that divide these two periods, perhaps implying that Victorian poetry becomes too caught up in the material of ideology to respond to a reading that aims to reassert the significance and resistance to signification of other kinds of materiality. This being so, it becomes necessary to move beyond (or, as I will suggest, before) Kant in order to include post-Romantic poetry in methodological rapprochement between history and form.

A second solution to the problem posed by Levinson would be to reconsider the critical and philosophical assumptions that divide the material of ideology from the materiality of aesthetic textuality in the first place. Armstrong and Levinson name Kant as the originator of this division. Kant's establishment of the aesthetic as an independent mode of knowing in the *Critique of Judgement* (1790) coincides happily with the early years of Romanticism in a way that has proved irresistible both to the narrative drive of literary history, which views the poetry of the late eighteenth and early nineteenth centuries as the practice or achievement of Kantian theory, and to the discipline of literary study, the inalienable value of which a Kantian aesthetic reassuringly corroborates. So far, so new historicist. From Jerome McGann (1983) onwards, criticism has required readers to look to the materials of history out of which Romantic and post-Romantic poetry and its readers build their palaces of art. This critical turn, towards (in Levinson's terms) one kind of material (political, ideological) and away from the other (the aesthetic) maintains, indeed insists upon, the incommensurability of the two. At the hands of new historicism, aestheticism bites the materialist dust.

This is the loss that New Formalism seeks to recuperate by incorporating the materials of the aesthetic into its ideologically conscientious practices, either by proposing form not just as the object of, but also as part of the practice of theory and criticism,[3] by proposing formalism as a 'particular freeing perspective' continuous with and always returning to the material realities of history and culture (Loesberg, 1999: 54),[4] or, related to this, by calling for a renewed 'attention to the formal means that establish the conditions of possibility for experience – textual, aesthetic, and every other kind' (Levinson, 2007: 562). This last redefinition of form, one that allows it to expand beyond the narrow, self-containment of the aesthetic, has proved most appealing to recent scholars of Victorian poetry, who have taken advantage of its capacity to accommodate what Caroline Levine describes as Victorian poetry's 'excess': its failure to adhere to the standards of traditional formalism that manifests as an 'unnecessary prolixity', a refusal to 'fit...each word into a compact and tense totality' (Levine, 2007: 1249). Scholars, including Levine and Herbert Tucker have begun to consider how the language of aesthetic/poetic form interacts with the forms that organise, shape and demarcate the physical and ideological spaces of politics and culture. Levine asserts that 'literary forms participate in a destabilizing relation to social formations, often colliding with social hierarchies rather than reflecting or foreshadowing them', imagining form as the means of a radical and productive rapprochement between the two kinds of materialist methodology described by Levinson, rather than as the cause of their division, a rapprochement that might, therefore, rescue Victorian poetry from its posthumous condition and place it at the vanguard of poetry scholarship (Levine, 2006: 86).

In so far as it constitutes a return to form that is not a turn away from history, this manifestation of New Formalism decentres the Kantian moment for literary history and criticism, and rescues Victorian poetry from that 'supreme condition of posthumousness' identified by Armstrong. The claims that New Formalism make for the broader application and cross-fertilisation of form within and between the realms of art, culture, politics and history are frequently founded on a productive alertness to the vocabulary of form as employed in nineteenth-century non-literary texts: philosophical writings, religious tracts and political treatises. As Angela Leighton and Kirstie Blair have shown, in spite of Kant's insistence on the purity of aesthetic form, form develops as a promiscuous, porous term throughout the nineteenth century, one that appears to insist upon the continuing relevance of aesthetic materiality.[5] A question remains, however, about the theoretical basis for Victorian poetry's doubly material practice. In other words, if not Kant, then who?

One possible answer to this question is Kant. Recent readings of *Critique of Judgement*, which reassess the assimilation of Kant's aesthetic theory into Romantic poetics and New Critical practice, put a Kantian aesthetic back in touch with its material context. Jonathan Loesberg's revisionist interpretation argues that the Kantian formulation, 'purposiveness without purpose', describes: 'not an internal order but a design with an end outside that order. Only such a design makes the terms purpose and purposiveness meaningful' (Loesberg, 2005: 25). Loesberg makes a persuasive case for the operation of the Kantian aesthetic within the materialist systems of capitalism and industrialism and his work poses a significant challenge to the received account of Kant that originates, for the British critical tradition, with Samuel Taylor Coleridge.[6] However, because Loesberg identifies Coleridge as the origin of literary criticism's powerful misreading of Kant, his return to Kant is problematic for a reading of Romantic and post-Romantic poetry because it requires that we interpret it against the grain of its own mistaken engagement with German metaphysics. At the same time, Loesberg's work is instructive in the nuanced attention that it pays to the reception of Kant in Britain, making way for further re-examination of Kant's influence on British literature at the beginning of the nineteenth century.

This leads to my interest in John Locke, the philosopher whose 'sandy sophisms' were, for Coleridge and many of his Romantic contemporaries, overthrown by the less grainy forms of Kantian aestheticism (Coleridge, 1959: 969), and a second possible answer to my question about a philosophical foundation for Victorian poetry's double materialism. In many senses, Locke is an unlikely candidate for the role. Not only is his work published a century before Kant's *Critique*, it is also regarded by conventional accounts of the history of philosophy as the figurehead of the other side of the divided philosophical tradition that New Formalism aims to resolve. Bernard Bosanquet's *History of Aesthetic*, first published at the end of the nineteenth century, understands that history in teleological terms, offering Kant and then Hegel as the answer or solution to the question: '"how can a pleasurable feeling partake of the character of reason?"' (Bosanquet, 2011: 173). According to Bosanquet, this question is raised by the apparently incommensurable ontologies of, on the one hand, Descartes Spinoza, Leibniz, Wolff and Baumgarten, which he describes as 'universal' and 'intellectual', and, on the other, Locke, Shaftesbury, Berkeley, Hume and Rousseau, which he associates with the 'individual' and with 'feeling' (Bosanquet, 2011: 173). It is worth noting how closely Bosanquet's question resembles the questions raised by Levinson, Levine and others about the divided state of modern literary criticism, a resemblance that might suggest something about the form of critical metanarratives and the persistent appeal of accounts of division and reconciliation. Bosanquet differs from Levinson et al. in that he views the Kantian aesthetic as one that unites the ideal and the material, but his understanding of Locke and his followers as thinkers who 'do not give much attention to the phenomena of the beautiful', but instead: 'throw themselves at once into what seem the most urgent and central issues of man's position in the world – into questions relating to human freedom, the nature of God, the extension of knowledge, the nature of the mind of society' (Bosanquet, 2011: 176), associates Locke with the materials of history, politics and culture and divides him from the materiality of the aesthetic. A return to Locke would, in these terms, impede more than it would legitimate the exchange between literary forms and social formations that New Formalism seeks to achieve.

Nevertheless, there is evidence that Locke continues to be a significant influence for nineteenth-century poetry. The best-known example of Locke's persistence after Kant is his impact on the work of William Wordsworth. Wordsworth's materialism is conventionally read, following Coleridge's assessment of his one-time collaborator and friend, as the sign of an aging poet's artistic decline. According to this account, Wordsworth becomes the embodiment of a failing empiricism, and his late poem *The Excursion* is an easy target for critics of the excesses of a materialist poetic.[7] A less familiar example, perhaps because it does not so readily lend itself to the narrative of empiricism's declining fortunes at the hands of German idealism, is provided by the work of a young Elizabeth Barrett, the writer from whom the second epigraph to this essay is taken. The quotation comes from notes on 'Kant's Philosophy', which are included in a juvenile notebook and dated 1824 and which summarise her understanding of the key points of Kant's idealism. Barrett's notes indicate that she is working from an encyclopaedia of philosophy rather than from the original text and so her strong rejection of Kant is not necessarily based on a thorough knowledge of his work. Nevertheless, the short shrift that she pays the German metaphysician indicates something of his significance in the formation of her identity and her poetics. Her notes, which begin with a description of a priori and a posteriori knowledge and move on to consider Kant's scepticism regarding the existence of a divine author, read Kant through the lens of empiricism. Her objections focus on contradictions that she perceives in Kant's reasoning about the existence of material objects. She allows that 'our author does not go to the lengths of Berkeley' but goes on: 'Nevertheless, our author denies space, while he believes [in] the existence of external objects, which is a manifest contradiction, as to the thinking mind, this non-reality of the former, must bring with it the non-reality of the latter' (Barrett, 1824–26). At one point, she expresses her incredulity at Kant's assertion that no idea is possible without experience by calling the translation into question: 'I cannot help thinking that this last line is a mis-construction of the original author. Surely experience is not necessary for the reception of simple ideas!' (Barrett, 1824–26). This exclamation betrays Barrett's philosophical bias. She takes the term 'simple ideas' not from Kant, but from Locke. Rather than understanding Kantian idealism as the philosophical movement that supplants materialism, Barrett uses Locke as the measure by which Kant is tested and found wanting.

The same notebook contains a second essay, dated 1 March 1825, which bears the title: 'A Short Analysis of Locke's Essay Concerning Human Understanding'. This is a more extended study of Locke's theory of mind, which offers a methodical account of the different faculties of the understanding and refrains from making the kind of evaluative comments that pepper her essay on Kant, except to remark that Locke's description of the faculty of memory is full of 'beautiful and I have almost said poetic imagery' (Barrett, 1824–26). This single piece of editorial is significant because it signals Barrett's alertness to the poetry of Locke's philosophy and so implies that she understands poetry, and beauty more generally, to be categories relevant to, not isolated from, the epistemological concerns of Locke's essay. By describing Locke's philosophical prose as 'almost' poetic, Barrett perhaps indicates her sense that a statement of this kind involves a measure of intellectual risk. She takes this risk because it is important that philosophy can be poetry (and vice versa) and that the aesthetic therefore remain part both of the work of sensation and reflection and of the production of knowledge.

This concern becomes the focus of Barrett's essay towards its conclusion, when it outlines Locke's theory of complex ideas:

> In the reception of simple ideas mind is merely passive, but in the formation of complex ones 'it exerts several acts of its own. These acts of mind [influence] its simple ideas and are chiefly these three 1 – Combining simple ideas into complex ones, whence all complex ideas are found: Instance beauty.'

> Modes are mixed when compounded of different ideas combined to form a complex one, as beauty &c. (Barrett, 1824-26)

Barrett's account returns to her quarrel with Kant on the reception of simple ideas, reinforcing the sense that her knowledge of Lockean empiricism is the thing that informs her rejection of Kantian aestheticism. Simple ideas are received by the passive mind rather than formed, as Kant would have it, by the experienced mind. Barrett takes beauty as her example of a complex idea, once more indicating her sense of what is at stake in her reading of Locke. Beauty, a complex idea that is created through the combination of simple ideas, which are in turn received by the passive mind, is once again anchored to the material world beyond the mind, demanding that the aesthetic (and, by implication, poetry) participate in the real.

If Locke's theory of mind allows the young Barrett to constitute her poetic identity in direct relation to lived experience, his theory of language describes a contractual relationship between word and world that places the materials of her art at the service of political life. In a comic essay, intended for publication in the *New Monthly Magazine* in 1823, Barrett imagines the relationship between language and mind as a family feud between the family of Thoughts and the family of Words. In this essay, words are described as 'a younger branch of the family, and, tho' repleat with pride, quite divested of natural talent' (*Essay on Mind* in Barrett Browning, 2010: 4.281). Words, having been at one time 'the most intimate friend of the Thoughts' are described as having become estranged from them (4.281).

Barrett's poetic *Essay* shows her once more to be a disciple of Locke, who asserts that words have 'naturally no signification' (Locke, 1979: 477). Locke's theory of language is one of the aspects of his metaphysics that recalls the liberal political philosophy of *Two Treatises of Government*, also published in 1689. In Part III of *Essay Concerning Human Understanding*, Locke describes language as doubly material in that its purpose is the achievement of social bonds: 'God having designed Man for a sociable Creature...furnished him with Language, which was to be the great Instrument and common Tye of Society', and that it belongs to the inscrutable materiality of the body: '*Man* therefore had by Nature his Organs so fashioned, as to be *fit to frame articulate Sounds*, which we call Words' (Locke, 1979: 402). As such, the development of language is understood as a synecdoche for the development of liberal society. Language is both the means to the social contract that he theorises in *Two Treatises* and is itself contractual: an agreement that particular sounds and marks be made to stand for particular ideas:

> Men learn Names, and use them in talk with others, only that they may be understood: which is then only done, when by <u>Use or Consent</u>, the Sound I make by the Organs of Speech, excites in another Man's Mind, who hears it, the *Idea* I apply it to in mine, when I speak it. (Locke, 1979: 407, emphasis mine)

> [E]very man has so inviolable a <u>Liberty</u>, to make Words stand for what *Ideas* he pleases, that no one hath the Power to make others have the same *Ideas* in their minds, that he has, when they use the same Words that he does. (Locke, 1979: 408, underlined emphases mine)

The political character of language, implied here in the vocabulary Locke uses to describe its development, is stated more explicitly when Locke considers the benefits of a clearer understanding of language's uses and limitations:

> I am apt to imagine, that were the imperfections of language, as the Instrument of Knowledge, more thoroughly weighed, a great many of the Controversies that make such noise in the World, would themselves cease, and the way to Knowledge, and, perhaps Peace too, lie a great deal opener than it does. (Locke, 1979: 489)

Just as liberal government is an imperfect system created to serve the free and sovereign individuals that make up the state, language is likewise secondary in that it is subordinate to the ideas that it expresses.

According to Barrett, the only member of the Thought family to remain on cordial terms with the Words is 'Mrs Poetical Thought', who 'flirts away valiantly with the Words, who continue her humble servants though at variance with the rest of the family' (Barrett Browning, 2010: 4.282). This goes beyond Locke, who allows that words can also generate and enable the creation of knowledge and understanding, becoming a formal mechanism by which thought is accomplished, but regards this as the work of philosophy and not poetry, which he tends to see as an imprecise rather than a creative use of language: 'Man should *use the same Word constantly in the same sense*. If this were done many of the...Poets Works...might be contained in a nut-shell' (Locke, 1979) By laying claim to language on behalf of poetry and to the exclusion of other kinds of thought (especially philosophy), Barrett departs from Locke, granting poetry both a 'mind' of its own and suggesting it as the successor of philosophy in its ability to employ language to mediate between mind and world.[8] Poetical Thought's valiant flirtation with words also re-imagines the political exchange of Locke's linguistic contract as the embodied exchange of a sexual contract, a second departure that shows Barrett's alertness to the possibility that the mind of poetry might gain its advantage over philosophical thought through its exploitation of pleasurable form. Empiricism is thereby shown to have an appeal for Barrett as a woman poet in her development of an embodied, avowedly feminine poetic.

'*An Essay on Mind*', the title poem of EBB's first collection, published in 1826 (Barrett Browning, 2010, Vol. 4: 82–131), puts these questions of contractual language and pleasurable form to the test. The poem rehearses some of the major tenets of Locke's *Essay* in a long sequence of Popean couplets. Its argument so closely resembles that of the *Essay Concerning Human Understanding*, that it might – with some justification – be dismissed as a work of slavish imitation. Indeed, in a letter of 1828, written to Hugh Stuart Boyd, Barrett expresses a desire to remove two of the most gushing lines from the poem that suggests her later embarrassment about the extent of her devotion to the philosopher: 'Two of the lines on Locke I would wish omitted. He is neither "first in my heart" nor "noblest in my song" and I cannot conceive why I should have said so' (in Kelley and Hudson, 1984: 138). However, in translating Locke into pentameter couplets, *An Essay on Mind* encourages the reader to reflect on the relationship between Locke's philosophy and poetic composition, and concludes with a defence of poetry that rehearses at greater length Barrett's significant variance with and development of Locke's philosophy of language.

The poem is divided into two parts: the first explores Mind's relationship to individual man; the second focuses on the nature and work of language. Questions about the identity and role of the poet press on the poem throughout. 'Form', for example, is a word that appears repeatedly throughout Barrett's rehearsal of Locke's philosophy in Part 1 of her *Essay*. Employed to signify the material, embodied nature of selfhood, the word also gestures towards a relationship between forms human and poetic that is instructive for an understanding of Barrett's developing philosophical aesthetic. A reference to 'various mind in various forms' follows a liberal metaphysics of individuation, whereas another, to the 'unequal forms' that receive the 'equal light' of Genius, position individual variety, after Locke, within the context of a single divine power. Considering the figures of the distant and of the more recent past, the speaker asks 'why a like mass of atoms should combine / To form a Tully, and a Catiline?' (ll. 25–6). She continues:

> Or why, with flesh perchance of equal weight,
> One cheers a prize-fight and one frees a state?
> Why do I not the muse of Homer call,
> Or why, indeed, did Homer sing at all?
> Why wrote not Blackstone upon love's delusion,
> Or Moore, a libel on the Constitution?
> Why must the faithful page refuse to tell
> That Dante, Laura sang, and Petrarch, Hell –
> That Tom Paine argued in the throne's defence –
> That Byron nonsense wrote, and Thurlow sense –
> That Southey sigh'd with all a patriot's cares
> While Locke gave utterance to Hexameters? (ll. 27–38)

This set of reversals, which Barrett employs to illustrate the puzzle of individuality (why is this person himself and not somebody else?), also introduces politics and poetry as the interrelated subtexts that are never all that far from EBB's philosophical discourse. We are made aware that her own identity and vocation are a significant part of what is at stake here and that the work of the individual body may be political ('one frees a state') or it may be literary. The final reversal exchanges conservative poet for liberal philosopher in a way that is intended to associate Locke's political philosophy with English national identity. Locke, along with Byron and Paine becomes a national hero.

Barrett's reference to the hexameter line is itself political. The hexameter is singled out as an unpatriotic verse form, poetic evidence of Southey's political shortcomings. This political formalism is obviously something that appeals to Barrett, who returns to Southey towards the end of Book 1 to demonstrate how his 'gross faults buy deep experience':

> What thousand scribblers of our age, would choose
> To throw a toga round the English muse;
> Rending her garb of ease, which graceful grew
> From Dryden's loom, besprankt with varied hue!
> Is that dull aim, by Mind unsanctified.
> What thousand Wits would have their wits belied
> Devoted Southey! If thou had'st not tried! (520–6)

The hexameter, a classical form, is imagined as an inappropriate item of clothing for the English muse, whose 'garb of ease' is the pentameter line, which Barrett identifies with Dryden and which, we cannot fail to notice, is adopted by Barrett herself.[9]

In Book 2 of Barrett's essay, words become the object of investigation. The binary of individual, material form and universal mind that shapes the discussion in Book 1 is repeated, but this time the material body is replaced by the material of language. Words, being man-made, are a less satisfactory kind of body for Mind. They are a 'gross' but 'needful' solution to the problem of communication. Nevertheless, Barrett's language acknowledges and consolidates the connections between the two kinds of form. She employs the Icarus myth, describing words as 'Mind's winged strength, wherewith the height is won, / Unless she trust their frailty to the sun' and warns:

> Destroy the wings – let Mind their aid forgo
> Do not Icarian billows yawn below?
> Ah! spurn not words with reckless insolence;
> But still admit their influence with the sense,
> And fear to slight their laws! Perchance we find
> No perfect code transmitted to mankind.
> And yet mankind, till life's dark sands are run
> Prefers imperfect government to none.
> Thus Thought must bend to words! (651–9)

Words, the artificial wings by which man takes flight, bolster him against the elemental void. Here again Barrett seems to forget the conclusion of the Icarus myth in which the wings themselves are destroyed by the heat of the sun. She reinterprets the story so that flight no longer symbolises disobedience of the limits imposed on man by divine law and in so doing betrays a more libertarian impulse. But the lines that follow rein this impulse back in using the language of government and law so that Icarus's fate is re-imagined as the outcome of a failure to heed the laws to which his use of these material forms contracted him. Barrett then writes about the application of linguistic law, which once more seeks to achieve a balance between freedom and obedience: 'Respect the technicality of terms! / Yet not in base submission – lest we find / That, aiding clay, we crouch too low for Mind; / Too apt conception's essence to forget, / And place all wisdom in the alphabet' (676–80). Mirroring the relationship between social matter and individual mind, literary forms are understood to enable rather than hinder free communication and the development of ideas.

Barrett goes on to provide a role-call of writers and thinkers who have, in her opinion, achieved the balance of word and mind most effectively: Plato, Bacon, Pope, Burke, Price, Knight and, of course, Locke himself, who Barrett apostrophises with the enthusiasm that she later regrets in her letter to Boyd: 'Oh! Ever thus, immortal Locke, belong, / First in my heart and noblest in my song;' (892–3). And yet, this rapturous address to the philosopher who she describes as 'the Columbus of the Mind', is, in part, an attempt to ingratiate herself with her parent thinker at the point of her departure from him. The concluding section of her Essay expresses a cautious desire to exceed his philosophical achievements through the work of poetry. It does not constitute a rejection of what has gone before, but it identifies in poetry the ability to extend beyond the reach of the reasoning mind into the inspired, invisible realms of fancy: 'But where Philosophy would fear to soar, / Young Poesy's elastic steps explore!' (900–1). The 'fairy feet' of 'tiptoe fancy' that make these elastic steps are of central importance to Barrett, who, in making this special case for poetry, engages in a direct discussion of poetic form, a theme which, as I have attempted to suggest, presses on the essay throughout.

According to Barrett, poetry achieves that subordination of the constraining legality of Lockean philosophy to the impulse of freedom, the desire for which she has hinted at elsewhere. Poetry roams further and sees more plainly than Reason, bestowing 'living radiance' on its 'cold form' and 'sculptured grace' (*An Essay on Mind*, ll. 940–1). In another list, this time of poetic rather than philosophical and political heroes, Barrett keeps returning to the relationship between material, metrical form and inspired Mind. She refers to the 'overflowing line' and 'full cadence' of Milton's poetry (ll. 1049–50); describes the 'sportive measures' of Horace (l. 1052); and Pope's 'didactic page', on which 'sound' is 'ruled by sense, and sense made clear by sound' (ll. 1057–8). Over-formality is identified as characteristically French: Racine reduces the woes of Nero's mother to a matter of 'two hundred lines' and, in his translation of the Oresteia, Orestes, 'maddened by his crime, / Forgets life, joy, and every thing – but rhyme'. Like much of the poem, this epigrammatic criticism is partly to do with showing off. This is Barrett performing as Pope or Byron, acting up to a particular kind of witty, lettered sophistication. However, this movement in Part 2 of her essay towards comment on literary specifics also represents the culmination of Barrett's philosophical musings. The figurative references to form in her discussion of empiricist philosophy in Part 1 are rewritten here in literal terms so that matters political become the figures and metaphors for poetic composition. The two parts of Barrett's poem bind poetic and political form together so intimately that their relationship with one another exceeds the metaphorical. For Barrett, strong disciple of Locke, the drama of form and freedom that poetry enacts is both essentially political and essential to the progress of political (meaning social or communal) society.

Critical reflections

It is a drama that is repeated in Barrett Browning's most famous poem:

How do I love thee? Let me count the ways.
I love thee to the depth and breadth and height
My soul can reach, when feeling out of sight
For ends of Being and ideal Grace.
I love thee to the level of everyday's
Most quiet need, by sun and candle-light.
I love thee freely, as men strive for Right:
I love thee purely, as they turn from Praise.
I love thee with the passions put to use
In my old griefs, and with my childhood's faith.
I love thee with a love I seemed to lose
With my lost saints, – I love thee with the breath,
Smiles, tears, of all my life! – and, if God choose,
I shall but love thee better after death.

Read with Barrett's juvenile essays and poetry in mind, Sonnet XLIII begins to sound less sentimental and more cerebral, less a rhetorical performance of courtship, more a carefully worked through solution to a philosophical conundrum. Elizabeth's speaker begins by repeating a question, posed by her lover. Traditionally, the response she goes on to provide, 'let me count the ways' (l. 1) is a rhetorical flourish that makes a mockery of the question: love measured to show that it is immeasurable, or, in the words of Sonnet VIII, love told to prove that it is untold. However, taken as part of a post-Lockean poetic discourse, these measures become more precise expressions of the material economy of human emotion. The sonnet invokes this discourse in line 7, which compares love to the struggle of liberal politics, the 'men who strive for right'. The speaker loves freely, but, as Locke teaches us, that freedom is not absolute, bound as it is by human contract.

Taking this simile as a starting point, we can begin to recognise the contingency of the lyric speaker's expansive measures. 'Depth and breadth and height' (l. 2) sounds as though it describes a multidimensional vast, giving the impression of emotional idealism; but the next lines tell the reader that the soul reaches blindly ('out of sight') *for* an ideal grace that is therefore not quite attained. The remaining lines of the sonnet describe a love that confines itself within the limits of mortal, material experience and that conforms to a doctrine of Lockean selfhood whereby an individual's identity is the product of their past experience: she loves 'to the level of every day's most quiet need' and 'with passions put to use / In my old griefs and with my childhood's faith' (ll. 10–12). In the sonnet's final quatrain the breadth and depth and height of the soul is exchanged for the 'breath, / Smiles, tears of all my life' (ll. 12–13), an 'all' that diminishes as the ebullient exclamation is checked by the acknowledgement of divine law; and the end rhyme leads from 'faith' to 'breath' to 'death'. The conditional mood of the last two lines reinforces the limited reach of the speaker both by drawing a comparison between mortal and immortal love and by alluding to a future state that cannot be counted and for which she cannot be held to account.

It is therefore appropriate that this sonnet is obedient to the material fetters of poetic form. Rhymes are generally complete – with the exception of 'Grace' (l. 4) and 'faith' (l. 10), both words that gesture beyond the material confines of the sonnet world; the argument conforms to the shape of the line; and, although the iambic pattern is initially troubled by the dactyl and spondee that make up the opening question, the response is immediately more measured, performing the kind of responsible liberty that it describes. The progress of the sequence is, therefore, from an untold love, which the speaker cannot responsibly accept, to a measured relationship in which each party can be held to account. This is also a poetic/linguistic progress. The reciprocal, responsible relationship to which the speaker contracts herself is likewise a linguistic contract, so that love told, is love counted and held to account through the formal language of lyric poetry. In Barrett Browning's sonnet sequence the doubly material dogma of the juvenile *Essay* is developed into a mature poetic practice that takes the politics of form for granted so that her youthful worship of Locke tacitly (in)forms the adult poet's love for her husband.

This essay has aimed to show that Victorian poetry's sustained engagement with the philosophy of the English empiricist tradition reconfigures that poetry's relationship with the philosophical and literary traditions that immediately precede it. Victorian poetry's sceptical relationship with a Kantian aesthetic therefore need not be read in terms of decline or disappointment and might instead be understood as part of an active interdisciplinary discussion about the material forms of life and art in which all was still to play for. My reading also has significant implications for the relationship between Victorian poetry and its twentieth-century successors, the modernism that is often credited with reinvigorating the posthumous poetics of the previous generations. A full discussion of this aspect of my argument is beyond the scope of this essay, but a sense of the kinds of continuities that it might uncover is provided by the following extract from T. S. Eliot's doctoral thesis, *Knowledge and Experience in the Philosophy of F. H. Bradley*:

> When the poet says 'I lived with shadows for my company' she is announcing at once the defect and the superiority of the world she lived in. The defect, in that it was a vaguer, less of an idea than the world of others; the superiority in that the shadows pointed towards a reality, which, if it had been realised would have been, in some respects [a] higher type of reality than the ordinary world. (Eliot, 1989: 55)

Eliot's thesis is interested in Bradley's attempt to reconcile the world of ideas (knowledge) with the world of the real (experience). In order to illustrate the distinction between these two worlds Eliot (mis)quotes Sonnet 26 of *Sonnets from the Portuguese*:

> I lived with visions for my company,
> Instead of men and women, years ago,
> And found them gentle mates, nor thought to know
> A sweeter music than they played to me.
> But soon their trailing purple was not free
> Of this world's dust, – their lutes did silent grow,
> And I myself grew faint and blind below
> Their vanishing eyes.

Eliot's reading views Barrett Browning as a posthumous idealist, a characterisation that is more sharply defined in the original poem, in which 'shadows' are exchanged for the more optimistic 'visions', which contrast all the more starkly with the grainy materialism of 'this world's dust'. But Eliot's conveniently vague account of his Victorian forebear forgets the conclusion of the sonnet:

> Then THOU didst come – to be,
> Belovèd, what they seemed. Their shining fronts,
> Their songs, their splendours (better, yet the same,
> As river-water hallowed into fonts)
> Met in thee, and from out thee overcame
> My soul with satisfaction of all wants –
> Because God's gifts put man's best dreams to shame.

Rather than elegising the loss of the ideal, as modernist memory would have it, Barrett Browning's poem makes a deliberate turn to the real as an embodied manifestation of the divine. It is this, not the world of the shadow/vision, that constitutes a 'higher reality' for Barrett. Eliot's choice of quotation is therefore perhaps more apt than he means it to be, in that Barrett's sonnet stages the reconciliation that Bradley's

Victorian idealism attempts by finding the ideal within the flesh and blood of material experience. This is, on the one hand, just one more example of the modernist misrepresentation of Victorian poetry that is partly to blame for its posthumous condition; but, by burying Barrett's sonnet within what is a foundational working-through of his own poetic philosophy, Eliot allows it to participate in the on-going development of a modern aesthetics, modelling a means by which the material forms of Victorian poetry might inform the aesthetic thought of the twentieth century.

Notes

1 In a later article, one that acts as an illuminating post-script to her book, Armstrong asserts that 'we now need to jettison the term [Victorian] altogether. It is an irrelevant if not a misleading category' and suggests 'antemodern' as a possible alternative (Armstrong, 2001: 281).
2 See also Angela Leighton, *On Form* (2007), which identifies a related paradox in the definition of form itself, which 'is both "essential", yet becomes visible or "manifest" in "material things". It is an abstraction from matter, removed and immaterial; but it is also subtly inflected towards matter' (p. 1).
3 This is the proposal of two important essays published as part of a special issue of *MLQ* in 2000. Robert Kaufman argues that 'aesthetic form, which formalist theories regularly shorthand as "art," is an ongoing and foundational practice calling forth constant (re)projection of form, thereby contributing to the possibilities of critical thought and agency.' (Kaufman, 2000: 155). A similar argument is made by Ellen Rooney: 'form is both the enabling condition and the product of reading' (Rooney, 2000: 18).
4 See also Jonathan Loesberg, *A Return to Aesthetics* (2005), which is discussed at greater length later in this chapter.
5 'Form, which seems self-denying, is restless, tendentious, a noun lying in wait for its object.' (Leighton, 2007: 1). Kirstie Blair's excellent study of Victorian religious poetry is most successful in pinning down the precise nature of the relationship between the different kinds of form that her work addresses, making and substantiating the claim that 'in relation to these particular literary and social formations there is nothing "as if" about their interlacing. Victorian writers...sometimes start from a position of comparing poetry and religion, but often end up by assuming that the two are equivalents, operating by the same methods and under the strictures of divine law.' (Blair, 2012: 10).
6 '[T]he problems that [Cleanth] Brooks's essay raises about organicism, and that he, Wimsatt and Beardsley and Krieger struggle with, had emerged even more clearly in Coleridge's articulation of the concept, from which they all more or less draw.' (Loesberg, 2005: 20).

7 Herbert Tucker's recent account of *The Excursion* as 'a transcendental vision broken to mundane harness for its own good' is one of the more forgiving recent accounts of the poem (Tucker, 2008: 178).
8 A later version of the essay, published in *The Athenaeum* in 1836, restates the power of poetry in stronger terms: 'Poetical Thought! – how the Words serve her! Their malice and their meanness do not dare to slacken their obedience: she "holds them with a glittering eye," and, if they wrong her, it is rather by belying than denying.' In this second version, Poetical Thought, an Ancient Marineress with 'mystical' vision, seems drawn from a Coleridgean idealist poetics, creating an association that complicates Barrett's earlier rejection of Kant (Barrett Browning, 2010: 279). The developing image of Poetical Thought, from matronly flirt to high priestess, perhaps expresses Barrett's growing ambition as a poet and a developing faith in poetry as the highest order of thought.
9 Barrett may have in mind Johnson's description of Dryden as 'the father of English criticism', a writer who, rather than forcing the English language into classical forms, translated the classics into English.

References

Armstrong, Isobel (1993). *Victorian Poetry: Poetry, Poetics, Politics*. London: Routledge.

────── (2001). 'When is a Victorian Poet Not a Victorian Poet? Poetry and the Politics of Subjectivity in the Long Nineteenth Century'. *Victorian Studies* 43(2): 279–92.

Barrett, Elizabeth (1824–26). Notebook. Browning Collection. Boston, MA: Wellesley College Special Collections. Reproduced with kind permission.

Barrett Browning, Elizabeth (2010). *The Works of Elizabeth Barrett Browning*, 5 vols, ed. Sandra Donaldson, Rita Patteson, Marjorie Stone and Beverley Taylor. London: Pickering and Chatto.

Blair, Kirstie (2012). *Form and Faith in Victorian Poetry and Religion*. Oxford: Oxford University Press.

Bloom, Harold (1971). *The Ringers in the Tower: Studies in Romantic Tradition*. Chicago, IL: University of Chicago Press.

Bosanquet, Bernard (2011 [1892]). *A History of the Aesthetic*. Cambridge: Cambridge University Press.

Chapman, Alison (2015). *Networking the Nation: British and American Woman's Poetry and Italy*. Oxford: Oxford University Press.

Coleridge, S. T. (1959). *Collected Letters of Samuel Taylor Coleridge*, ed. E. L. Griggs. Oxford: Oxford University Press.

Douglas-Fairhurst, Robert (2002). *Victorian Afterlives: The Shaping Influence of Nineteenth-Century Poetry*. Oxford: Oxford University Press.

Eliot, T. S. (1989). *Knowledge and Experience in the Philosophy of F. H. Bradley*. New York: Columbia University Press.

Kaufman, Robert (2000). 'Everybody Hates Kant: Blakean Formalism and the Symmetries of Laura Moriarty'. *Modern Language Quarterly* 61(1): 131–55.

Kelley, Philip and Ronald Hudson (1984–2016). Ed., *The Brownings' Correspondence*, 23 vols. Winfield, KS: Wedgestone Press.

Leighton, Angela (2007). *On Form*. Oxford: Oxford University Press.

Levine, Caroline (2006). 'Strategic Formalism: Towards a New Method in Cultural Studies'. *Victorian Studies* 48: 85–95.

——— (2007). 'Formal Pasts and Formal Possibilities in Victorian Studies'. *Literature Compass* 4: 1241–56.

Levinson, Marjorie (1998). 'Posthumous Critique', in *In Near Ruins: Cultural Theory at the End of the Century*, ed. Nicholas B. Dirks. Minneapolis: University of Minnesota Press, pp. 257–95.

——— (2007). 'What is New Formalism?'. *Publications of the Modern Language Association* 122(2): 558–70.

Locke, John (1979). *Essay Concerning Human Understanding*, ed. Peter H. Nidditch. Oxford: Clarendon.

Loesberg, Jonathan (1999). 'Cultural Studies, Victorian Studies and Formalism'. *Victorian Literature and Culture* 27(2): 537–44.

——— (2005). *A Return to Aesthetics*. Stanford, CA: Stanford University Press.

McGann, Jerome (1983). *The Romantic Ideology*. Chicago, IL: University of Chicago Press.

Mellor, Anne K. (1993). *Romanticism and Gender*. New York: Routledge.

Rooney, Ellen (2000). 'Form and Contentment'. *Modern Language Quarterly* 61(1): 17–40.

Tucker, Herbert (1988). *Tennyson and the Doom of Romanticism*. Cambridge MA: Harvard University Press.

——— (2008). *Epic: Britain's Heroic Muse*. Oxford: Oxford University Press.

4

Reading the Gothic and Gothic readers

Andrew Smith

The contribution that scholarship on the Gothic has made to our understanding of the long nineteenth century has developed exponentially from the resurgent scholarly interest in the form that emerged in the 1980s into what now represents a small publishing industry dedicated to the Gothic (including, of course, Gothic from the twentieth and twenty-first centuries).[1] There is a critical consensus that reading the Gothic enables an engagement with alternative cultural narratives about desire, race, class and colonialism. Such a position has meant embracing works that once would have been considered as pulp fictions beyond the academic pale, such as those by Bram Stoker, Arthur Machen, Henry Rider Haggard, and Florence Marryat (amongst many others). This also indicates a tacit critical acknowledgement that the populist bears complex, because so often ambivalent, witness to the anxieties of an age. This may be more true of the fin de siècle Gothic than of the Gothic of the late eighteenth century which has historically been accorded a culturally assured position within Romanticism, in part because so many of the Romantics, such as Coleridge, Percy Shelley and Keats wrote in the Gothic form.[2] Whilst reading the Gothic might have proved a critically profitable manoeuvre on the part of the academy, it is also noteworthy that the fin de siècle Gothic expresses a level of self-consciousness about reading practices that also invites critical scrutiny. By looking at readers and writers within the Gothic we gain a new insight into how the Gothic engages with the interpretive procedures that underpinned the putatively analytical discourses of the period. This chapter addresses how looking at readers and writers within fin de siècle Gothic texts enables us to reconsider the Gothic's critique of the dominant culture. As we shall also see, the Gothic often undertakes self-consciously aware forms of critical analysis. The critical journey that the fin de siècle Gothic takes us on is an unusual odyssey which, in the instance of readers and writers, leads towards animals. The contribution that recent work in animal studies can make to our rethinking about the Gothic at the end of the nineteenth century will be explored in depth in an account of *Dracula* (1897), but first it is important to observe how these critical self-reflections are manifested in images of readers and writers that pervade the fin de siècle Gothic text.

Gothic readers in the Gothic

Towards the end of Arthur Machen's *The Great God Pan* (1894) we encounter an eye-witness account of the death of Helen Vaughan, the novella's femme fatale, written by Dr Robert Matheson. Helen has been persuaded to hang herself when confronted by evidence of her crimes (she has driven several men to suicide, apparently for financial gain). We know at this stage that Helen is the daughter of Pan and Mary (a seventeen-year-old who has been used in an experiment by one Dr Raymond, which has resulted in Helen's birth). Matheson, however, is baffled by what he sees and in a chapter tellingly titled 'Fragments' he records the peculiar transformations that Helen is subject to in her final dissolution:

> I saw the form waver from sex to sex, dividing itself from itself, and then again reunited. Then I saw the body descend to the beasts whence it ascended, and that which was on the heights go down to the depths, even to the abyss of all being. The principle of life, which makes organism, always remained, while the outward form changed. (Machen, 2010: 70)

As Helen dies so she recapitulates all of life. Matheson, a medical doctor, reads this moment in a certain way, although one which confounds his professional ability to make coherent sense of what he sees. At one level Matheson is a failed reader because his adherence to the principles of medical science places him beyond the capacity to read Gothically. Nevertheless his document incorporates a reference which implicitly acknowledges that writing and interpretation are linked. Matheson describes Helen's form as 'lying there black like ink' as he watches her 'melt and dissolve' (Machen, 2010: 69). The editorial prefatory note to Matheson's document also recounts a problem with textual fragments when stating that Matheson's 'notes were in Latin, much abbreviated, and had evidently been made in great haste. The MS was only deciphered

Critical reflections

with great difficulty, and some words have up to the present time evaded all the efforts of the expert employed' (Machen, 2010: 68–9). The bodily fragments of Helen are elided with the textual fragments of Matheson's narrative, which nervously, and cryptically, conceal what he has seen whilst also reflecting his incredulity. If Matheson's medical analysis lies in fragments, the same cannot be said for Clarke who pulls many of the disparate narratives of the novella into some semblance of coherence.

Clarke, a friend of Dr Raymond, was present at the experiment on Mary and is a more conventionally Gothic reader than Matheson, one who 'knew that he still pined for the unseen' (Machen, 2010: 14). The ostensibly polite and charming Clarke has a concealed interest in the Gothic. He possesses a bureau, which 'teemed with documents on the most morbid subjects' and is the proud owner of 'a large manuscript volume, in which he had painfully entered the gems of his collection' (Machen, 2010: 14). The narratives which constitute this volume are all unpublished and form a secret archive that he titles 'Memoirs to Prove the Existence of the Devil' and 'his sole pleasure was in the reading, compiling, arranging and rearranging' of these documents (Machen, 2010: 15). The narratives within the novella compose a significant part of these 'Memoirs' so that Clarke effectively becomes the compiler of the novella itself. Clarke's pursuit of evidence is different in kind to that of Matheson whose pursuit of reason is clearly at odds with Clarke's editorial ambitions. Nevertheless, Clarke's reconstruction of evidence into a narrative form emulates the scientific approach of Matheson and constitutes an alternative taxonomic process – one that is intended to prove the presence of the supernatural via an alternative cultural commentary which revels in the limitations of mainstream scientific analysis. Read in this way *The Great God Pan* demonstrates a level of self-reflection which celebrates the counter-cultural virtues of the Gothic.

The presence of self-reflection is a feature of many fin de siècle Gothic texts and it indicates that the dominant culture was subjected to a radical rethinking. How to discover evidence for the type of truth that our Gothic narrators assert is also a key feature of these texts and is evident in the various multi-vocal inter-textual forms which characterise *The Strange Case of Dr Jekyll and Mr Hyde* (1886) and *Dracula*. The Gothic writings of Stevenson and Stoker might seem far removed from an earlier Romantic Gothic tradition, but an example of how to critically read early Gothic narratives can be found in Conan Doyle's *The Hound of the Baskervilles* (1902), which also evidences a fascination with facts, secrets, and forms of interpretation.

The legend of the hound of the Baskervilles is an eighteenth-century narrative which comments on an incident during the civil war in which the rapacious Hugo Baskerville is providentially killed by, according to Dr Mortimer '"a foul thing, a great, black beast, shaped like a hound yet larger than any hound that ever mortal eye has rested upon'" (Doyle, 1996: 18). With the recent death of Sir Charles Baskerville this family curse has seemingly become activated once more. Holmes, however, indicates to Mortimer that the tale is only of interest '"To a collector of fairy-tales'" (Doyle, 1996: 18), and is quick to set aside any supernatural explanation. Holmes realises that the solution to the crime involves identifying the person responsible for bringing this Gothic tale to life. The older Gothic narrative might be defeated by Holmes's pragmatism, but in reality the tale is replaced by a contemporary Gothic narrative about degeneration and disease in which true genetic identities are ultimately exposed. Holmes is thus correct to interpret the myth of the hound as a false, because fanciful, Gothic story. He is also able to read Gothically in a fin de siècle sense because he is skilled in the art of reading the signs of atavism when he notes Stapleton's similarity to a family portrait of, tellingly, Hugo Baskerville. Stapleton is revealed as '"an interesting instance of a throwback, which appears to be both physical and spiritual'", who is trying to murder his way into the inheritance of the estate (Doyle, 1996: 145). Stapleton is indeed like Hugo, but is a modern Gothic horror defined by his degenerative traits. Whilst Holmes successfully reads the signs of Stapleton's biological stigmata he is also open to like interpretation when the anthropologically-minded Mortimer, who collects Neolithic human remains found on the moor, tells Holmes '"I confess that I covert your skull'" because '"I had hardly expected so dolichocephalic a skull or such well-marked supra-orbital development'" (Doyle, 1996: 12). Biology will out, and even the fierce hound who has been smeared with phosphorous to render it unearthly will also give up its genetic identity after death, with Watson noting 'It was not a pure bloodhound and it was not a pure mastiff; but it appeared to be a combination of the two' (Doyle, 1996: 157).[3] Disguises cannot in the end conceal true identities as interpreters such as Holmes and Mortimer read the signs of physical abnormality to decode the presence of Gothic horrors concerning degeneration (with even the cocaine-taking Holmes placed on the scale of 'abnormal' types).[4]

At one level this focus on reading: of myths, minds and bodies might appear to gloss the scientific practice of the period, but again it is noteworthy that the novel includes within it readers (such as Holmes) who look for the new Gothic presence suggested in the theories of degeneration championed by Lombroso and Nordau.[5] Gothic readers are not, however, always as astute as Machen's Clarke or Doyle's Holmes and *Dracula* provides some interesting examples of how readers make errors of interpretation, albeit ones which are helpfully corrected by more knowing readers of the Gothic.

Jonathan Harker's opening journal initially represents a tourist's view of Transylvania as he records the apparently peculiar sights, customs, and meals eaten by its colourful inhabitants. The tone becomes much darker as he becomes progressively pulled into the world of Castle Dracula – a place which appears to be subject to alternative metaphysical laws. This leads Harker, a solicitor, to desperately try and maintain a fact-based analysis of what he confronts 'Let me begin with facts – bare, meagre facts, verified by books and figures, and of which there can be no doubt' (Stoker, 1996: 30). The problem is that he has the wrong kind of books in mind as the novel suggests that it is Harker's western rationality that blinds him to the presence of vampirism. Harker is positioned as a writer, as his journal suggests, although one who is baffled by his experiences at Castle Dracula but who records enough instances about the presence of vampirism for more knowing readers to interpret.

At one level *Dracula* associates reading and writing with health. As Harker notes 'I turn to my diary for repose. The habit of entering accurately must help to sooth me' (Stoker, 1996: 36). Later Van Helsing will urge the vampire hunters to keep a record even of their 'doubts and surmises' (Stoker, 1996: 119) which can be textually scrutinised for any clues about the Count that they might contain – which suggests that the vampire is, paradoxically, to some degree produced from within the intuitive epistemologies of those hunting the vampire. The issue of reading and health in the novel can also be located historically. Maggie Kilgour has suggested that the figure of the Count can be read as a gloss on Oscar Wilde who, as Michael Foldy notes, was imaged in the British reactionary press during the trials as a predatory quasi-aristocratic figure whose corruption was partially compounded due to an interest in apparently dissolute French literature (Kilgour, 1998; Foldy, 1997).[6] Wilde therefore becomes figured as an unhealthy reader and this has implicit points of contact with Nordau's account of illness and the consumption of Art in *Degeneration* (1895), when he notes the emasculating potential of reading badly. For Nordau the overly emotional, and so feminised, man:

> laughs until he sheds tears, or weeps copiously without adequate occasion; a commonplace line of poetry or prose sends a shudder down his back; he falls into raptures before indifferent pictures of statues; and music,

especially, even the most insipid and least commendable, arouses in him the most vehement emotions. (Nordau, 1993: 19)

Reading badly becomes supplanted in *Dracula* by healthy reading which, in decoding the Count's vampirism, identifies the presence of degenerative disease, with Mina Harker observing after one of her textual analyses that '"The Count is a criminal and of criminal type. Nordau and Lombroso would so classify him"' (Stoker, 1996: 342). Although Harker's journal provides enough clues about the degenerate Count (even if Harker is unable to read them), Nordau's concern about effeminacy and reading becomes linked to Harker when Harker aligns himself with a projected female writer, noting that 'Here I am, sitting at a little oak table where in old times possibly some fair lady sat to pen, with much thought and many blushes, her ill-spelt love-letter' (Stoker, 1996: 36). The transformation of Harker from a feminised writer to a man of action requires him to become a more active, because self-aware, reader and writer who can contribute to the connected narrative that *Dracula* becomes as it forces writers out of their individual subject positions and into dialogue with one another – a process which depends upon 'healthy' textual scrutiny. Even the initially confused Harker appears to anticipate this possibility when he is seemingly seduced by the three female vampires at Castle Dracula, a moment in which he recalls 'I felt a desire that they would kiss me with those red lips. It is not good to note this down, lest some day it should meet Mina's eyes and cause her pain; but it is the truth' (Stoker, 1996: 37). Mina's personal pain is well hidden behind a professional pursuit of the clues about the nature of the vampire, which leads to Van Helsing extolling the strength of her '"man's brain"' (Stoker, 1996: 234), which sits in ironic contrast to the passivity recorded in Jonathan Harker's journal. Mina, according to Van Helsing, reads and writes like a man and it is tempting to see this as a cultural response to the supposedly degenerate reading practices which might, according to Nordau, infect emotionally susceptible men like Harker.

In *Dracula* writing also has an oblique, but ultimately revealing, association with vampirism. The Count's link to writing is recalled in Van Helsing's comment that Dracula is '"the author of all this our sorrow"' (p. 203). Later, Van Helsing notes that the Count is vulnerable when '"He is confined within the limitations of his earthly envelope"' (p. 271). That the Count represents a threat to textuality is also suggested in his destruction of one of the copies of their complete manuscript. Dracula also appears to have an influence over the infected Lucy when, whilst asleep, she retrieves her recent written account 'from her breast and tore it in two' (p. 143), before Van Helsing intervenes and takes the pieces from her. Renfield also plays a crucial role in this with Seward acknowledging that Renfield functions as 'a sort of index to the coming and going of the Count' (p. 210). Later, Harker also refers to Renfield as 'mixed up with the Count in an indexy way' (p. 231). The Count and Renfield represent texts that require decoding and this brings back into focus an idea of taxonomy, which was discussed earlier in relation to Machen.

Dr Seward acknowledges a fascination with Renfield, an inmate of Seward's asylum, in part because Renfield's behaviour appears to be unique – leading Seward 'to invent a new classification for him, and [to] call him a zoophagous (life-eating) maniac' (Stoker, 1996: 70). Renfield is a petty would-be vampire who is intent on creating a food chain which progresses from flies to spiders to birds, but which comes to an end when Seward refuses him a cat. This refusal is perhaps prescient given that a later journal entry notes a 'Strange and sudden change in Renfield last night. About eight o'clock he began to get excited and to sniff about as a dog does when setting' (Stoker, 1996: 100). Van Helsing encourages a more nuanced response to such seemingly abnormal behaviour when he tells Seward '"it is the fault of our science that it wants to explain all; and if it explain not, then it says there is nothing to explain"' (Stoker, 1996: 191). Seward's desire to place Renfield within a taxonomy fails because the scientific designation 'zoophagus' does not help locate Renfield within the system of manias. Van Helsing stresses the need to understand Renfield rather than to allocate him a place (if a new one) within a pre-existing system. The sense that Renfield functions as an 'index' to the Count is central to this reconsideration as it suggests that reading Renfield will provide an insight into the Count. Consideration of his strange dog-like behaviour opens up the novel for a different type of analysis – one that is indebted to recent research on animal studies.[7]

Locating the animal

The Count is variously associated with animals, he can morph into a bat or a dog and he is seen in the daylight by the Keeper of the Zoological Gardens in London, when Dracula uses his powers to influence the captive wolf, Bersicker. The Count is part human and part animal and this ability to move between these states raises questions about the scientific taxonomies of the time, an analysis of which enables a reconsideration of the cultural engagements of the Gothic and how it relates to the wider fin de siècle world.

Theories of evolution are key here, but in a precise way. Darwin may seem to be the obvious figure but Virginia Richter has noted how Aristotle's notion of a great chain of being influenced theories of species development from the eighteenth century. A central concern in such theories was how to evidence apparent biological morphologies when no obvious missing link could be found to bridge these interstitial spaces. Darwin, for example, would be taxed by the apparent lack of physical evidence for the creature which bridged the ape and human worlds, but Richter also acknowledges how in 1740 the discovery, by Abraham Trembley, of the freshwater polyp, Hydra, seemed to provide the link between plants and animals (Richter, 2011: 40). Richter notes that similarly 'The discovery of a life form conjoining the features of two different species would clinch Darwin's argument' (Richter, 2011: 40). In *Dracula* vampirism functions as this missing link between the human world and the animal kingdom. The Count can appear as both human and animal and vampirism is the liminal condition which functions as the missing interstitial realm. The idea of 'indexy' links between the vampire and vampire hunters explains why Renfield occupies such an important position in the novel. It also explains why the novel implies, largely via Van Helsing, that the key to vampirism is to be found within themselves which suggests that they harbour a vestigial animal nature which links them all to the Count.

As Matheson in *The Great God Pan* would note the biological inheritance that he witnesses in the dissolution of Helen Vaughan, so Van Helsing observes the biological complexity of the Count '"he can command all the meaner things: the rat, and the owl, and the bat – the moth, and the fox, and the wolf; he can grow and become small; and he can at times vanish and come unknown"', so that the problem they confront is '"How then are we to begin our strife to destroy him?"' (Stoker, 1996: 237), especially given that he can also masquerade as a person. The Count includes within him a history of evolutionary experience and his Darwinian ability to adapt to his environment is seen by Van Helsing as an extension of these evolutionary principles. Van Helsing claims of the Count '"In some faculties of mind he has been, and is, only a child; but he is growing, and some things that were childish at the first are now of man's stature"' (Stoker, 1996: 302). Van Helsing also notes that the Count has applied a quasi-scientific approach to their world so that '"this monster has been creeping into knowledge experimentally"' (Stoker, 1996: 302), by using Renfield as a way of understanding the human, meaning that the Count's '"great child-brain...was growing"' (Stoker, 1996: 303). The task confronted by the vampire hunters is to use these links, such as that provided by Renfield, in order to reverse the lines of communication to gain access to the world of the vampire.

A complicating factor is the obvious fascination that the vampire hunters have with vampirism. This is clear from Harker's account of the three female vampires discussed earlier, but is also reflected in how the blood transfusions with the infected Lucy Westenra turn the vampire hunters into symbolic vampires (by replacing her blood with theirs). The vampire hunters are thus attracted to that which should repel them and the true lesson provided by Renfield is that the human possesses an urge to release their inner animal. These themes are not specific to *Dracula* and we can witness them in *Jekyll and Hyde*, although arguably they are challenged in Wells's *The Island of Doctor Moreau* (1896). Wells's novel has been much discussed by scholars working in animal studies as it explores the manufacturing of a 'humanity' from animals parts – one which is undermined by the lingering forceful presence of the beast that lurks within. The novel also suggests the proximity of the animal to the amoral humans who largely populate the novel. Philip Armstrong notes the function of the Ape-Man in *Moreau*, whose presence appals Prendick because the Ape-Man understands 'that the basis of their kinship [is] their shared taxonomic position as primates' (Armstrong, 2008: 79), something which Prendick is keen to deny. The animal within creates this unusual frisson in *Dracula* which explains why the vampire is such an ambivalent figure, at one level heroic, masterful, free from social constraints and at another is diseased, pathologised, and monstrous. Ultimately the vampire cannot be restored to the human order and remains cut off from 'humanity', although, paradoxically, retaining an unsettling emotional presence within it. Richter, in a discussion of Conan Doyle's *The Lost World* (1912), notes of the 'missing link' that it

> refuses to play along with the project of restoring plenitude. It is not comforting; it neither closes the gap between man and animal, civilisation and nature, present and past, nor does it affirm man's splendid isolation. Rather it remains suspended in a liminal space, always out of reach. Accordingly, the effect of the missing link as a literary device is itself uncanny, a pulsation between fascination and fear, desire and disgust. (Richter, 2011: 59)

The Gothic provides a privileged space in which this revisioning of the subject takes place and therefore enables a rethinking of models of subjectivity at the time, which were shaped by these post-Darwinian considerations. The incorporation of the animal within the human and the human within the animal also has a specific inflection in *Dracula*, which centres on images of food and cannibalism.

Eating the animal – defining the animal

Carrie Rohman in *Stalking the Subject: Modernism and the Animal* (2009) follows a Derridean line when asserting that meat eating is conditioned by a social and ontological hierarchy. To eat meat is to gain mastery over animals because this asserts that animals, unlike people, are 'things' to be consumed (Rohman, 2009: 15).[8] The consumption of food is a recurrent theme of Harker's opening journal as he records a number of local recipes (not all of them including meat), which he would like Mina to attempt when they get married. More widely the novel makes repeated references to the consumption of food and drink which aligns the activities of the non-vampire world with the images of consumption that are associated with the vampire. Later, at Castle Dracula, Harker encounters the Count who has recently dined and notes of the now sleeping figure that:

> Even the deep, burning eyes seemed set amongst swollen flesh, for the lids and pouches underneath were bloated. It seemed as if the whole awful creature were simply gorged with blood; he lay like a filthy leech exhausted with repletion. (Stoker, 1996: 51)

Harker's horror is caused by the realisation that the Count has consumed human blood. When Harker is attacked by the three female vampires, the Count gives them a baby to drain instead (the mother of which is subsequently attacked and eaten by a pack of wolves, under the command of the Count). Harker's concern is therefore that after the Count leaves the next day, 'The coming night might see my own body a banquet' when he is fed to the three vampires (Stoker, 1996: 51). A similar horror is registered by Wells in *The War of the Worlds* (1898) where the Martians drain humans of their blood. The idea that humans might become food makes them thing-like within this gastronomic economy and the idea of humans as food gained some cultural traction in contemporary accounts of cannibalism. Richter has noted that it is important to consider the imperial context of these literary narratives which evidence a horror of cross-racial encounters combined with fears of cannibalism. In adventure stories set in jungle-like lost worlds 'Cannibalism and miscegenation epitomise the ultimate horror of cultural contact: the Other invading, assimilating and swallowing, literally, the body of the European traveller' (Richter, 2011: 120). However, these points of contact are also touched

Critical reflections

by ambivalence. As noted above, vampirism has its implicit allure for the vampire hunters, who struggle with their own inner needs and appetites, which the vampire seemingly awakens so that the essential paradox is that 'the *anxiety* of assimilation goes hand in hand with the *desire* for dissolution, diffusion, amalgamation' (Richter, 2011: 120, italics in original). This is not the articulation of a death drive, but a confused acknowledgement that in the post-Darwinian world what it means to be a human is subject to biological and emotional confusion. It also means that modernity cannot be fully trusted.

Dracula seems to pit the modern world of bourgeois (scientific and legal) knowledge against that of the Count whose feudal past aligns him with older forms of understanding. However, as Harker acknowledges in his journal 'the old centuries had, and have powers of their own which mere 'modernity' cannot kill' (Stoker, 1996: 36). Rohman has claimed that in the 1870s and 1880s Victorians implicitly countered a view of simian proximity by asserting that developments in science and culture suggested mental progress rather than troubling reversion. However, by the 1890s 'What the late literature of the Victorian…era reveals…is the lurking anxiety that this view of human privilege cannot be maintained' (Rohman, 2009: 5). In *Dracula* this is in part manifested as an epistemological uncertainty as the novel explores the competing claims on comprehending, and controlling, vampirism. Scientific and religious solutions are advanced in the novel, but ultimately it is a folkloric understanding of vampirism that proves most helpful in accounting for the physical and temporal prohibitions imposed on the vampire. The claims of modernity are undermined, as they are in *Jekyll and Hyde* and *Moreau*, as these texts bear witness to the limitations of medical and legal knowledge. These narratives are also characterised by an air of incompletion because although they ostensibly conclude on moments of apparent triumph for the dominant order, in reality we cannot be so sure of these resolutions. At the end of *Jekyll and Hyde*, for example, it is unclear whether Jekyll kills Hyde (and so restores an idea of 'human privilege') or Hyde kills Jekyll (and so represents the overthrow of such 'privilege'). We only have Utterson's claim that 'he was looking upon the body of a self-destroyer' (Stevenson, 1984: 70), which does not clarify the matter.[9] Prendick on his return to England, after the trials of Moreau's island, cannot quite return to civilisation because:

> I could not persuade myself that the men and women I met were not also another, still passably human, Beast People, animals half-wrought into the

outward images of human souls, and that they would presently begin to revert, to show first this bestial mark and then that. (Wells, 2000: 128)

The ending of *Dracula* is equally unclear as the concluding 'Note' erases the very textual authority that had been so crucial in the defeat of the Count with Jonathan Harker asserting that 'in all the mass of material of which the record is composed, there is hardly one authentic document! nothing but a mass of type-writing' so that 'We could hardly ask anyone, even did we wish to, to accept these proofs of so wild a story' (Stoker, 1996: 378). Reading and writing in the end do not appear to amount to much; even whilst the potential traces of vampirism that could have lurked within Mina may have been inherited by the baby, Quincey, that Van Helsing dandles on his knee. Any triumph of order is therefore provisional and in part this is due to the insistent presence of the denied animal, but it can also be related to the wider context of empire that the fin de siècle Gothic repeatedly engages with.

In *Empire and the Animal Body* (2012), John Miller theorises the possible points of convergence between ecocriticism and postcolonialism and how they relate to the context of late-Victorian adventure stories set in Africa (and beyond). Territory is invaded, colonised, and lost within a number of adventure narratives which bear witness to often ambivalent, and so fragile, imperial endeavours. Miller also notes a counter story to this in publications such as the *Boy's Own Paper* (established by the Religious Tract Society in 1879) which encouraged a number of similar literary narratives that corrected this possible ambivalence by asserting 'a form of literary hygiene that aim[ed] to lead the nation away from degradation and towards a re-installation of the human, and in particular the white, colonial human, un-imperilled by the degenerative effects of 'lower' forms of literature' (Miller, 2012: 152). Whilst Baden-Powell's *Scouting for Boys* (1908) would seem to represent the apogee of this movement, *Dracula* can also be read as engaging with these issues about textual hygiene, although in a complex way.

Dracula reads like a boy's own story with its focus on the defeat of Otherness and the triumph of masculine endeavour. However, it also incorporates adult themes about sexuality, money, and class that complicate the simplicity of that narrative. Nevertheless, it too, as we have seen, is interested in the idea of literary hygiene, as writing becomes a means by which one demonstrates health. To that degree we can read the novel as trying to work against the Gothic presence of the Count, so that his feudal past (and animal-like nature) can finally be laid to rest.

Critical reflections

The problem is that in the end (as witnessed by Harker's 'Note'), the text does not quite believe in itself. Writing and forms of hygiene are linked in numerous ways at the fin de siècle. In the wider context of the postcolonial and theories of the animal, for example, writing and reading healthily represent a form of mastery that works against the idea of the human as a source of food. The ability to write, so the novel suggests, demonstrates a capacity for self-reflection, which implies self-presence and self-control – values which take the subject out of the animal kingdom. The ability to use language is central to this because the illness of vampirism removes the subject from the written text. Towards the end of the novel when Mina's infection appears to be spreading, Van Helsing notes 'She make no entry into her little diary, she who write so faithful at every pause. Something whisper to me that all is not well' (Stoker, 1996: 363). Language is also central to the dictates of empire as Miller notes of the Victorian naturalist who reflects the linguistic bafflement so typical of the aphasiac in which 'For the colonial naturalist, the vast array of unassimilated organisms outside language...mirrors this bewilderment: a proliferation that demands order, yet seems to defy it' (Miller, 2012: 67). Whilst this references a specific problem with taxonomic designation, one which Van Helsing had critiqued in Seward's use of 'zoophagus', it also points towards the notion that it is only when events, objects, and exotic encounters have been turned into discourse that they gain intellectual, cultural, and moral legibility. Such an issue is notably acute within the scientific context because 'Science's effect is to make wordless bodies eloquent with reflexes, mechanisms and behaviours, to produce a body of knowledge from the uncertainty of animal behaviours' (Miller, 2012: 57). The links between writing and reading in the Gothic thus address various levels of experience (personal, scientific, ethical), which all coalesce around the idea of what it means to be a person – a topic of considerable debate at the time.

The taxonomic ambitions of nineteenth-century naturalists indicate one epistemic strand that tries to identify and locate plants and animals within a scientific system. Where to place the 'person' is another complex taxonomic strand and the example of the British Association for the Advancement of Science (BAAS), which was established in 1831, is instructive in that regard.[10] It is clear from the structure of the BAAS's annually published *Proceedings* that whilst there was scientific agreement about the presence of 'life' (which at various times created links between botany, zoology and human physiology) there is no clear conception of a 'person'. Indeed, by the 1890s where you place the 'person' is subject to considerable disciplinary instability because at various points in the *Proceedings* the lines between 'Physiology', 'Anatomy', 'Zoology' and 'Botany' were highly fragile. By the 1890s 'Physiology' included a subcategory on 'Experimental Psychology', but nevertheless where to scientifically locate the person is still unclear in part due to the consolidation of 'Anthropology' as a distinct scientific category – although one which developed out of the older category of 'Ethnology' from the 1840s. However, there are slippages with other categories, most frequently between animals and humans. In 1894, for example, a report on animal responses to changes in temperature was included under 'Physiology' whilst under 'Anthropology' there were reports on 'the Mental and Physical Condition of Children' and 'The Heredity of Acquired Characters'. The section also included a report that brought the medical and the anthropological together titled 'On the Anthropological Significance of Ticklishness' – with many of these scientific reports written by MDs rather than MAs.[11]

The question is, how can we relate this to Stoker? One intriguing possible link is to the German Max Müller, the Oxford Professor and well-known orientalist that Stoker met in the Beefsteak Room at the Lyceum and later at Oxford University. Critics such as Robert Eighteen-Bisang and Elizabeth Miller, following the work of David B. Dickens, have claimed that Müller provided the template for Van Helsing (Dickens, 1998; Eighteen-Bisang and Miller, 2008: 283). Stoker's early working notes on *Dracula* suggest that Van Helsing was an amalgam of a philosophic historian, a German professor of history, and a detective inspector and the reference to a 'German Professor' appears later in the notes as a reasserted model for Van Helsing, with the suggestion that this character would provide the necessary anthropological history of the vampire.

Max Müller was President of the Anthropological section of the BAAS and the 1892 edition of the *Proceedings*, somewhat unusually, includes the full script of his presidential address delivered in Cardiff on 20 August 1891. In it he revisited a BAAS paper from 1847 by C. J. Bunsen in which Bunsen outlined a pre-Darwinian theory that humans may be descended from animals. The points of contact between humans and animals are emotional ones so that Müller notes (following Bunsen) that 'in the vocal expression of feelings, whether of joy or pain, and in the imitation of external sounds, animals are on a level with man' (Müller, 1892: 784). The key distinguishing feature is the possession of language and for Müller it is the analysis of language that constitutes the means of understanding a culture's formation. Such an assertion is intended as a rebuke to those anthropologists who attempted to account for culture in either racial terms, or via accounts of cranial morphology – measuring heads, for Müller, just takes us back to the animals and away from the culturally specific formations of 'humanity' that language articulates. In one respect we may say that this pursuit of the language of the Other lies at the heart of a novel such as *Dracula*. Van Helsing provides some sense of the anthropology of the vampire, but the Count remains essentially like an animal – one who tellingly is not prone to the textual loquacity of the vampire hunters.

Readers and writers in *Dracula* point towards the importance of self-reflection. The novel indicates ways in which this breaks down as vampirism functions as a missing link between the human and the animal. These themes are not specific to Stoker's novel as we can see further examples in the wider culture of the fin de siècle Gothic. The limitations of science are clear in these examples, but so is just how fragile the notion of the 'human' was at the end of the nineteenth century. The Gothic is a form that so often, despite its frequently superficial political reactions, rethinks the dominant culture in complex ways. The contribution that animal studies can make to both scholarship on the Gothic and to accounts of the nineteenth century provides us with one way in which we, as critics, can radically revision the period.

Notes

1 Publishing developments include 'Gothic Literary Studies' and 'Gothic Authors: Critical Revisions' published by the University of Wales Press, the 'International Gothic' imprint published by Manchester University Press and 'The Edinburgh Companions to the Gothic' series published by Edinburgh University Press. There are also several journals dedicated to the Gothic including the long standing *Gothic Studies*, published by Manchester University Press and *Horror Studies*, published by Intellect. There are also several online journals such as *Gothic Fiction Studies*, *Diegesis*, and the *Irish Journal of Gothic and Horror Studies*, to name but a few. Key critical publications on the Gothic from the 1980s include David Punter's *The Literature of Terror* (1980), Rosemary Jackson's *Fantasy: the Literature of Subversion* (1981), and Christine Brooke-Rose's *The Rhetoric of the Unreal* (1981).
2 See Coleridge's *Christabel* (1798–1801), Shelley's *Zastrozzi* (1810), *St. Irvyne; or, The Rosicrucian* (1811) and *The Cenci* (1819), and Keats's *Lamia* (1820). An early critical text that explored the place of the Gothic within Romanticism is Mario Praz's *The Romantic Agony* (1933).
3 For an account of dog breeding and *Hound of the Baskervilles* see Pemberton, 2012.

4 Reference to degeneration is also applied to Selden the escaped criminal who is hiding on the moor and who is described as having 'an evil yellow face, a terrible animal face, all seamed and scored with vile passions' (Doyle, 1996: 102). Holmes appears on the spectrum of abnormality due to his apparent 'genius'.
5 See Cesare Lombroso, *Criminal Man* (1876) and Max Nordau, *Degeneration* (1993 [1892, first English translation 1895]).
6 The topic of reading healthily in *Dracula* was explored in a seminar I led on the novel with MA students at the University of Sheffield, and I would particularly like to acknowledge the contribution of Ellen Nicholls to that discussion which has stimulated the following reading of health.
7 For an interesting account of how the representations of dogs in *Dracula* draw upon the rabies scare of the 1870s, see McKechnie, 2013.
8 Rohman draws upon Derrida, 1991. Other important texts which discuss meat eating include Fiddes, 1992 and Fudge, 2010.
9 The narrative 'Henry Jekyll's Full Statement of the Case' does not clarify the issue either, as the tenses shift throughout the document leaving it unclear who narrates the final line 'Here, then, as I lay down the pen, and proceed to seal up my confession, I bring the life of that unhappy Henry Jekyll to an end' (Stevenson, 1984: 97). By this point it could be either Jekyll or Hyde who narrates.
10 The British Association for the Advancement of Science produced annual *Proceedings* until 1938. The association still exists in the form of the British Science Association.
11 See *The Proceedings of the British Association for the Advancement of Science*, 1894: 776, 778.

References

Armstrong, Philip (2008). *What Animals Mean in the Fiction of Modernity*. London and New York: Routledge.
Derrida, Jacques (1991). '"Eating Well," or "The Calculation of the Subject": An Interview with Jacques Derrida', in *Who Comes After the Subject?* ed. Eduardo Cadava, Peter Connor and Jean-Luc Nancy. New York: Routledge, pp. 96–119.
Dickens, David B. (1998). 'The German Matrix of Stoker's Dracula', in *Dracula: The Shade and the Shadow*, ed. Elizabeth Miller. Westcliffe-on-Sea: Desert Island Books, pp. 31–40.
Doyle, Arthur Conan (1996). *The Hound of the Baskervilles*. Harmondsworth: Penguin.
Eighteen-Bisang, Robert and Elizabeth Miller (2008). Eds., *Bram Stoker's Notes for* Dracula: *A Facsimile Edition*. Jefferson, NC: McFarland.
Fiddes, Nick (1992). *Meat: A Natural Symbol*. New York and London: Routledge.

Foldy, Michael (1997). *The Trials of Oscar Wilde: Deviance, Morality, and Late-Victorian Society*. New Haven, CT and London: Yale University Press.

Fudge, Erica (2010). 'Why it's easy being a vegetarian', *Textual Practice* 24(1): 149–66.

Kilgour, Maggie (1998). 'Vampiric Arts: Stoker's Defense of Poetry', in *Bram Stoker: History, Psychoanalysis and the Gothic*, eds. William Hughes and Andrew Smith. Basingstoke: Macmillan, pp. 47–61.

Lombroso, Cesare (1876). *Criminal Man*. Milan: Ulricho Hoepli.

Machen, Arthur (2010). *The Great God Pan*. Cardigan: Parthian.

McKechnie, Claire Charlotte (2013). 'Man's Best Friend: Evolution, Rabies, and the Gothic Dog.' *Nineteenth-Century Prose* 40(1): 115–40.

Miller, John (2012). *Empire and the Animal: Violence, Identity and Ecology in Victorian Adventure Fiction*. London: Anthem.

Müller, Max (1892). 'Presidential Address', in *The Proceedings of the British Association for the Advancement of Science*. London: John Murray, pp. 782–96.

Nordau, Max (1993 [1892]) *Degeneration*. Intro., George L. Mosse. Lincoln, NE and London: University of Nebraska Press.

Pemberton, Neil (2012). 'Hounding Holmes, Arthur Conan Doyle Bloodhounds and Sleuthing in the Late-Victorian Imagination'. Special issue on 'Victorian Animals', eds, Claire Charlotte McKechnie and John Miller. *Journal of Victorian Culture* 17(4): 454–67.

Praz, Mario (1933). *The Romantic Agony*. Oxford: Oxford University Press.

Richter, Virginia (2011). *Literature After Darwin: Human Beasts in Western Fiction, 1859–1939*. Basingstoke: Palgrave.

Rohman, Carrie (2009). *Stalking the Subject: Modernism and the Animal*. New York: Columbia University Press.

Stevenson, Robert Louis (1984). *The Strange Case of Dr Jekyll and Mr Hyde and Other Stories*, ed. and intro. Jenni Calder. Harmondsworth: Penguin.

Stoker, Bram (1996). *Dracula*, intro. Maud Ellmann. Oxford: Oxford University Press.

Wells, H. G. (2000). *The Island of Doctor Moreau*, ed. Brain Aldiss. London: Everyman.

Part II

Rethinking national contexts and exchanges

5

The global circulation of Victorian actants and ideas: liberalism and liberalisation in the niche of nature, culture, and technology

Regenia Gagnier

Global processes, local niches

The study of world literature is rapidly growing in contested terrains: world literature as the best; as bearer of universal values; as circulating in translation/remediation; in relation to power and domination (in relation to postcolonial studies, for example); in relation to globalisation; in relation to commodification. Central to current debates about the value of world literature is the relation of world, a place or lifeworld that we inhabit, to globalisation, a process or transformation that often acts upon us. This suggests the positive, cosmopolitan, diversity-friendly connotations of world literature, while also showing the pitfalls of its analysis, that is, historical and present inequalities.

While the globalisation of literature is ancient and the globalisation of literary studies inevitable, there is often presumed division between the generalisers with larger hypotheses, comparisons and perspectives, and the particularisers, devoted to the local, thick description, and cultural difference (Felski and Friedman, 2009). The particularisers see the dangers of homogenising processes allegedly rooted in the encyclopedic ambitions and evolutionary models of nineteenth-century European thought, distorting the uniqueness of the objects compared; reducing them to variants on a common standard; often devaluing some cultures in relation to others. The generalisers claim that the larger perspectives serve as a jolt to consciousness, initiating a destabilising, even humbling, awareness of the limits and contingency of one's own perspective.

This chapter will consider some implications for Victorian Studies suggested by recent developments in the fields of world literatures and globalisation studies. It will draw attention to the global scope of Victorian literature as an actant in world affairs, as in processes of liberalisation, democratisation, and trade, but also to the specificity of each local environment and moment of transculturation. It hopes to make a methodological intervention on behalf of interdisciplinary and intercultural studies by providing a framework to address two current problems. First, how may we, in language and literature studies, best trace global processes of modernisation, democratisation, and liberalisation without losing the specificity of the local? Global processes transform local environments, yet each locality is transformed distinctively, depending on its unique indigenous traditions. Second, how may we best study the uniqueness of distinct locales where the forces of tradition and modernisation meet? If the first problem requires translators and transculturalists who know literary history and history of genres, the second requires the disciplines relating to environment: nature (natural sciences), culture (the humanities), and technology (social sciences, engineering, and medicine). And indeed in producing this chapter I have been able to draw on multilingual collaborators including The Global Circulation Project and an interdisciplinary research centre: Egenis, The Centre for the Study of Life Sciences.[1]

Egenis was founded in 2002, roughly coinciding with the first mapping of the human genome in 2003, to study the social implications of science. Through it, we have developed a symbiological approach that allows us to focus on specific environments at moments of change and transformation:

> Recent developments in molecular biology imply that classic distinctions between nature and nurture or biology and culture are not applicable to the human ecological niche. Research in epigenetics shows that the effects of culture on nature go all the way down to the gene and up to the stratosphere, and the effects of biology on culture are similarly inextricable. Living systems almost invariably involve the interaction of many kinds of organisms with a diversity of technologies. The anthropocene – the age of human cultures and technologies impacting on natural environments – changes rapidly, and to understand and manage its functioning requires perspectives from each domain. Symbiology is the post-organismic study

of relations-in-process. The kinds of relations we study include symmetric mutuality (relations among equals in power or status), asymmetric mutuality (relations among unequals – parents/offspring, teacher/pupil, human/nonhuman animals), recognition, reciprocity, solubility, domination, parasitism, alienation, isolation, and so forth, and these relations are discernible throughout nature and all cultures. (Gagnier in Egenis, 2002-)

This chapter will argue that the intercultural transvaluation of actants and ideas often associated with Victorian Britain will be central not only to the development of Victorian Studies in global contexts made possible by new media, but also to other disciplines concerned with globalisation, transculturation, and liberalisation. The actants I discuss here include Victorian geopolitical ideologies such as individualism, collectivism, nationalism, internationalism, and cosmopolitanism, but with more space we could include geopolitical institutions and state apparatuses such as modes of government, trade, legal systems, armed services, and geopolitical commodities and technologies such as cotton, tea, water, transport and sanitation systems, around which lives and literatures are built. We ask what is in the specific niche that is crossed by global processes, and what are the salient actants in these relations-in-process.

Liberal individualism

The Qing Dynasty collapsed in 1911 with formal submission in 1912. The reforming literati, often associated with the May Fourth or New Culture Movements, experimented widely with western and other models that they might use in reforming China. In Lu Xun's term (拿来主义, *nalai zhuyi*) they translated, 'grabbed', or borrowed what they needed from western works and rejected what they could not use. They translated and intensely debated Charles Darwin's theory of evolution via Thomas Huxley's 'Evolution and Ethics' (trans. 1898), Adam Smith's *Wealth of Nations* (trans. 1902), J. S. Mill's *On Liberty* (trans. 1903), and Herbert Spencer's *Study of Sociology* (trans. 1903). As they were concerned about China's relation to expanding and emerging British, American and Japanese empires, they emphasised Spencer's social Darwinism rather more than Darwinian evolutionary theory. Freud was translated in 1907, and by 1900 the term 'geren' (个人, individual) meaning something like the western sense of individualism, entered Chinese (Liu, 1995; Shih, 2001). Today among sinologists this period of experimentation with external models primarily from Britain is often termed 'The History of Modern Critical Consciousness'.

Rethinking national contexts and exchanges

While the reforming literati were often critical of western materialism and domination over other cultures, they were interested in forms of liberal individualism as developed by Mill, as well as the challenges to Millian progressivism launched by Freud and Nietzsche in the forms of unconscious motivation and the critical transvaluation of liberal values. They were also interested in Darwinism as a critique of human exceptionalism (which resonated with Daoism; see Yang, 2013), Malthusianism as competition for scarce natural resources, and, as mentioned, social Darwinism, the survival of the fittest, as competition between nations and empires. Above all, they were interested in models of scientific and technological progress and its effects on human subjectivity, rather as Marx and Engels had been in their understanding of human freedom as beginning with labour and technology and unfreedom with their alienation.

Specialists in transculturation frequently emphasise the two-way, triangulated, or even multilateral nature of exchange when cultures come in contact. When we turn to cultural translation of specific works we are no longer engaged in literary appreciation, which focuses on the ontology of the masterpiece, the way that the masterpiece unfolds creatively and fits together as a whole or *gestalt*. Rather, we are looking at the phenomenology of a work's circulation, including the structure of the field of transnational cultural exchanges, political or economic constraints that influence the exchanges, the agents or actants (in Bruno Latour's sense of actants as human or nonhuman agents with causal effects – Latour, 1997; 2004) of intermediation, and the processes of export and import. We think in terms less of genius and originality than in terms of circulation, appropriation, use, transtextuality, revoicing, reaccentuation, indigenisation, mediation.

In the case of J. S. Mill's *On Liberty* (1859) in China, as translated by the polymath Yan Fu who had been trained as a naval engineer at Greenwich in Britain, we can see the processes of transculturation at work. Mill's work is the *locus classicus* of the western liberal tradition. Written to protect the individual not only against a strong State but especially against a growing 'marketplace of ideas' within an increasingly powerful commercial press, Mill emphasised tolerance of individual diversity in the face of mass society; absolute liberty of thought and discussion; and critique of dogmatism, authoritarianism, and intolerance at all costs except injury to others. Mill emphasised critique, debate, and tolerance because, for him, seeking out the truth amid the many competing interests of modern society was difficult, and only by the widest possible attention to different perspectives might one be able to discern the path best for the many. This was the closest that we could come to the pursuit of truth as the Utilitarians understood it.

When Yan Fu (严复》) translated *On Liberty* into wenyan or classical Chinese (a script only accessible to well-educated peers), his interest was less in epistemology and the rights of the individual and more in the relation of the individual's responsibilities to the collective, a basic problem that exercised the Chinese reformers. Translated as *The Boundary between Self and Group*《群己权界论》(1903), Yan's work, unlike Mill's, maintained objective social norms that in most cases derived from long established Confucian teachings, including clear boundaries between self and group, and a clear moral and social order. In Yan's translation, Mill's epistemological pessimism was de-emphasised (Huang, 2008). Yan Fu writes:

> If people formed a group in which everyone was free to do as one liked without restriction, it would be mired in conflict, and the world would be dominated by might. Therefore, even if one has freedom, its limit must arise out of the right others equally have to freedom. This is the principle of *xieju* from the Great Learning, with which scholar-officials are able to pacify the world. The purpose of Mill's book is to distinguish between the extent to which one may be free and that to which one should be unfree. (Huang, 2008: 92)

Max Ko-wu Huang has studied the translation and dissemination of *On Liberty* in detail. At one point, in the turmoil of early Republican China, Yan lost the manuscript, rather like Mill's maid allegedly burning Mill's copy of Carlyle's *French Revolution*. When the lost manuscript of the translation was returned to Yan, he wrote 'The future of my 400,000,000 compatriots truly relies on it…Heaven was unable to bear the sorrow of its loss' (Huang, 2008: 94–5). When Yan Fu was dying of opium addiction – opium being arguably a transcultural actant between British trade policy and a Chinese government too weak to resist it – he committed his last words on the boundary between the self and group. While he credited Mill's significance (see below), his emphasis was no longer Mill's. Yan instructed his son in his will (1921) to respect tradition as well as change and not to put the individual before the group:

> Keep in mind that China will not perish and that ancient principles can be reformed, but must not be abandoned. Keep in mind that, to lead an enjoyable life, staying healthy is the most important condition. Keep in mind that one has to work hard, and understand that time passes and will never

return. Keep in mind that one must constantly reflect and think about things in a systematic way. Keep in mind that one must forever learn and absorb new kinds of knowledge, but understand that the perfect achievement of a goal in one's moral and intellectual pursuits is never easy. *As for the relations between self and group, remember that the group is of greater importance than the self.* (Huang, 2008: 107, italics added)

Yan was concerned that individual freedom in the West was not balanced with a moral order and social justice. His Confucian ideals of 'depending on the self', 'completing the developments of the self', 'seeking value within oneself', Daoism's 'freedom', and Yan, Zhu's 'acting to benefit oneself' made him appreciate Mill's belief in the individual as a distinct moral subject endowed with freedom, but this was within a balanced relationship between self and group, not the Faustian-Promethean individualism of much western literature. Yet Mill's *On Liberty* had an afterlife well beyond Yan Fu. In 1961, the scientist Mao Zishu wrote, 'Since the creation of writing, Mill's book stands out as one of the most precious works ever written' for its positive freedom, correlating freedom with a moral concern with others (Huang, 2008: 94–5). And in 1989, echoes of Mill, now much closer to the original, were among the voices of the protestors in Tiananmen Square 'to wrench from the state its monopoly on truth and the moral way and to open up a space for the individual subject' (cited in Kelly and Reid, 1998: 106).

Perhaps the most far-reaching afterlife was in the great modernist Lao She's thought experiment on the suitability of western individualism in China's modernisation in *Rickshaw Boy* (Lao, 2010). Lao She's (1899–1966) *Rickshaw Boy* (骆驼祥子, Luòtuo Xiángzi [Camel Lucky Lad] 1936–39) is a modern classic attributed with establishing the vernacular and common people in Chinese literature. The novel has been translated into 30 languages, and has sold 70 million copies in Russian alone; the numbers in sinophone languages have yet to be calculated (Shu, 2011). The plot is of an orphaned peasant, Xiangzi, who comes to Beijing (then Beiping, the name 'northern peace' used during the Republican era) from the countryside to make his way in the world. He is a model of a competitively fit specimen of humanity in a situation of self-reliant autonomy: '[Xiangzi] did not smoke, he did not drink, and he did not gamble. With no bad habits and no family burdens, there was nothing to keep him from his goal as long as he persevered' (Lao, 2010). He is healthy, strong, intelligent, capable, and willing to work for self-advancement, and he arrives with the goal of buying a rickshaw to make his living:

Xiangzi's hands trembled more than ever as he tucked the warranty away and pulled the rickshaw out, nearly in tears. He took it to a remote spot to look it over, his very own rickshaw. He could see his face in the lacquer finish...It occurred to him that he was twenty-two years old. Since his parents had died when he was very young, he had forgotten the day of his birth and had not celebrated a birthday since coming to the city. All right, he said to himself, I bought a new rickshaw today, so this will count as a birthday, mine and the rickshaw's. There was nothing to stop him from considering man and rickshaw as one. (Lao, 2010: 12)

Initially he identifies with his rickshaw, even physically works as one with it, each as an extension of the power of the other:

> Xiangzi did not notice [the cold], for his resolve pointed to a bright future...Sometimes a strong headwind made it hard to breathe, but he lowered his head, clenched his teeth, and forged ahead, like a fish swimming upstream. Strong winds stiffened his resistance, as if he were locked in a fight to the death...When he laid down the shafts, he straightened up, exhaled grandly, and wiped the dust from the corner of his mouth, feeling invincible. (Lao, 2010: 94)

Xiangzi sees the desperate condition of the old rickshaw men but pursues his individual goal heartened by his own capacities.

Yet with repeated setbacks and misfortunes, Xiangzi begins to adjust to the daily life of struggle, becoming less and less ambitious. He becomes alienated from his labour and his rickshaw becomes merely instrumental:

> A rickshaw was nothing to be pampered. No longer did he fancy buying one of his own, nor did he care about those owned by others. They were just rickshaws. When he pulled one, he ate and paid the rent; when he didn't, he paid no rent...That was the relationship – the only relationship – between man and rickshaw. (Lao, 2010: 259)

He takes some consolation with others and begins to feel solidarity. Yet with more misfortune, he turns to crime, violence, apathy, and anomie. He quits feeling, talking, becomes more and more alienated and isolated. The last chapter shows a brilliant Beiping in summer, full of life and colour, but also of cruelty, betrayal, and sadism, a people entertained by state killings. Lao She said that the moral was that 'Individualism cannot be of use in a corrupt society.' The development of each and of all are interdependent. The last lines are:

> Respectable, ambitious, idealistic, self-serving, individualist, robust, and mighty, Xiangzi took part in untold numbers of burial processions but could not predict when he would bury himself, when he would lay this

Rethinking national contexts and exchanges

degenerate, selfish, hapless product of a sick society, this miserable ghost of individualism, to rest. (Lao, 2010: 300)

We have discussed how the modernisers like Lao She transformed the genre of the novel in introducing common people and vernacular. A symbiological approach also considers the specific niche in which the story takes place, the environment in which the literature evolves. In the case of *Rickshaw Boy*, we can trace the liberalisation of the rickshaw itself as actant. From Japanese *jinrikisha* (人力車, literally 'human-powered vehicle'), pulled rickshaws appeared in Tokyo in 1868. By 1874, 300 were imported to Shanghai. By 1879, there were 2500 in Shanghai, and by the 1920s, one sixth of all males in Beijing were pullers. By the time of the novel the rickshaw had become the rural immigrant's door to independence. Yet in 1949 hand-pulled rickshaws were abandoned by the PRC as undignified labour. In the 1990s cycle rickshaws, no longer hand-pulled, had become a tourist attraction, and in Dhaka, Bangladesh hand-decorated 'expressive rickshaws' advertised their owners as individual performers as well as transporters. In 2006 the Communist mayor of Kolkata declared that 'We cannot imagine one man sweating to pull another.' And in the latest – green – revolution, the cycle rickshaw in New York City, now called a pedicab, has become the choice for sustainable transport, with owners being commuters and shoppers rather than labourers (Banu, 2011; Strand, 1989).

Liberalisation and caste

If we turn to India in the nineteenth century after the Napoleonic invasions, global liberals participated in transregional or global spheres of liberal discourse. Rammohan Roy (from the 1820s), Romesh Chunder Dutt (1870s), Dadabhai Naoroji (1880s), G. K. Gokhale (1900s), to B. R. Ambedkar (from the 1920s) criticised the Raj from within it, and the liberal writings of Tagore, Gandhi, Nehru and novelists Bankim Chatterjee and Mulk Raj Anand continued the debates up to and through independence. They sympathised with Chartists, Mazzini's republican radicalism, American and Irish struggles against Britain, and others who had experienced slavery and racial prejudice. They deployed arguments from *Uncle Tom's Cabin* (1852), Byron, Mill, Dickens, and Ruskin. Even when they were ignored by their intended European interlocutors, they were raising consciousness among home audiences of liberalism even under conditions of exploitation and humiliation. (Mulk Raj Anand would later say that humiliation was the cause of nationalism in India – Kochler, 1978). The Indian liberals developed a sophisticated mathematical rhetoric of statistics that they deployed against the metrics of the Raj. They referred to indigenous traditions of Vedantic continuity, in other words, revelation stressing self-realisation, as a nation as well as individuals, and over time multicultural India revealed relations of individual rights to group beliefs that problematised liberalism to its core (Bayly, 2012; Guha, 2007; Khilnani, 2012).

At the same time as Lao She's *Rickshaw Boy*, Mulk Raj Anand's *Untouchable* (1935) also took up the problem of the individual, now in relation to caste, beginning with the untouchable's labour in the latrines. Anand was taken as the social novelist, the 'Dickens of India', and the novel was legendarily edited by Gandhi as part of his assault on caste. Like Xiangzi, the young male protagonist Bakha is a model of an individual, entirely capable, self-reliant, and confident:

> [Bakha] worked away earnestly, quickly, without loss of effort. Brisk, yet steady, his capacity for active application to the task he had in hand seemed to flow like constant water from a natural spring. Each muscle of his body, hard as a rock when it came into play, seemed to shine forth like glass. He must have had immense pent-up resources lying deep, deep in his body, for as he rushed along with considerable skill and alacrity from one door-less latrine to another, cleaning, brushing, pouring phenol, he seemed as easy as a wave sailing away on a deep-bedded river…Though his job was dirty he remained clean. He didn't even soil his sleeves, handling the commodes, sweeping and scrubbing them…It was perhaps his absorption in his task that gave him the look of distinction. (Anand, 1940: 15)

Whereas Xiangzi's nemesis is social corruption, Bakha's and the climax of the novel is the catastrophic touching (Anand, 1940: 47–8), when Bakha accidentally brushes against an upper caste merchant and causes a scandal on the streets:

> His first impulse was to run, just to shoot across the throng, away, away, far away from the torment. But then he realisised that he was surrounded by a barrier, not a physical barrier, because one push from his hefty shoulders would have been enough to unbalance the skeleton-like bodies of the Hindu merchants, but a moral one. He knew that contact with him if he pushed through would defile a great many more of these men. (pp. 47–8)

On the run now, Bakha's life begins to unravel. The final scenes of the novel find him running from the defilement he has unwittingly caused and coming upon Gandhi, who is addressing the multitude. Listening to the Mahatma, those nearest Bakha begin to debate the possible solutions to the problem of caste and untouchability.

The first possibility is that of Christianity and its premise of the sacredness of each individual soul. This is appealing for its egalitarianism, but Christianity cannot be communicated by the missionary in the novel, who is arrogant and smug in his promotion of the Bible over the Gita. Then there are Gandhi's own solutions of *Swaraj* (freedom, self-rule, what in African emerging nations was known as *Uhuru*, independence) and the conservative *Swadeshi* (economic self-sufficiency). The last solution proposed is that of technology: flush toilets and sanitation systems, which in the novel are associated with the poet Iqbal Nath Sarshar, editor of *New Era*, and, of course, Jawaharlal Nehru.

Mulk Raj Anand had studied and worked with London liberals and democratic socialists E. M. Forster and George Orwell at the offices of the *Criterion*, University College London, Cambridge, and in Bloomsbury. In July 1974, Anand contributed a lecture and essay 'The Search for National Identity in India' to UNESCO's (United Nations Educational, Scientific and Cultural Organisation) International Progress Organisation: 'The Cultural Self-comprehension of Nations' at Innsbruck, Austria. In his essay (in Kochler, 1978), Anand traces a history of multicultural and modernising India through key figures: in the sixteenth century Akbar ('The Great') wanted to unite Hindus, Muslims, Christians, Zoroastrians, and aboriginals. His grandson Aurangzeb wanted one religion, Muslim, so the great dream of one Hindustan was eclipsed. Cultural self-comprehension came to the fore only at the end of the nineteenth century, what Anand calls 'humiliation as the cause of nationalism' under British political unification. Raja Ram Mohan Roy was just one of the intellectuals who thought that the West and India could combine to benefit both, and welcomed English for arts and sciences. The elite Rabindranath Tagore, mindful of the peasants, also looked to the present, modern world rather than transcendent time, and emphasised individual freedom in both western and Brahmanic senses of autonomy. His nationalism of one's own country as part of one harmonious world partook of global hopes for internationalism. His friend Gandhi sought to unite India in complete political freedom, *Purna Swaraj*, through non-violence (non-cooperation), and *Swadeshi* (as in cotton manufacture). Nehru furthered modern economic India, combining practical science and technology with Gandhian vision. Seeing historical unity in the diversity of India's history, Nehru developed Parliamentary democracy and discarded East/West polarities altogether (Kochler, 1978). He accepted the Muslim theocracy of Pakistan but not the two-nation theory. *Untouchable* ends with Gandhi's invocation and Nehru's science and technology. Today a spokesperson for the Dalitbahujans (not only untouchables, Dalits, but now also tribals, poor women, and the so-called OBCs [Other Backward Communities]), Kancha Ilaiah claims that the persistence of caste is attributable to the fact that the Indian Liberals were abstract liberals, constructing nationalism within their own caste (Brahmanic) image, and thus could not remove caste from the national (Hindu) religion. Referring to the image from the Vedas – 'His mouth became the Brahmin [the priest or intellectual caste]; his arms were made into the warrior [*kshatriya*], his thighs the people [*vaishiya* or merchants/tradespeople], and from his feet the servants [*shudra*] were born' (Khilnani, 2012: loc. 545–7) – Ilaiah claims that 'the brahmanical interaction with nature is anti-production as the brahmanical forces interact with the forces of nature only to consume or destroy them' (Ilaiah, 2010: loc. 503–4). He argues that Brahmanic book knowledge is merely 'idealist' and must be counterpoised with the techno-economic knowledge of the Dalitbahujans, whom he describes as more empirically oriented, like applied scientists and engineers, within their own specific niches:

> While confronting nature, the Dalitbahujans show enormous courage and confidence but while confronting people [of higher caste] who look different and claim to be superior, they suffer from historical diffidence. This diffidence is constructed over a period of centuries. They study very carefully what is available in nature. They are very comfortable in dealing with animals, birds and their human essence has been consistently expressed in feeding animals and in training many of them to be human friendly. They have more of an investigative psychology than an imaginative ability like the Brahmans have. For example, most of the Dalitbahujans know the whole range of mineral wealth underground and overground. They have an ability to grasp the smells of soil, animals and they know how to test metals, stones, trees, plants, leaves and so on. (Ilaiah, 2010: loc. 438–46)

Ilaiah concludes 'the Dalitbahujans call their hands *matti chetulu* (meant for soil) whereas the brahmanical forces call their hands *pooja chetulu* (meant for worship)' (loc. 544–5) and 'The Dalitbahujan...evolved a culture of 'labour as life' as against the brahmanical method of 'eat and worship', which in effect means a life of leisure' (loc. 3452–4).

Ilaiah traces Hindu caste back to the Vedas and contrasts it with western philosophy: 'European thinkers...went back to nature and productive social forces, but not to the Bible as the Indian nationalists have gone back to the Vedas' (loc. 380). Such internal debates in India highlight the extent of communitarianism underlying any individualisms. 'Will someone in the social sciences write a dissertation on how the rise of individualism in Bengal (in contrast to the West) destroyed rather than energised entrepreneurship. How, in India, caste and community drive capital and the free market?' asked Amit Chaudhuri in 2013 in *Calcutta: Two Years in the City* (Chaudhuri, 2013: 18), his reflection on the intense transformations of the city of his birth. And the historian of *India After Gandhi*, Ramachandra Guha, writes about the difference between Indian and British forms of individualism, a difference entrenched by the British:

> Within England the growth of liberal values placed a premium on the sovereignty of the individual; but in the colonies the individual was always seen as subordinate to the community. This was evident in government employment, where care was taken to balance numbers of Muslim and Hindu staff, and in politics, where the British introduced communal electorates, such that Muslims voted exclusively for other Muslims. Most British officials were predisposed to prefer Muslims, for, compared with Hindus, their forms of worship and ways of life were less alien. Overall, colonial policy deepened religious divisions, which helped consolidate the white man's rule. (Guha, 2007: loc. 804–9)

Today, caste continues to play a role in Indian democracy, often less 'one person, one vote' than communitarian politics.

Socialist individualism, national internationalism

Our final example of transcultural transvaluations of actants and ideas associated with Victorian liberalism and liberalisation begins with Oscar Wilde's 'The Soul of Man Under Socialism' (1982 [1891]), an essay that was often taken lightly in London (and subsequently in Victorian Studies) but circulated widely throughout the Communist world. Wilde had argued in characteristically brilliant fashion that in order for individualism to flourish, society would first have to institute a level playing field through socialist redistribution. Only from an initial basis of equality would people then be able to develop in accordance with their different and unique talents and capacities. In his 'Défense de la culture' speech at the 1935 International Writers' Conference in Paris, the young, anti-fascist André Gide, long an admirer of Wilde, used Wilde's ideas to promote international universality through national particularity. Gide addressed the confederation:

> There are, for peoples as for individuals, certain indices of particular refractions, and this is precisely the great interest of our cosmopolitan meeting… the culture that we aspire to defend is the sum of the particular cultures of each nation. This culture is our common good. It is common to all of us. It is international. (qtd in Tran, 2012: 370)

Like Wilde, William Morris, Edward Carpenter, Eleanor Marx, and others of the *Fin de Siècle*, Gide was working his way into being that Victorian-inspired combination of socialist individualist and national Internationalist (Gagnier, 2010). He said:

> For my part, I claim to be strongly internationalist while remaining intensely French. In like manner, I am a fervent individualist, though I am in full agreement with the communist outlook, and am actually helped in my individualism by communism. (qtd in Tran, 2012: 370).

On the topic of World Literatures, Gide spoke out for universalism through particularity: 'What could be more particularly Spanish than Cervantes, English than Shakespeare, Russian than Gogol, French than Rabelais or Voltaire – at the same time what could be more general and more profoundly human' (qtd in Tran, 2012: 371).

Gide's remarks at the International Writers' Conference then appear in the Art for Art's Sake Debates of 1935–39 in colonial Annam (French *Indochine*; today Vietnam), so the relevant empire in which the Victorian Wilde's ideas were translated was the French and the relevant movement was the Communist International. Gide was attractive to the Vietnamese for what they called his 'romanticism' (for them, the value he placed on individual subjective expression) and his 'realism' (for them, his representation of the real struggles of the masses). In the Art for Art's Sake debates, the critic and activist Hoài Thanh cited Gide in developing a cosmopolitan outlook:

> Gide expresses his complete commitment to individualism. Individualism does not contradict communism, but rather individualism needs communism in order to reach complete fruition. The more an individual develops his character the more the collective benefits, Gide claims. The same is true for each national culture: the more each enunciates its distinctiveness, the more [hu]mankind benefits. (cited in Tran, 2012: 374)

While Hoài Thanh was rebutted and his cause ultimately defeated by 'realist' Marxists, Gide's model of universality through particularity broke with the Confucian instrumental use of literature for the State in favour of creative and personal expression. Hoài Thanh thought that this would lead to ethically autonomous individuals who would benefit the collective. The free development and articulation of the individual could only be realised by the free development and articulation of all, as Wilde had proposed.

We could continue with other examples of transculturation between the Victorians and other modernising cultures. During Korea's colonial period under the Japanese, the Theatre Arts Research Association (TARA 1931–39) leaders Yu Ch'ijin and Ham Sedŏk drew on the Irish Renaissance/Celtic Twilight 'to establish a New Drama in Korea' (Hwang, 2012). Between 1910 and 1945, they introduced the poet-dramatists of the Irish uprising against Britain – Augusta Lady Gregory, John Millington Synge, Edward Plunkett, Lord Dunsany, Sean O'Casey, and W. B. Yeats – whose drama provided objective correlatives for Korea under colonisation: mad mothers whose sons do not return, deserted fields, hopeless symbolic seas. They developed both romantic realism that provided symbols for the emotions of colonisation, such as that that Neil Lazarus calls 'inconsolability' (Lazarus, 2011: 30–1, 214, and passim), and classic realisms opening the drama to the life of common people. We could go on to compare the literatures of other rebellions and civil wars, such as Lee Kyun-Young's striking *The Other Side of Dark Remembrance* (2001 [1979, trans.1983]), in which Lee deals with the Korean War only mediated through memory. Comparative studies of specific niches such as the literatures of civil war (English, American, Irish, Korean); the literature of the village in Bengal and in the south-west of England; the literature of the mines in Sichuan and in Wales; the literature of the plantation in Haiti, the southern USA, and the manor house in Yorkshire; or the New Woman literature in London and Shanghai, are another way to approach the transculturaltion processes that we can expect in future scholarship.

Asian freedoms

In *Asian Freedoms: the Idea of Freedom in East and Southeast Asia* (Kelly and Reid, 1998), the contributors, mostly Asian area studies social scientists and political theorists, claim that western ideas of freedom have circulated widely in Asia but have had radically different careers depending on the local stock of concepts or practices onto which they have been grafted. One common stock has been manifest in the tension between western individual freedoms and Buddhist and Confucian concepts of a well-ordered society, subject to rules. Beginning with slavery in Athens and Rome, over the last 2,500 years the western end of Eurasia developed notions of freedom in contrast to slavery. In contrast with the West, where freedom was the opposite of slavery, in many Asian cultures it only became so in the nineteenth and twentieth centuries under colonisation; it was then contrasted with external domination. Before that, freedom denoted hierarchical privileges exercised according to one's rank or status in a family, community, or in the service of the king. (Hence Hegel's notorious dictum in *The Philosophy of History* [1837], 'the east knew and to the present day knows only that *one* is free; the Greek and Roman world, that *some* are free; the German world knows that *all* are free' [Teggart, 1949: 405–6]. However, Hegel's idea that the end of history would come about through the progressive disciplining of the self-consciousness of 'uncontrolled natural will' conferring modern freedom, or freedom under constraint, producing the self-regulating modern western individual might be better achieved in 'Confucian' social relations of respect than in the hedonism of mass consumer society in the West.) China had had bureaucratic absolutism for 2,000 years, and freedom (*ziyou)* implied licence, doing what you liked at everyone else's expense, at least until the nineteenth century. Freedom in Asian societies is often a stage, a product of development and education, rather than opposed to slavery or related to 'class.' In Thai, for example, according to Thanet Aphornsuvan, the concept of the social does not begin with individuals, abstracting them into a totality (that is, 'society'), but rather with the concrete relations operating between members of the social order (Kelly and Reid, 1998: 164), much closer, in fact, to Kantian ideas of autonomy as against heteronomy, or Mill's of education as bringing one's heteronomous desires into the service of the social good.

A careful reading of *Asian Freedoms* throws up many distinct but often overlapping ideas of freedom throughout Asia:

- Freedom as a value or status to be prized for its own sake, including rights to be involved in making political, economic, philosophic, and cultural/lifestyle decisions about oneself and one's society: 'freedoms to'.
- Freedom as hierarchical privilege or status in a family, community, or service (Confucian: Kung Fu 551 BCE–479 BCE): generated not from an opposite – slavery – but from a relationship of recognition, respect, and duty.
- Freedom (*ziyou*) as licence, doing what one liked at everyone else's expense.
- Freedom from suffering, pain and poverty (Buddhism).

- Freedom from poverty, pain, ignorance (socialism).
- Freedom from claims of family, State, property and ties (Buddhism).
- Freedom from State control (SE Asia) or foreign control (China).
- Freedom as revolutionary liberation from despots or foreign control.
- Freedom as a stage of development, a school rather than a market. Individual freedom only after an education guided by elites had instilled virtue and wisdom.
- Meritocratic civil service exam premissing liberty on equality (in Vietnam since the 11th century and called in 1874 an 'academic democracy').

In the Burmese treatise 'In Quest of Democracy' (1990–91), Aung San Suu Kyi combined western tolerance (Mill) and progress (Darwin) with Buddhist order, dissent with conservation, individual rights with respect, law, and order, pointing out that 'law and order' is often misused as an excuse for oppression. She contrasted *Nyein-wut-pi-pyar* (quiet-crouched-crushed-flattened) with a poem on Buddhist order:

> The shade of the tree is cool indeed
> The shade of parents is cooler
> The shade of teachers is cooler still
> The shade of the ruler is yet more cool
> But coolest of all is the shade of Buddha's teachings. (*Asian Freedoms*: Kelly and Reid, 1998: 199)

Obviously, as we approach multiple nuanced notions of freedom, individuals, rights, and responsibilities in translation, Victorianists must defer to linguists in specific area studies. Yet as we study the processes of transculturation, we may conclude with one of the more productive articulations of nineteenth-century western philosophy, the idea of human underdetermination.

Human underdetermination

This idea has held that there is no essence of humankind other than our exceptional ability to interact self-consciously with our environments. While many species transform their environments (beavers build dams, bees make hives, birds make [and even steal] nests, microbes change the colours of the seas), humans have an exceptional ability to transform nature through our use of technology, which in turn transforms us. The Frankfurt School called this the dialectic of enlightenment, the ways that human evolution and development are in a ceaseless loop in which we create technology that in turn returns to recreate us (Adorno and Horkheimer, 1997 [1947]). The salient factor in human development is not what is in your genes, but what specific niche or environment your genes are in. And the ability of humans to reflect on this natural history of change and difference tells us that things can and will change; so that hope, so central to modern identities, is the natural consequence of human underdetermination.

In the fifteenth century, Giovanni Pico della Mirandola defended a conception of the human as the animal whose nature was not to have a nature, the Proteus who could sculpt itself into whatever shape it preferred. The eighteenth- and nineteenth-century philosophical anthropologists from Kant, Hegel, Feuerbach, Marx/Engels and Nietzsche to Arnold Gehlen and Helmuth Plessner in the twentieth century also found that humans are exceptionally malleable. Schopenhauer had written that you know the species when you know one non-human animal, but humans have choice and in their choice consists their individuality and diversity, their unique identities. This exitless individuality or unfinishedness, our being presented at every moment with choices, being thrown into metaphysical unfoundedness, was the source of Sartre's notorious *Nausea*. More extreme and hubristic than the philosophical anthropologists – who, like Buddhists, understood that freedom was always within constraints – Transhumanists today argue that precisely because humans have the freedom to alter themselves and their environments through their use of technologies, we must mobilise every enhancement and augmentation in our power to overcome what used to be considered the limits of human freedom: ageing, sickness and death. Transhumanists consider it their task to confront ageing, sickness and death with whatever enhancements (rational self-manipulations) and augmentations (mechanical enhancements) they can, from pharmaceuticals or biotechnical neuroplasty to mechanical or digital extensions. (Their neoliberal leader is mnemonically named Max More, alluding to the Transhumanists' maximal ambition.) Without sharing the Transhumanists' ambitions, we concur that humans are developmentally plastic, with the capacity to be both creative and destructive, rational and irrational, active and passive in their diverse niches.

If we consider literature or other cultural products in their specific niches, we can see certain geopolitical ideologies linking the production and reproduction of life, such as individualisms, communisms, religions, liberalisms, neoliberalisms, and so forth. Elsewhere I have also focused on forms of biodiversity around which lives and literatures are built – cotton, coffee, tea, rice, bananas, tobacco, sugar – and imaginative literatures about total environments of banana wilt, rice blast, waste management, sustainable transport, e.g., novels called *Rice, Yeast, Oil, Water, Men of Maize, Wolf Totem, Untouchable, Rickshaw Boy*. Symbiological studies locate the salient actants – human or nonhuman – and relations within particular niches in which humans make their own identities. For humans do make their own identities. This is universal, in a well-known Victorian formulation: 'but they do not make them as they please…but under circumstances existing already, given and transmitted from the past' (Marx, 'Eighteenth Brumaire' quoted in Tucker, 1978: 595.) Yet Marx was probably too deterministic. An immanent as well as an historical materialism would allow for a wider and more diverse range of actants and the emergence of more possibilities within the specificities of distinct niches.

Note

1 *The Global Circulation Project* can be found at: http://literature-compass.com/global-circulation-project/). Egenis, The Centre for the Study of Life Sciences can be found at: http://socialsciences.exeter.ac.uk/sociology/research/sts/egenis/.

References

Adorno, Theodor W. and Max Horkheimer (1997 [1947]). *Dialectic of Enlightenment*. London: Verso.

Anand, Mulk Raj (1940 [1935]). *Untouchable*. London: Penguin.

—— (1974). 'The Search for National Identity in India' (July), in *The Cultural Self-Comprehension of Nations: In co-operation with the United Nations Educational, Scientific and Cultural Organization (UNESCO)*, ed. Hans Kochler (1978). Tubingen: Erdmann, pp. 73–98. (Conference Innsbruck, Austria, 27–29 July 1974).

Aung San, Suu Kyi (1995). 'In Quest of Democracy(1990–91)', in *Freedom from Fear*. London: Penguin, pp. 167–79.

Banu, Lisa (2011). 'The Rickshaw: Transport of Oppression or Expression?' *South Asian Arts: An Online Journal of Cultural Expression in South Asia*. Available at www.southasianarts.org/2011/11/rickshaw-transport-of-oppression-or.html (accessed 1 November 2011).

Bayly, C. A. (2012). *Recovering Liberties: Indian Thought in the Age of Liberalism and Empire*. Cambridge: Cambridge University Press.

Chaudhuri, Amit (2013). *Calcutta: Two Years in the City*. London: Union Books.

Egenis: Centre for the Study of Life Sciences (2002-) Available at http://socialsciences.exeter.ac.uk/sociology/research/sts/egenis/ (accessed 27 June 2015).

Felski, Rita and Susan Stanford Friedman (2009). 'On Comparison: Introduction'. *New Literary History* 40(3): i–v.

Gagnier, Regenia (2010). *Individualism, Decadence, and Globalization: On the Relationship of Part to Whole*. Basingstoke: Palgrave Macmillan.

Gide, André (1950 [1935]). 'Défence de la culture.' *Littérature engagée*, ed. Yvonne Davet. Paris: Gallimard, pp. 85–96.

Global Circulation Project. (2009-). Available at http://literature-compass.com/global-circulation-project/ (accessed 27 June 2015).

Guha, Ramachandra (2007). *India After Gandhi: The History of the World's Largest Democracy* (e-reader edition). London: Pan Macmillan.

Huang, Max Ko-wu (2008). *The Meaning of Freedom: Yan Fu and the Origins of Chinese Liberalism*. Hong Kong: The Chinese University Press.

Hwang, Yuh. J. (2012). 'A Mad Mother and Her Dead Son: The Impact of the Irish Theatre on Modern Korean Theatre'. *Global Circulation Project* 9. Available at http://onlinelibrary.wiley.com/doi/10.1111/j.1741-4113.2012.00896.x/abstract (accessed 1 August 2012).

Ilaiah, Kancha (2010). *The Weapon of the Other: Dalitbahujan Writings and the Remaking of Indian Nationalist Thought* (e-reader edition). Delhi: Pearson.

Kelly, David and Anthony Reid (1998). Eds., *Asian Freedoms: The Idea of Freedom in East and Southeast Asia*. Cambridge: Cambridge University Press.

Khilnani, Sunil (2012). *The Idea of India*. London: Penguin.

Kochler, Hans (1978). Ed., *The Cultural Self-Comprehension of Nations: In co-operation with the United Nations Educational, Scientific and Cultural Organization (UNESCO)*. Tubingen: Erdmann. (Conference, Innsbruck, Austria, 27–29 July 1974.)

Lao, She (2010). *Rickshaw Boy*, tr. Howard Goldblatt. London: Harper Collins.

Latour, Bruno (1997). 'On Actor-Network Theory: A Few Clarifications'. *CSI-Paris*. Available at www.bruno-latour.fr/sites/default/files/P-67%20 ACTOR-NETWORK.pdf (accessed 10 October 2014).

——— (2004). *The Politics of Nature*. Cambridge, MA: Harvard University Press.

Lazarus, Neil (2011). *The Postcolonial Unconscious*. Cambridge: Cambridge University Press.

Lee, Kyun-Young (2001 [1979; trans.1983]) *The Other Side of Dark Remembrance*. Seoul: Jimoondang Publishing Company. (See https://openlibrary.org/publishers/Jimoondang_Publishing_Company.)

Liu, Lydia (1995). *Translingual Practice: Literature, National Culture, and Translated Modernity – China, 1900–1937*. Palo Alto, CA: Stanford University Press.

Shih, Shu-Mei (2001). *The Lure of the Modern: Writing Modernism in Semicolonial China 1917–1937*. Berkeley: University of California Press.

Shu, Yi (2011). 'Interview with Lao She's son Shu Yi'. Formerly on www.ruiwen. com/news/55072.htm (accessed 22 March 2011, later accessed 21 May 2012. Site is no longer available).

Strand, David (1989). *Rickshaw Beijing: City, People, and Politics in the 1920s*. Berkeley and Los Angeles: University of California Press.

Teggart, J. (1949). Ed., *The Idea of Progress: A Collection of Readings*. Berkeley: University of California Press.

Tran, Ben (2012). 'Queer Internationalism and Modern Vietnamese Aesthetics', in *The Oxford Handbook of Global Modernisms*, eds. Mark Wollaeger with Matt Eatough. Oxford: Oxford University Press, pp. 367–84.

Tucker, Robert C. (1978). Ed., *The Marx-Engels Reader*. 2nd edition. New York: W. W. Norton.

Wilde, Oscar (1982 [1891]). 'The Soul of Man Under Socialism', in *The Artist as Critic: Critical Writings of Oscar Wilde*, ed. Richard Ellmann. Chicago, IL: University of Chicago Press, pp. 255–89.

Yang, Haiyan (2013). 'Knowledge across Borders: The Early Communication of Evolution in China', in *The Circulation of Knowledge between Britain, India, and China: The Early-Modern World to the Twentieth Century*, eds. Bernard Lightman, Gordon McOuat and Larry Stewart. Leiden: Brill, pp. 181–208.

6

Literary folk: writing popular culture in colonial Punjab, 1885–1905

Churnjeet Mahn

In the wake of the annexation of the Punjab in 1849, the creep of colonial infrastructure facilitated the work of a diverse range of administrators, archaeologists, travellers and various kinds of amateur scholar, who sought to compile, categorise and understand this religiously and linguistically diverse region. The borders of Punjab would change dramatically throughout the colonial period, finally leading to partition in 1947 when the new national border between India and Pakistan was used to cut through diverse communities that had historically characterised the area. Recent scholarship on the broad idea of *Punjabiyat* or 'Punjabiness' practises a historiography that reads beyond partition to understand the ways in which cultural practice, memory and identity persist post-partition. Although Punjabi is a language shared by a number of faiths and cultures, studies of the history of Punjabi language and its management have demonstrated how it has become increasingly synonymous with the Sikh faith (Mir, 2010). Faith, rather than language, acted as the axiom of difference when it came to constructing the basis of new national imaginaries. This chapter identifies some of the ways a Punjabi literary sphere was (mis)understood in the late-Victorian empire through the curation of a canon of Punjabi folk-culture by R. C. Temple (1850–1931), Flora Annie Steel (1847–1929) and C. F. Usborne (1874–1919), all of whom lived and worked in Punjab as an extension of colonial administration. Examples of a diverse and rich Punjabi literary culture were translated into English under the banner of 'folklore' which delegitimised the diversity of prose and verse in Punjabi with origins in religious, spiritual and genres of the epic derived from Persian. While this chapter does not aim to assess the literary merits of the translations against the originals (an impossible task due to the fact that the originals existed as performed texts), it does question the ways in which Punjabi literary culture was filtered in British writing. This literary culture was transmitted in print, but also in performances and through the work of performers and artists who would creatively adapt the orally transmitted poetic epics, lyrics and ballads of the region.

Part of the premise of this argument relies on a broader understanding of early anthropological work and research as an important variety of literary activity in the late nineteenth-century. This is not a controversial point in itself: the work of James Clifford, Ruth Benedict and Clifford Geertz was part of a wave of revisionist thinking about how anthropology constructed and understood method, evidence and the production of knowledge, 'No longer a marginal, or occulted dimension, writing has emerged as central to what anthropologists do both in the field and thereafter' (Clifford and Marcus, 2010: 2). The influence of this work in literary studies has primarily been in the field of travel writing where the work of James Clifford (1997) and Mary Louise Pratt (1992) on the relationship between the traveller and the people/cultures they describe, especially in 'exotic' contexts, has become part of the critical canon. However, the anthropological debate has offered a larger epistemological challenge, which has failed fully to permeate branches of literary and historical colonial scholarship, partially due to the difficulty in labelling early amateur anthropologists and ethnographers. The writers under consideration here have been of minor interest within the fields of archaeology, South Asian studies and English literary fiction. At the fringes of different spheres of expertise, the accumulation of their knowledge about Punjab has been dispersed.

The past decade has offered more nuanced methodological approaches to understanding the relevancy of different kinds of discourse for South Asian literary research. Multi-disciplinary approaches based in literary studies have illuminated a series of networks of influence and impact across the Empire.[1] However, the study of colonial Indian literary culture continues to be divided between disciplines including history, English-based literary studies and South Asian studies. In a recent special edition of *Victorian Literature and Culture* Mary Ellis Gibson summarised the problem with discussing English writing in the context of India: 'which Victorian India? Whose Victorian India?' (Gibson, 2014: 325). This line of questioning could be taken further in order to consider what counts as fictional writing, and how useful the term 'literary' is in this context. Sukanya Bannerjee's *Becoming Imperial Citizens: Indians in the Late-Victorian Empire* (2010) is a good example of this issue as it considers literary sources alongside governmental sources and historical material to offer a different kind of framing for literary culture that relies on Hayden White's theorisations of narrative.[2] The strength of this view is its approach to seeking similar levels of cultural value between a variety of discursive types; Patrick Brantlinger argues against the sceptical reaction of historians to postcolonial literary studies because: 'a literary text is just as much fact as a government document…It may even be epistemologically more reliable than a government document' (Brantlinger, 2009: 56). Gayatri Gopinath's *Impossible Desires: Queer Diasporas and South Asian Public Cultures* (2005) is another example of a recent critical study which weaves together colonial-era texts with Bollywood films and Caribbean texts to queer the understanding of race and sexuality by deliberately writing around existing historical genealogies. Part of the impact of transperipheral research has been to disrupt disciplinary conventions, especially in the literary and historical study of empire, alongside an interest in 'narratives that trace historical ruptures rather than teleological trajectories' (Gibson, 2014: 325). The loose definition of narrative and discourse here offers an opportunity and problem: what are the new types of ring-fencing being put in place to make manageable the sheer volume of material that falls under the category of narrative? And what kinds of geo-historical specificities are effaced in transperipheral research?

Connecting narratives across geographical contexts has made a powerful impact on contemporary literary scholarship, but it does raise questions about the relevancy and importance of this medium in areas like Punjab which have had exceptionally low rates of literacy. Farina Mir has argued that oral performance allowed Punjabi literary cultures to develop outside the formal and informal apparatuses of colonial power (Mir, 2010), especially as Urdu persisted as the official language of colonial administration in the area. By analysing the boundary between oral culture and print culture, this chapter offers an overview of a partial and incomplete project to variously transcribe, translate, curate and analyse a version of 'common' Punjabi culture conventionally divorced from official literary contexts.

By bringing together three figures who formed an interface between English-language print culture and Punjabi vernacular culture in the decades after Punjab's annexation, this chapter's response to the 'which Victorian India?' dilemma is to make an argument for more devolution

Rethinking national contexts and exchanges

in literary and cultural politics in order to examine literary formations in more focused contexts. R. C. Temple, Flora Annie Steel and C. F. Usborne all relayed accounts of forms of popular 'legends', 'ballads', 'fairy tales' and 'folktales' that decontextualised Punjabi literary culture, especially in terms of genre and performance, through labelling a diverse set of practices as 'folk' and 'folklore'. Important studies by Jennifer Schacker (2003) and Caroline Sumpter (2008) have discussed the ideological contexts for the classification of 'folk' in the Victorian period and its relationship to social movements based in racial origin theories or forms of nascent socialism. The loose interchange between these terms is an issue that was partially addressed as folklore studies professionalised in the latter part of the century through the establishment of the Folklore Society in 1878. A criterion that spanned the genres was a degree of 'popular' or 'oral' circulation that at times translated into an interest in primitivism or antique survival. Debates about folklore's role in destroying its object of study is well debated, as Sumpter points out: 'print's role in the supposed death of folklore has been lamented since (at least) the seventeenth century' (Sumpter, 2008: 9). Arjun Appadurai reminds us that, 'the idea of "folk" in South Asia creates an illusion not just of synchronic homogeneity but also of historical and geographical fixity' (Appadurai, 1991: 468–9). This chapter does not attempt to define who the 'folk' of Punjab were; rather, the focus remains on how 'folk' is constructed and transmitted by Temple, Steel and Usborne.

The distinction between folklore and literary studies becomes important for the context of Punjab precisely because Punjabi was positioned as the vernacular or 'folk' language of an area that had a rich history of oral and literary material in Punjabi, albeit published in a variety of local scripts including Shahmukhi and Gurmukhi. Through the instituting of Urdu as the official language of government, Punjabi was relegated from literary culture as its legitimacy as the most commonly spoken language in the region was undermined. According to Farina Mir, this created a social space for Punjabi's print cultures and performed literary cultures to develop and circulate with relative autonomy from the kind of colonial influence and regulation seen in other South Asian languages: 'Punjabi literary culture offers, therefore, a particular instance of stability through a period usually marked for its ruptures, as people and institutions traversed the divide between precolonial and colonial rule' (Mir, 2010: 4). From Temple's use of local legends to understand the shrines and monuments of the Punjab, to the translation and adaptation of localised forms of lyric poetry into English fairy tales, this chapter offers a snapshot of how Punjabi literary culture was translated into a variety of North Indian folklore in British writing. This chapter seeks to understand this process in the first instance by tracing the interest in 'classical' Punjab and its survivals in the work of Punjab's first colonial archaeological survey, which also collected anthropological and ethnographical material. It then looks at three different types of overlapping evidence of Punjabi literary culture in English through the 'collecting' of folklore, the adaptation and translation of children's tales, and the curation and translation of Punjabi lyrics.

Excavating cultures: colonial mythologies in Punjab

In 2013, sitting in the gardens of a retired military officer in Sirhind, Punjab, I was reliably informed that my surname, 'Mann' (transliterated in a variety of forms into English), entered Punjab with Alexander the Great's army. A less personalised version of this origin myth was repeated for me by a variety of local elders who regarded Alexander as one of many invaders including Jahangir and the British that northern India had been subject to. Alexander Cunningham also recorded hearing an origin story in his archaeological tour of this region of Punjab in 1863–64. Son of the Scottish poet Allan Cunningham, Alexander was a British Army engineer who in 1861 was appointed to organise archaeological reports across northern India thereby laying the foundations of the Archaeological Survey of India, which is now part of the Ministry of Culture in India. In Cunningham's first collation of reports, he prefaces his work with the minute by Charles John Canning, the then Governor General of India for whom, 'It is impossible to pass through that part, – or indeed, so far as my experience goes, any part – of the British territories in India without being struck by the neglect with which the greater portion of the architectural remains, and of the traces of by-gone civilization have been treated' (Cunningham, 1871: i). Although Canning was keen to highlight that the financial burden of conservation was beyond the reasonable expectation of the Indian government, the cataloguing of architectural remains generated the outline of a national and historical boundary line for what could be called heritage.

In the preface to his first collection of reports, Cunningham traces a lineage of Orientalists from William Jones through to James Prinsep and himself to establish a legacy of knowledge about remote periods of Indian history. The Greek influence in northern India is a particular point of interest because Bactrian, a middle-eastern language with a Greek-based script, had been spoken as far east as India. Cunningham identified himself with a move away from text-based studies of Indian civilisations to the study of architecture and other material culture. Dismissing the 'lying gabble' (Cunningham, 1871: xix) of Brahmin histories and traditions whose writings were consistently routed into Hindu mythology, archaeological observation opened a new field of evidence: 'Facts now poured in rapidly, but though many in number, they were still bare and unconnected facts, mere fossil fragments of the great skeletons of Indian history' (Cunningham, 1871: xix). The archaeological metaphor of the incomplete skeleton was a common trope for describing areas dense with historical architectural evidence (Mahn, 2012). With the skeleton metaphor came a privileging of specific strata of the region's history, a preference which was often ideologically loaded. In the case of Cunningham, his routes to Punjab were through Greece:

> In describing the ancient state of the Panjab [sic], the most interesting subject of enquiry is the identification of those famous peoples and cities, whose names have become familiar to the whole world through the expedition of Alexander the great. To find the descendants of those peoples and the ruined mounds of the present day, I propose, like Pliny, to follow the track of Alexander himself. (Cunningham, 1871: 1)

Cunningham later compared this to following Pausanias in Greece; his tour through the Punjab was mirrored in the rhetoric of scholars and archaeologists in Greece who sought to look past the recent remains of the Ottoman Empire to see ancient survivals. The irony of attempting a navigation based on the account of an invading army is somewhat lost on Cunningham and his interest in Alexander desensitises him to some of the value and diversity in the landscape he encounters. Historically, the region called Punjab in colonial India had been home to a range of civilisations, religions and tribes from Buddhists and Jains to Sufis, Sikhs and Muslims. While British historians of the Punjab used religion as a way of understanding historical architecture and cultural influence, what was lost was an understanding of how regional identities organised social relations beyond a narrower interpretation of faith-based communities. The linear view of history and lack of sensitivity to more intricate forms of syncretic religious practice led Cunningham to catalogue a Punjabi heritage that drew straight lines from ancient to modern and through communities along the lines of religion and tribe. In this view, Sikh Jats could be categorised as Hindu and mausoleums could be sites of Islamic practices of memorialisation and religious worship.[2]

Cunningham's ordering of the strata of Punjabi history and culture undergirded the assumptions made by colonial administrators about the status, quality and importance of contemporary Punjabi culture. Its most intrinsic value lay in its antiquity, as its present displayed a few fragments from the past in corrupted and decayed form. The rest of this chapter turns to how this derivative view of contemporary Punjabi culture from its 'collection' by folklorists, to the (mis)understanding of its circulation (in print and performance) and its context (social and cultural).

Varieties of Punjabi literature in R. C. Temple's *Legends of the Punjab*

Born in Allahabad and educated at Harrow and Cambridge, Temple was an army officer and colonial administrator who became an important part of the folklore and Indian antiquary movement in India, as well as Britain. He joined the Folklore Society in 1885 and was editor of *The Indian Antiquary* from 1872 until 1918, as well as being the founding editor of *Punjab Notes and Queries* in 1883. During his lifetime he worked to produce systematic records of folklore and archaeological evidence from a variety of regions in northern India, while encouraging the work of a range of writers including Flora Annie Steel and C. F. Usborne. As a member of the Royal Asiatic Society, the Asiatic Society of Bengal and the Anthropological Institute, he was connected to some of the leading societies concerned with South Asia at the time. Temple was keen to distinguish folklore studies from branches of comparative mythology or religious studies and to establish a Punjabi folk canon. His three-volume *The Legends of the Punjab* was partially derived from the work of other scholars in the field, including the Sikh historian Max Macauliffe, as well as hired local artists who were asked to perform for payment. While this broad range of sources and formats for collection illustrate a diversity in methods, Temple was confident that his collection would prove to be encyclopaedic.

What, exactly, could be counted as folklore was a tricky question which he addressed head-on in a contribution to the Folklore Society:

> *Folk-lore, then, is in the first place, popular learning, the embodiment, that is of the popular ideas on all matters connected with man and his surroundings...* A superstition as being an unreasonable and excessive belief, is a fact of Folk-lore so is a legend as unfounded history. (Temple, 1906: 2)

Temple takes a view which includes the majority of popular narratives in the Punjab that were not part of official religious scriptures or classical, recorded history. The relegation of Punjabi as an official language, alongside the disregard of local practices of historiography and the imposition of Eurocentric models for categorising heritage and culture, bracketed the diversity of Punjabi literary output under the singular heading of 'folklore'.

In *Legends of the Panjab*, Temple categorises the subjects of Punjabi folklore, drawing distinctions along the lines of gender and elements of religious culture deemed to be 'superstitious'. In relaying the legend of Dhruva, Temple comments on themes of daughter sacrifice or death:

> A desire so universal, so strong, so important to the peasantry necessarily finds not only frequent expression in their stories and legends, but also in the acts of daily life, sometimes of a very serious nature. Women have over and over again been guilty of murder and incendiarism due to wild superstitious attempts to gratify it, I can recall a case in which the ignorant low-class mother of daughters only has, with the assistance of her elder daughter, killed a little girl belonging to a neighbour by way of human sacrifice. (Temple, 1906: 78)

Colonial commentary on daughter sacrifice, wife immolation and son-preference in nineteenth-century South Asia has been widely covered in scholarship from Gayatri Spivak's famous analysis of sati (1988) to Navtej K. Purewal's recent work in the operation of son-preference in the colonial to postcolonial periods of India (Purewal, 2010). Purewal in particular highlights how the role and voice of women continued to be effaced in the debate around female infanticide. This view works to affirm Temple's own beliefs that folklore is a common kind of story or narrative used to underwrite local order and customs. However, it also relies on the apparent inability of the 'low-class' to correctly interpret the allegorical world of the folktale. Temple takes this observation further by marking the imaginative slippage between religion, folklore and superstition:

> the average villager one meets in the Panjab and Northern India is neither a Muhammadan, nor a Hindu, nor a Sikh, nor any other Religion, as such is understood by its orthodox – or to speak more correctly authorized – exponents, but that his 'Religion' is a confused unthinking worship of anything held to be holy, whether men or places. (Temple, 1885: xxi)

The 'confused' and 'unthinking' assumes an unsophisticated and indiscriminate system of worship in Punjab. For Temple, part of the importance of restoring order to the world of folk and religion was part of an international enterprise to make transparent the operations of different

Writing popular culture in colonial Punjab

social cultures, as well as offering colonial administrators a better way of understanding the population under their control. At an address delivered at the University of Cambridge in 1904, R. C. Temple, after decades of work in the field, argued for the international value of anthropology as an area of study:

> Lifelong neighbours among Hindus and Muhammadans living chock-a-block in the same street usually know nothing of each other's ways. Again, every Indian talks of 'caste,' but there is nothing more difficult than to get information of practical value from an Indian about any caste, except his own. (Temple, 1904 [1904]: 2)

Temple was consistent in reading Punjabi cultural practices as confused and based in ignorance, a reading that inevitably coloured his own appreciation and understanding of the material he collected under the term folklore. Farina Mir has argued that this view, 'ultimately, was one of colonial assimilation: colonial in its insistence on the prevalence – indeed, singularity – of a European epistemological framework' (Mir, 2010: 103). Unwittingly, and precisely because of his prejudice, what Temple actually accomplished was the collection and translation of a range of Punjabi literary forms.

Temple's three-volume *Legends of the Punjab* brought together texts that were mostly circulated through performance, but were also appearing in Punjabi print. The 'legend' of Puran Bhagat, 'As Sung by Some Jatts from the Patiala State' (Temple, 1885: 375) is presented as the conflation of two legends with heroes who are interchanged at the bard's pleasure. The legend is transliterated from Punjabi into roman characters alongside a full translation. The legend is a *qisse*, a type of epic poetry that evolved a regional sub-branch in Punjab through the introduction of the form from Iran and Afghanistan. The *qisse* is based in performance, with musicians becoming associated with particular types of *qisse* in different regions. As a form closely connected to Sufism, it developed with a strong philosophical basis, which often wove together historical fact with local legends, and regionalised practices of faith and worship. Because of their length in performance, *qisse* often take an epic form with rhyming couplets and repeated refrains or motifs and would be understood by their audience as quite distinct from simple localised ballads or children's songs. Anshu Malhotra and Farina Mir sketch out the difficulty in understanding the *qisse* in the context of literary history:

> As historical texts or sources, *qisse* are entirely enigmatic. They are clearly fictional narratives, sometimes even fantastical. We know little about

those who composed them, even less about those who performed the tales orally, and almost nothing about audience reception. (Malhotra and Mir, 2012: 223)

One of the few popular folk ballads in the collection, 'The Ballad of Chuhar Singh' ironically comes into Temple's possession through a Gurmukhi manuscript rather than a local performer or bard. Relating the immolation of Chuhar and Dal Singh in 1793, Temple's descriptive notes focus on the important role of the Jatts in the Punjab. Despite Urdu being the official language of the Punjab, a market for Punjabi literature was emerging in the nineteenth century, from the *qisse*, to religious and popular poetic forms. Temple's undifferentiated volume reveals his own limited framework for understanding the literary environment of the Punjab but it nevertheless continues to offer a valuable snapshot of the contact between Punjabi poetic forms and English during the nineteenth-century.

Translating Punjabi folk in Flora Annie Steel's *Tales of the Punjab*

Although greatly assisted by Temple in terms of research and access to local networks in the Punjab, Flora Annie Steel offered her own version of the popular tales of Punjab. Flora Annie Steel was the daughter of George Webster, a Scottish Parliamentary Agent and later the Sheriff-Clerk of Forfarshire, and Isabella MacCallum, an heiress to a Jamaican plantation. In 1867 she married Henry William Steel and followed him to Punjab where he undertook a number of positions for the Indian Civil Service, primarily in Punjab. Her literary output was prolific and included an Indian Mutiny novel, popular histories of India, non-fiction writing on women's suffrage, as well as cookery handbooks. Based on stories she had heard or collected, Steel published *Wide-Awake Stories* (1884), which was later published as *Tales of the Punjab* (1894) and *From the Five Rivers* (1893), both collections of local stories from her time in Punjab, accompanied by illustrations by John Lockwood Kipling. She accompanied her husband through many of his tours and assisted with the medical and educational needs of local populations, taking a keen interest in women's education. She also took an interest in Punjabi handicraft, especially *phulkari* (a traditional style of embroidery particular to Punjab), and later, through her interest in female education, became the Inspectress of Schools in Punjab. A number of critics have noted her as a woman in Punjab interested in enhancing and understanding the lives of women, a quality that distinguished her from a number of other British officials and their wives (Crane and Johnston, 2007; Patwardhan, 1963). However, ultimately, her views sat comfortably in a conservative colonial model, as Nancy Paxton points out: 'To her credit, Steel's affection for individual Indian women may have helped her overcome some of her racism when she supported limited franchise for Indian as well as English women' (Paxton, 1990: 338b).

Although Steel claims to be fluent in Punjabi in her autobiography, what remains unclear is what kind of dialect she spoke, and the nature of her opinions about the relationship between Hindi, Punjabi and Urdu in the region. Punjabi in this case becomes an imaginary geography or colonial territorial area rather than a language with its own complex rhythms and forms. Her preface to *Tales of the Punjab* was co-written with R. C. Temple who assisted with the notes and appendices:

> Many of the tales in this collection appeared either in the *Indian Antiquary*, the *Calcutta Review*, or the *Legends of the Punjab*. They were then in the form of literal translations, in many cases uncouth or even unpresentable to ears polite, in all scarcely intelligible to the untravelled English reader; for it must be remembered that, with the exception of the Adventures of Raja Rasâlu, all these stories are strictly folk-tales passing current among a people who can neither read nor write, and whose diction is full of colloquialisms, and, if we choose to call them so, vulgarisms. It would be manifestly unfair, for instance, to compare the literary standard of such tales with that of the *Arabian Nights*, the *Tales of a Parrot*, or similar works. (Steel, 1894)

Apart from the *qisse* of Raja Rasalu, what differentiates this collection from Temple's is a more deliberate attempt to collect more fantastical stories that do not have the kind of historical, political or philosophical resonances of the work collected in *Legends of Punjab*. In her discussion of colonial British collectors of folklore, Sadhana Naithani identifies a common tripartite structure of 'India', the folklore collector, and the lore itself (Naithani 2001). In the case of Steel, India becomes associated with the 'uncouth' 'vulgarisms' of what we assume to be colloquial Punjabi. While this helps to authenticate her own understanding of local languages and access to everyday life and tales, her volume is ultimately framed by Temple's work and research. Her own take on more minor forms of Punjabi culture ensure that her work is definitely relegated from the literary to the popular, as the reference to *Arabian Nights* makes clear. While Temple obtains his sources from hired bards and performers and local scholars, Steel claims to obtain her material from children: 'some child begins a story, others correct the details, emulation conquers shyness, and finally the story-teller is brought to the front with acclamations: for there is always a story-teller *par excellence* in every village – generally a boy' (Steel, 1894). Steel's canon of folktales is largely divided between two types of output: stories and songs that can be performed by children, and the inclusion of selected *qisse*, some of which come from local manuscripts. In stark contrast to Temple, Steel attempts to fashion herself as an observer of semi-organic performance rather than a professional collector who would elicit work for his archive. She is aware that her presence may produce a temporary reluctance, but the apparent inevitability of organic performance prevails. In her translations she experimented with a variety of forms from epic ballad to conventional nursery stories and fairy tales. Despite her literary intervention Steel styles herself as a collector rather than translator of the tales:

> That is neither a transliteration–which would have needed a whole dictionary to be intelligible–nor a version orientalised to suit English tastes. It is an attempt to translate one colloquialism by another, and thus to preserve the aroma of rough ready wit existing side by side with that perfume of pure poesy which every now and again contrasts so strangely with the other. Nothing would have been easier than to alter the style; but to do so would, in the collector's opinion, have robbed the stories of all human value. (Steel, 1894)

Steel uses a variety of strategies to authenticate her translations. She begins by self-consciously identifying herself against orientalism: her desire is not to play on the exotic, but to draw her readers into a closer identification with the tales and naturalise them for English tastes. In maintaining the 'rough ready wit' she attempts to reaffirm the unsophisticated quality of expression, although she does credit some elementary level of poetic value. She rules out a straight translation, which is something Temple attempted to do in his own *Legends of Punjab*. This results in a very different kind of output:

> Once upon a time a soldier died, leaving a widow and one son. They were dreadfully poor, and at last matters became so bad that they had nothing left in the house to eat.
>
> 'Mother,' said the son, 'give me four shillings, and I will go and seek my fortune in the wide world.'
>
> 'Alas!' answered the mother, 'and where am I, who haven't a farthing wherewith to buy bread, to find four shillings?'

'There is that old coat of my father's,' returned the lad; 'look in the pocket – perchance there is something there.' (Steel, 1894)

The tales that Steel hears are adapted for the British nursery. Shillings, farthings, and coat-pockets make up some of the small details that help to bridge the context of Punjab and Britain. Without the benefit of the transliteration into roman characters and with some key identifiers missing, it is difficult to ascertain the origin of the tales, the manner of their circulation, and the context of their performance, leaving them to slot easily into Temple's systems of classification. Ralph Crane and Anna Johnston argue that Steel's, 'life and writing sit uncomfortably on the boundaries of Empire, revealing the complex personal and textual negotiations that occur at the margins of anthropology' (Crane and Johnston, 2007: 92). It may be that part of the reason Steel has been relatively neglected in English literary studies is because of her pseudo-anthropological work and collaboration. However, her work with Temple and her reading of what she called local, vernacular Punjabi tales, effaced some of the political, social and economic specificities of the region to sanitise and universalise her material for an English-speaking colonial audience. Indian women and children, supposed repositories of these tales, become reduced to vehicles for a translatable and consumable heritage. Shampa Roy has discussed Steel's efforts to give Indian women a voice in her short fiction:

> this concern and the irony that it produces – the staple and great alibi of bourgeois liberal politics – also stops short of identifying concrete and meaningful directions with actually liberating and empowering possibilities for these women which might even entail more radical questionings of prevalent social and political structures. (Roy, 2010: 73)

Steel's contribution to the circulation of Punjabi literary culture is important: she collected, translated and adapted material from her time in Punjab which then went on to circulate in India, Britain and beyond. While she may have used some sleight of hand with her abilities in Punjabi and the context of the performances she encountered, she still offers an important contrast to Temple's indiscriminate reading of popular Punjabi forms in the context of folklore studies through creative adaptation.

C. F. Usborne's *Hir and Ranjha* and *Punjabi Proverbs and Lyrics*

A graduate of Bailliol College, Charles Frederick Usborne joined the Indian Civil Service in 1898, serving at a variety of stations and eventually becoming the Deputy Commisioner of Hissar. He was trained to communicate in Punjabi shortly after arriving in India which faciliated an enduring interest in Punjabi-language literature. One of his best-known publications is a translation of Waris Shah's *Hir and Ranjha* (1766) published in 1901, and the collection *Punjabi Lyrics and Proverbs* published in 1905. Like Steel, Usborne benefited from Temple's knowledge of Punjabi culture, but his departure from Temple was through an interest in what he defined as literary culture:

> Captain R. C. Temple, who was for some time Cantonment Magistrate at Ambala, has written several articles on Panjab ballads and folklore in the *Calcutta Review* and *Indian Notes and Queries*; but the author is more interested in folklore than in literature, and the few lyrics he has collected are not of much value...Mr. Swinnerton and Mrs. Steel have both translated fairy tales and stories current in the Panjab, but they have not collected many examples of lyric poetry, and it was mainly lyric poetry which I have been trying to discover. (Usborne, 1905: i)

Usborne further evidences some of the ways in which British models of literary taste and culture were being used to partition a complex Punjabi literary sphere that developed alongside classical forms of Persian and Sanskrit writing that Usborne identifies as acceptable literary forms among the Punjabi elite. What Usborne does not do is identify or discuss the ethno-religious and linguistic dispositions of the educated Punjabis that he meets. Usborne appears to be aware of language prejudice without fully outlining or comprehending its socio-political implications:

> What the poets of the cultivated few admire and what their readers expect is an elegant and rather far-fatched ode in Persian or Sanskrit...Indeed, it is not an exaggeration to say that if a Panjabi Burns, Beranger or Mistral were to arise tomorrow he would get very little encouragement from the educated native of the Panjab. (Usborne, 1905: ii)

The difficulty in understanding exactly what Usborne classifies as a literary lyric, albeit one in vernacular form, proves as confusing to Punjabi poets as it does to him. When he launched a competition in one of the 'leading native newspapers of the Punjab' (Usborne, 1905: ii) for a compilation of Punjabi lyrics, he did not receive any entries. When he eventually began to arrange his own anthology, he found difficulty in forming a consensus about what 'good' poetry may be: 'None of the natives could understand exactly what I wanted. Poems they thought good I thought intolerable. What I thought worth copying and translating, they usually thought childish' (Usborne, 1905: iii). Farina Mir's work has demonstrated a thriving Punjabi-language print culture in the period; Usborne's difficulty in putting together a collection was not because of a lack of material, but a disconnection between the understanding of literary value in English and Punjabi writing.

Usborne's apparently full translation of Waris Shah's *Hir and Ranjha* presented one of Punjab's most famous *qisse* with some basic explanatory notes, although this translation has been criticised for being poor and filled with errors and misinterpretations (Shackle and Snell, 1992: 262). The narrative broadly follows the tragic lives of Hir and Ranjha who fall in love despite Hir subsequently being married to another man. *Hir and Ranjha* had been 'collected' by R. C. Temple but Usborne's interest in the literary vernacular culture demonstrates the difficulty in identifying an adequate approach to interpreting the work. For Malhotra and Mir, the difficulty in defining the form is tied up with the difficulty in understanding the formation of Punjabi-ness in the period:

> In terms of genre, it blends Perso-Islamic and local aesthetics into a coherent and recognizable regional genre. In their representations of devotional practice, Punjabi *qisse* emphasize a kind of piety that was shared across religious traditions as opposed to one affiliated to a single religion. In both realms of genre and devotional practice, Punjabi *qisse* represent ideas that do not fit comfortably within existing categories or taxonomies whether literary/aesthetic or relgious. (Malhotra and Mir, 2012: 226)

Malhotra and Mir point out that while the broad form of the epic-length verse romance persisted from a Persian tradition, what regionalised the *qisse* was the use of indigenous forms of poetic metre (Malhotra and Mir, 2012: 232). Usborne's translation of Shah is in prose, but an extract of a lyrical rendition in *Punjabi Lyrics* does utilise rhyming couplets although the *qisse* is adapted into stanzas. The relaying of some of these formal qualities allows features of the performed verisons of *Hir and Ranjha* to filter into English. However, without the context of the performance and without the context of devotional practices in the Punjab, the reading of *Hir and Ranjha* falls into the model of a romance and fails to resonate as a variety of popular literary, print and oral narrative which transcended the conventional borders of devotional practice, faith and genre imposed by figures such as Temple.

To conclude, the political and polemical potential of elevating 'folk' to the realms of the literary was not lost on Indian writers. Lal Behari Day and Rabindranath Tagore both turned to collections of Bengali folklore as a way of understanding the relationship between 'folk' and nationalism (Crane and Johnston, 2007: 89). In different ways, Temple, Steel and Usborne incorporated a range of genres and forms of Punjabi in their work which through the labels of folk, vernacular and popular lost their relation to each other as part of a complex literary world based on performance and making increasing inroads into Punjabi-language print. The distinction that Sudipta Kaviraj draws between a 'fuzzy' and an 'enumerated' community has become an important model for understanding South Asian social formations:

> Communities were fuzzy in two senses. Rarely, if ever, would people belong to a community which would claim to represent or exhaust all the layers of their complex selfhood…On the appropriate occasion, every individual would use his cognitive apparatus to classify any single person he interacted with and place him quite exactly. (Kaviraj, 2010)

The difficulty of pulling apart the folk, vernacular and the popular rests in the difficulty of establishing stable boundaries of genre and value without a fuller understanding of the context of performance and circulation. This difficulty and contradiction was translated by Temple as native confusion and ignorance, entirely side-stepped by Steel through a focus on children's writing, and met with puzzlement by an Usborne unable to identify traditions of poetry he could understand. Beginning the project of considering their work in English literary studies opens a route into understanding one of the most important strategic areas of the British Empire as a site of vibrant creative practice that failed to be fully 'enumerated' by British interests.

Notes

1 An excellent example of this has been *Making Britain: South Asian Visions of Home and Abroad, 1870–1950*. For more details on this project see www.open.ac.uk/arts/research/asianbritain/making-britain (Open University, 2017).
2 For more detailed discussions of White's analysis of historical and literary narrative see White (1987).
3 The recent work of South Asian scholars such as Hussain Ahmed Khan (2015) and Anne Murphy (2012) have highlighted the ways in which colonialism facilitated religious sectarianism, aggravating existing underlying tensions.

References

Appadurai, Arjun (1991). 'Afterword', in *Gender, Genre and Power in South Asian Expressive Traditions*, eds. Arjun Appadurai, Frank J. Korom and Margaret Ann Mills. Philadelphia: University of Pennsylvania Press, pp. 467–76.

Bannerjee, Sukanya (2010). *Becoming Imperial Citizens: Indian in the Late-Victorian Empire*. Durham, NC: Duke University Press.

Brantlinger, Patrick (2009). *Victorian Literature and Postcolonial Studies*. Edinburgh: Edinburgh University Press.

Clifford, James (1997). *Routes: Travel and Translation in the Late Twentieth Century*. Cambridge, MA: Harvard University Press.

Clifford, James and George E. Marcus (2010). Eds., *Writing Culture: The Poetics and Politics of Ethnography*. Berkeley and Los Angeles: University of California Press.

Crane, Ralph and Anna Johnston (2007). 'Flora Annie Steel in the Punjab', in *Writing, Travel, and Empire: In the Margins of Anthropology*, eds. Peter Hulme and Russell McDougall. London and New York: I. B. Taurus, pp. 71–95.

Cunningham, Alexander (1871). *Archaeological Survey of India. Four Reports Made During the Years 1862–63–64–65*. Simla: Government Central Press.

Gibson, Mary Ellis (2014). 'Introduction: English in India, India in England'. *Victorian Literature and Culture* 42(3): 325–33.

Gopinath, Gayatri (2005). *Impossible Desires: Queer Diasporas and South Asian Public Cultures*. Durham, NC: Duke University Press.

Kaviraj, Sudipta (2010). *The Imaginary Institution of India: Politics and Ideas*. New York: Columbia University Press. Ebook.

Khan, Hussain Ahmed (2015). *Artisans, Sufis, Shrines: Colonial Architecture in Nineteenth-Century Punjab*. London: I. B. Tauris.

Mahn, Churnjeet (2012). *British Women's Travel to Greece, 1840–1914: Travels in the Palimpsest*. Burlington, VT: Ashgate.

Malhotra, Anshu and Farina Mir (2012). 'Genre and Devotion in Punjabi Popular Narratives. Rethinking Cultural and Religious Syncretism', in *Punjab Reconsidered: History, Culture and Practice*, eds. Anshu Malhotra and Farina Mir. Oxford: Oxford University Press, pp. 221–54.

Mir, Farina (2010). *The Social Space of Language: Vernacular Culture in British Colonial Punjab*. Berkeley and London: University of California Press.

Murphy, Anne (2012). *The Materiality of the Past: History and Representation in Sikh Tradition*. New York: Oxford University Press.

Naithani, Sadhana (2001). 'Prefaced Space: Tales of the Colonial British Collectors of Indian Folklore', in *Imagined States: Nationalism, Utopia and the Longing in Oral Cultures*, eds. Luisa Del Guidice and Gerald Porter. Logan: Utah State University Press, pp. 64–79.

Open University (2017). 'Making Britain'. Available at www.open.ac.uk/arts/research/asianbritain/making-britain (accessed 22 January 2017).

Patwardhan, Daya (1963). *A Star of India: Flora Annie Steel, Her Works and Times*. Bombay: Daya Patwardhan.

Paxton, Nancy (1990). 'Feminism Under the Raj: Complicity and Resistance in the Writings of Flora Annie Steel and Annie Besant'. *Women's Writing International Forum* 13(4): 333–46.

Pratt, Mary Louise (1992). *Imperial Eyes: Travel Writing and Transculturation*. London and New York: Routledge.

Purewal, Navtej K. (2010). *Son Preference: Sex Selection, Gender and Culture in South Asia*. Oxford: Berg.

Roy, Shampa (2010). '"A Miserable Sham": Flora Annie Steel's Short Fictions and the Question of Indian Women's Reform'. *Feminist Review* 94: 55–74.

Schacker, Jennifer (2003). *National Dreams: The Remaking of Fairy Tales in Nineteenth-Century England*. Philadelphia: University of Pennsylvania Press.

Shackle, Christopher and Rupert Snell (1992). Eds., *The Indian Narrative: Perspectives and Patterns*. Wiesbaden: Harrassowitz.

Spivak, Gayatri Chakravorty (1988). 'Can the Subaltern Speak?' in *Marxism and the Interpretation of Culture*, eds. Cary Nelson and Lawrence Grossberg. Urbana: University of Illinois Press, pp. 271–313.

Steel, Flora Annie (1894). *Tales of the Punjab*. UPenn Digital Library. University of Pennsylvania. Available at http://digital.library.upenn.edu/women/steel/punjab/punjab.html (accessed 11 December 2014).

Sumpter, Caroline (2008). *The Victorian Press and the Fairy Tale*. Basingstoke: Palgrave Macmillan.

Temple, R. C. (1885). *The Legends of the Panjab*. Vol. 2. Bombay: Education Society's Press.

Temple, R. C. (1905 [1904]). 'The Practical Value of Anthropology', reprinted from *The Indian Antiquary, Vol. XXXIV*. Bombay: Bombay Education Society's Press, p. 132.

Temple, R. C. (1906). *A Collection of Papers from the Indian Antiquary 1891–1906*. Bombay: Bombay Educational Press.

Usborne, C. F. (1905). *Panjabi Lyrics and Proverbs*. Lahore: Civil and Military Gazette Press.

Usborne, C. F. (1973) [1901]. *The Adventures of Hir and Ranjha*. London: Peter Owen.

White, Hayden (1987). *The Content of Form: Narrative Discourse and Historical Representation*. Baltimore, MD: Johns Hopkins University Press.

7

'Across the waters of this disputed ocean': the material production of American literature in nineteenth-century Britain

Katie McGettigan

In September 1867, the American author Oliver Wendell Holmes wrote to his British publisher, Sampson Low, to complain about Low and his colleagues making material alterations to the American books they printed. Holmes proposes that 'an American author is on the whole more acceptable to an English public when his work is served au naturel than when it is hacked and flavoured'. Holmes's desire for direct discourse with a public broad enough to include 'those who only want to be entertained' as well as a 'small clan of more careful readers' frames his book as a democratic address from across the Atlantic. To facilitate communication with his English public, Holmes strongly requests that the preface to his forthcoming novel, *The Guardian Angel*, be retained in Low's edition so that readers properly understand the story: 'it is a part of the book as much as the porch is a part of a house'.[1] His comparison of a book to a house both imagines the book as a physical space, and resonates with the two meanings of 'domestic' by echoing the symbolic domestic spaces in *The Guardian Angel* itself, within discussions of American literature being circulated abroad. Holmes's letter suggests that a British edition of an American book might construct an American space outside of the nation itself, and that these American books could create transatlantic communication.

Holmes perceives the interventions of British publishers as antithetical to this aim; this chapter, however, argues the opposite. It suggests the

129

material interventions of British publishers – decisions about publishing formats, illustrations, and prefaces, amongst other things – could mark American books as both distinctly national and as participants in a transatlantic print culture. These British reprints are thus spatialised objects, in which the local architecture of the book manifests transatlantic circulations of ideas and goods, and constructs a national space outside of the nation itself. I begin by outlining the presence of the American book in Britain from the 1820s onwards, arguing that a print culture in which multiple imports and reprints circulated alongside one another led to the British perception of American literature as radically material. I then examine reprints of James Fenimore Cooper's *The Pilot* and Charles Brockden Brown's *Edgar Huntly* in the early numbers of Henry Colburn and Richard Bentley's influential 'Standard Novels' series (1831–55), whose illustrations and prefaces amplify connections between transatlantic circulation and the American nationhood articulated in the texts themselves. The spaces created by these books and by the series fashion an American culture which expands the boundaries of literature in English and complicates the national identity of the series itself.

Repositioning the 'Standard Novels' as a transatlantic publishing venture, the chapter provides a starting point from which to rethink cultural relations between America and Britain in the nineteenth century and to reconsider how national literatures, quite literally, materialise. It seeks to complicate the relatively recent national histories of the book that have codified the field of scholarship but can only accommodate transatlantic circulations of print in 'limited and awkward ways', as Michael Winship observes (1999: 99). For example David McKitterick states that *The Cambridge History of the Book in Britain, 1830 to 1914* is concerned with 'the book in Britain, rather than the British book' and takes 'a global perspective' (2008: 22). However, transnational aspects of the book trade are given a single chapter, making them appear marginal rather than integral to the trade. Repositioning the transatlantic trade at the centre of British and American print culture reveals that 'literary producers in Britain and America inhabited an interconnected field whose networks of circulation have yet to be fully described', as Joseph Rezek suggests (2013: 582).

The chapter also frames connections between nineteenth-century British and American literary traditions as material as well as imaginative. Transatlantic approaches to nineteenth-century literature have conceptualised British and American literary traditions as intertwined with and mirroring one another, rather than forming in opposition.[2] However, by concentrating on generic, thematic and intertextual connections between texts, the field has neglected the material exchanges of transatlantic culture. This lacuna in scholarship is only now beginning to be filled. Recently, Rezek has argued that 'it was through success in London that Irish, Scottish, and American fiction were consecrated', and Jessica DeSpain has suggested that transatlantic reprints after 1840 articulate the instability of individual and national identities, and challenge disembodied notions of citizenship with their material forms (DeSpain, 2014; Rezek, 2015: 3). Developing those arguments, I suggest that the spatialised material texts of British reprints intersect with complex discourses of nationhood within American literary texts, but also manifest their own transatlantic origins to fashion an American identity beyond the nation's boundaries.

* * *

Throughout the nineteenth century, fewer American books were imported into Britain than British books into America. Winship's study of customs records shows that while the USA exported $3,866 worth of books to Britain in 1828, they imported $75,807 from Britain: by 1868, these figures were $77,524 and $826,117 respectively (1999: 119). Nevertheless, as early as the 1820s, there were London booksellers who specialised in the importing of American books, including Obadiah Rich, Richard J. Kennett and John Miller. Sydney Smith might have famously asked 'who reads an American book?' in the *Edinburgh Review* of January 1820, but he did so within a review of a statistical work on the United States published in Philadelphia, suggesting that his question cannot be taken at face value.[3] Indeed, William St Clair describes an 1821 printing of Percy Shelley's *Queen Mab* (1813) as one of several books which 'masqueraded as imports from America [in this case, so the real publishers could avoid a prosecution for libel], a ruse which would not have succeeded if American books had not been a common sight' (2004: 391).

John Miller also published British editions of American books: for example, he received advanced sheets of James Fenimore Cooper's *The Pilot* in 1824, in return for splitting half the profits with Cooper.[4] Receiving advanced sheets meant that British publishers could issue editions just before or simultaneously with the American publication: at various times until 1854, British publishers had some legal claim (through case law) to copyright of these prior or simultaneous publications.[5] Even after the copyright window closed, some publishers would pay for advanced sheets in the hope of securing sales by issuing their edition more quickly, or tempting purchasers to buy the 'author's' or 'authorized' edition.

These editions faced competition from unauthorised reprints. Though they may not have been permitted by the author or original publisher, such publications were often not strictly piracies, as they did not break copyright law.[6] Even when it was possible to secure copyright through prior publication in England, many American authors did not do so, meaning that their works could be reprinted freely: Nathaniel Hawthorne's *The Scarlet Letter* (1850), for example, did not have a British copyright. Moreover, fluctuations in the interpretation of copyright law and difficulties in proving that a British publisher had published an American text prior to its appearance in the United States meant that protecting copyrights that did exist could be problematic. Furthermore, unauthorised reprints were attractive to publishers, allowing them to avoid payments to authors, and to issue texts that had already been tested on an American public. Publishers in Britain were thus split in their approaches to American literature: some, like Richard Bentley and John Murray (II and III), invested time and money in making arrangements with American authors; others, like George Routledge and Henry Bohn, gained reputations for issuing unauthorised editions, and still others, like Sampson Low, dealt in both kinds of publication.

Reprints of American books in Britain never reached the numbers of reprints of British books in America, in terms of either numbers of titles or size of editions. A larger literate population, small numbers of native authors, the restriction of copyright to American citizens and a book trade based in selling cheap books to readers rather than expensive volumes to circulating libraries made British books very attractive to American publishers and ensured this disparity remained throughout the nineteenth century. But whilst it is difficult to establish figures for American reprints in Britain, unauthorised reprints circulated in substantial numbers, even for only mildly popular literary works. James J. Barnes suggests that, during the 1840s, reprints of American works 'were run off in as many as 5,000 to 6,000 copies at a time. When one considers that every other reprinter could also have issued the same work this is not an insignificant number' (1974: 154). British and American texts were brought together in the pages of cheap sensation weeklies like *Cleave's Penny Gazette of Variety and Entertainment* whose editors, in an article published in 1843, 'frankly acknowledge that we have at times largely drawn from our American contemporaries' (Anon., 1843: 2). Marie Léger-St-Jean's *Price One Penny* database catalogues many such publications, showing the extent to which American literature was printed alongside British and French works in a thriving culture of weekly 'penny blood' periodicals from the 1830s onwards.[7] But the interest of prestigious publishers such as Bentley and Murray in American writers, and the publication of expensive illustrated books, like David Bogue's lavish 1849 edition of Longfellow's *Evangeline*, ensured that American literature was not only associated with cheap print for the masses.

The American reprint trade reached new heights with the mass unauthorised republication of Harriet Beecher Stowe's *Uncle Tom's Cabin* in 1852, which sold over a million copies in Britain. Although *Uncle Tom's Cabin* undoubtedly increased appetites for and sales of American books among British readers, to take it as a starting or a focal point for discussions of American books in Britain is to obscure three preceding decades of British publishers' engagement with American literature. Sarah Meer's detailed account of 'Uncle Tom Mania', for example, argues that the success of Stowe's novel 'evoked and inspired…transatlantic literature: books produced in Britain and America that were written for or about the other country and that assumed and sometimes created transatlantic connections' (2005: 197). Yet Meer only briefly mentions the transatlantic successes of slave narratives that preceded *Uncle Tom's Cabin*: for example, *The Narrative of the Life of Frederick Douglass* sold 4,500 copies in Britain between May and September of 1845 (Blackett, 2002: 26).

The possibility for multiple authorised and unauthorised reprints meant that American literature in Britain appeared in a wide range of material forms. During the 1820s, three unauthorised editions of Cooper's *The Pilot* appeared alongside Miller's authorised printing. An *English Review* article on 'The Emerson Mania' of December 1849 – a phenomenon whose existence suggests that *Uncle Tom* was not the first American literary 'mania' – observed that 'we find his works reproduced in every possible form, and at the most tempting prices'.[8] An 1853 article in British weekly *The Lady's Newspaper* by American actor and writer Howard Paul imagines a shop window containing 'multitudinous variations of [George William] Curtis's "Nile Notes", Edgar Poe's Arabesque Tales, and Oliver Holmes's Sparkling Poems, and each for a shilling' as well as '"Webster's Dictionary," in pompous maroon binding', implying that American literature attracted readers of different social classes (1853: 230). This attention to the vivid and various materiality of transatlantic American books suggests that the material presentation of American literature seems to have distinguished it as a national phenomenon as much as its subject matter, themes, or aesthetics.

As DeSpain suggests, 'the smooth patina of textual transmission and national identity was severely fractured by transatlantic reprinting, which called attention to the mediating role of the publisher and the many versions of any one book' (2014: 14). This 'fracturing' could occur at the hands of British publishers, who reframed American texts to make them British: DeSpain examines how British editions of Susan Warner's *The Wide, Wide World* (1850, published under the name Elizabeth Wetherell) transformed its evangelical American heroine to fit models of secular British womanhood.[9] But fracturing could also take place when British publishers framed American texts as distinctly American. Constructing the nation outside of its own boundaries complicated the mapping of the national culture onto a physical space and onto the imaginative work of authors, and instead rendered American literature as the product of transnational print circulations and the interplay between a text and its material form. British reprints of American books were therefore not only vividly material but also radically spatial objects, with the familiar architecture of the book – its bindings, title pages, frontispieces and prefaces – manifesting the transatlantic dynamics of nineteenth-century print.

* * *

One of the most common ways that American literature circulated in Britain was within a publisher's series or 'library', which Leslie Howsam defines as a 'named, sometimes numbered, group of books with a common theme, usually with a uniform binding, and often uniformly priced, appearing under a general title' (1992: 5). Series publication helped to sell books in a variety of ways: buyers would wish to complete a series, the series name acted as a brand to vouch for the value of a title, and the idea of a 'library' itself connoted prestige (Altick, 1958: 11). In Britain, they also gave publishers the opportunity to reach new audiences by offering cheaper editions of both their own titles and out-of-copyright works, which could be reprinted at a lower cost than new works. For this reason, uncopyrighted American works were attractive to publishers. In his study of American literature in nineteenth-century Britain, Clarence Gohdes suggests that the publisher's series was 'the most important' means of circulating American literature 'so far as the number of copies...is concerned', and that, over the course of the century 'almost every very popular American book not protected by copyright found its way into one or more of the series' (1944: 26, 31).

Despite their (imagined if not actual) continual expansion, series tend be understood as stabilising literary spaces. John Spiers emphasises this aspect of the form, arguing that series 'usually seek to fix texts by giving them the authority of permanence...They have often sought to be "canonical'" (2011: 28). The material text is seen as part of this stabilising process, with the uniform bindings of the series absorbing each number into the tradition it constructs. But this stabilising is offset by the open-endedness of the series, and the way that it reconstitutes its whole with each new number. The ideal series should never end, meaning that its uniform bindings must remain porous. Reprinting a book within a series is an act of relocation as well as reproduction: for the book, which now appears in relation to the series theme and its other titles, and for the series, whose space shifts in character as it expands. This tension between the rigid boundaries and labile space of the series is suggested by the term 'library' itself, which implies both the security and perhaps completeness of a private collection, and the rapid motion of a circulating library. The series is thus a space in which the cultural identity of a text can be both asserted and renegotiated, as titles are recontexualised through being presented in new material forms and positioned alongside other titles. In terms of American texts in British series, the relocation into a series accompanied and emphasised the circulation of the text away from its nation of origin and into a transatlantic print culture. On the one hand, printing American titles in series could function, as DeSpain argues in the case of Walt Whitman's publication in Walter Scott's 'Camelot Series' in the 1880s, to naturalise American texts within a British canon (2014: 144). On the other, as I will demonstrate in the case of Bentley and Colburn's 'Standard Novels', it could locate the British series as a space in which American cultural identity could be fashioned through material and imaginative transatlantic exchanges.

Until the 1830s, fiction series generally contained reprints of eighteenth-century titles, one exception being Robert Cadell's five-shilling edition of Walter Scott's 'Waverley' novels. The 'Standard Novels' (1831–55, later 'Bentley's Standard Novels' and hereafter BSN), published first by Henry Colburn and Richard Bentley, and then by Bentley alone after their partnership dissolved in 1832, was the first series to reprint a range of modern fiction.[10] Priced at six shillings per number, the series was at the upper end of the reprint series market and aimed at a middle-class audience, as St Clair shows (2004: 362–3). Each number contained a whole novel (there were a few exceptions to this) with two steel engravings: the series imitated and was advertised as being uniform with Cadell's 'Waverley' series. The publishers reprinted their own authors and bought copyrights from other firms, adding further value by commissioning the author to write new prefaces and notes, and to revise the text: if the author was dead, as with Charles Brockden Brown, a relative or a critic supplied this material. Such additions allowed the publishers to assert a new copyright, usually respected within the trade if not absolutely enforceable under the law. Arguing that it shaped both the market conditions for reprinting fiction and the canon of British literature, Michael Sadleir observes that BSN 'became a tradition almost as soon as it came into existence' (1951: II: 180). The series was, from the first, a transatlantic literary space as well as a national one, commencing with the republication of Cooper's *The Pilot* on 25 February 1831. Cooper went on to be the most published author in the series – his twenty-one novels represent nearly 15 per cent of its total titles – and one of its best-selling.

The Pilot is an unusual number in that it includes no new introductory materials or authorial revisions. Bentley and Colburn had not attempted to secure the copyright before publishing: no payment for the text was made to either Cooper or Miller.[11] For revisions and new introductory material for the rest of his novels in the series, Colburn and Bentley paid Cooper £50 per text. James Franklin Beard suggests that by informing Colburn and Bentley on or around 24 February that A. C. Baynes of Liverpool was also proposing an edition of his novels, and had already printed *The Spy*, Cooper strengthened his position in negotiations for payment for the additions to his works: Bentley and Colburn needed Cooper's notes to distinguish their edition (Beard, 1960: 2:56).

Baynes's edition may have also been responsible for *The Pilot* being the first number and for its appearance without notes or preface. Early advertisements for BSN suggest that beginning with *The Pilot* may not have always been Bentley and Colburn's plan. Four British newspapers and literary weeklies published between 13 and 19 February 1831 contain advertisements that announce William Godwin's *Caleb Williams* as the first number, with *The Pilot* as the second, and that each number will have 'a Biographical and Critical Essay'.[12] This is the reverse of the order in which the two volumes actually appeared. Listing Godwin first may have been simply an error by the author of the advertisement. But the fact that I cannot locate an earlier correct advertisement suggests that Bentley and Colburn may have changed their minds about beginning with Godwin, in favour of Cooper sometime in February 1831. Meanwhile, on 12 February, *The Literary Gazette* – part-owned by Colburn – noticed Baynes's edition of *The Spy* in a series of Cooper's novels priced at five shillings and, a later advertisement would claim, published 'uniformly with the Waverley novels' (Anon., 1831b: 108; Anon., 1831c: 159). Baynes's edition of *The Spy* contained a prospectus which announced that *The Pilot* would be the next in an 'elegant Series' of 'the exquisite novels of Mr. Cooper' (Anon., 1831d). Therefore, it is possible that Colburn and Bentley were aware of the threat to their plans before Cooper's letter. The timeline suggests that Bayne's edition could have prompted them to bring forward the publication of *The Pilot*, believing that it was more important to beat the competition than to have a new introduction, from Cooper or elsewhere. This would further explain why Bentley and Colburn were insistent that a revised edition of Cooper's *The Spy* would be their third number, advertising it from the 19 February in Colburn's *Literary Gazette* and the *Morning Chronicle*. This plan was maintained despite severe delays to the manuscript reaching Cooper in Paris that left him with only days in which to revise it.[13] While neither Bentley and Colburn's reordering of the series, nor their direct response to Baynes's publications can be absolutely verified, if competition from Baynes spurred Colburn and Bentley's decision to publish Cooper first, then the conditions of the transatlantic marketplace led to an American text fronting a series that was advertised as a 'National Library'.

The origins and plot of *The Pilot* are also transatlantic. In his preface to the 1849 edition issued by American publisher George Palmer Putnam, Cooper claimed that he was inspired to write the novel after discussing Scott's *The Pirate* (1822) and concluding that he might 'present truer pictures of the ocean' (Cooper, 1991: 5). Set in 1780 on the north-east coast of England and based on the exploits of Revolutionary War hero John Paul Jones, *The Pilot* narrates an attempt by the American navy to kidnap important British persons. This secret mission from Congress, which ends in failure, runs parallel to the efforts of American sailors Lieutenant Griffith and Captain Barnstable to liberate their fiancées, Cecilia Howard and Katherine Plowden, from their loyalist guardian, Colonel Howard, who brings them back to England after America's victory in the Revolutionary War. Readings of *The Pilot* have generally focused on the novel's treatment of American nationhood, even as more recent studies emphasise Cooper's anxieties over and conflicting opinions on the subject.[14] Jason Berger has argued that a fear of the masses that requires 'writing out a lower-class constituent who had risen too far for comfort' complicates Cooper's republican patriotism (2008: 647), and Cynthia Schoolar Williams suggests that the liminal coastal setting is the crucial space of *The Pilot*, contributing to the novel's presentation of US nationhood as contingent, and ensuring that the novel 'resist[s] the trope of the nation as organic' (2014: 98).

In *The Pilot*, transatlantic identity seems more stable than either British or American nationality. The pilot, based on Jones, is a British subject

Rethinking national contexts and exchanges

who allies himself with the American navy. The English loyalist Colonel Howard is, as Cecilia says, 'a stranger...in the land whose rule he upholds so blindly' (Cooper, 1831: 134): meanwhile his American estates 'had never been confiscated', and are claimed by Cecilia and Griffith at the novel's end, transplanting a hereditary lineage onto the newly republican landscape (1831: 418). On his deathbed, Howard partially converts back to America: 'perhaps I may have also mistaken my duty to America – but I was too old to change my politics or my religion' (p. 405). Although he then blesses the monarch, Howard's previous statement equivocates this: he dies on the fluid space of the ocean, and is buried in Holland, not England. However, markers of American national identity also emerge through these transatlantic encounters. One example is the system of flag signals that Katherine devises to communicate secretly with Barnstable, and which Cooper presents in terms of contemporary debates over the need for an American form of English: 'it's a fine thing to be able to invent names and make dictionaries' (p. 59). But it is the English environment that engenders Katherine's American dictionary. The sign system is not naturally of the American landscape, as Cecilia implicitly suggests when she mistakes Barnstable's flags for English leaves, claiming they 'want the vivid tints which grace the autumn of our own dear America!' (p. 305). The transatlantic production of American culture persists beyond the conflict with Britain. In the novel's conclusion, Griffith, domesticated by marriage and a return to America, learns the pilot's true identity by reading 'English prints' (p. 419): national histories arise from a transatlantic circulation of print that prefigures *The Pilot*'s own course.[15]

The material text of the BSN *Pilot* registers a similarly complex relationship between transatlantic interactions and American nationhood. Gesturing towards Cooper's native land – common knowledge to readers of this reprint edition – the frontispiece and vignette illustrations both point west (see Figure 7.1). In the frontispiece, Katherine looks out of a window to the left of the picture as the reader views it: west in cartographic conventions, an idea reinforced by a map that is visible in the background. Cecilia sits to Katherine's right, consulting Katherine's flag-signal dictionary. The presence of the book and the silk flags, designated in the text as specifically American forms of communication, means that the reader is presented immediately with an image of someone reading an American book. The frontispiece thus playfully mirrors the reader's own situation, providing an answer to Smith's question, 'who reads an American book?' In the vignette, a ship is sailing westward towards the edge of the frame. Looking towards America, these images send the

The material production of American literature

British reader in the opposite direction from the one in which Cooper's text promises to transport its assumed American reader: 'a single glance at the map will make the reader acquainted with the position of the eastern coast of the Island of Great Britain' (Cooper, 1831: 1). But this apparent misdirection, to an extent, works in harmony with the text. The westward-pointing illustrations anticipate the text, directing the British reader where Cooper has assumed his American audience will be so that he can then relocate them to England. Rather that Anglicising the American text, Colburn and Bentley's edition ships its British readership towards America.

Nevertheless, in gesturing westward, the images also encourage a misreading of Cooper's promise to 'conduct' his reader 'across the waters of this disputed ocean', dropping readers of the BSN edition somewhere in

7.1 Frontispiece and title page of the 'Standard Novels' edition of The Pilot by James Fenimore Cooper. London: Colburn and Bentley, 1831. (Source: Robarts Library, University of Toronto. Digitised for the Internet Archive and hosted at https://archive.org/details/pilotstandard00coopuoft)

the middle of the Atlantic rather than the North Sea (p. 9). But in doing so, the illustrations emphasise that Cooper's 'disputed ocean' might easily be mapped onto the Atlantic, especially as the novel details a conflict between America and Britain. Furthermore, towards the end of the novel, Katherine substitutes the North Sea for the Atlantic Ocean, imagined as an American space, proclaiming that its air seems 'as if it were wafted from our own dear distant America' (Cooper, 1831: 375). Enhancing the symbolic possibilities of Cooper's maritime setting, the images that commence the 'Standard Novels' reject any easy identification with a British literary tradition in favour of connoting an American identity forged through transatlantic movement. Despite being initially advertised as a 'National Library' and uniform with the 'Waverley' series, the first number of BSN evokes the series' own transatlantic circulation of texts, and foregrounds Cooper's American identity.

Pairing a household with the ocean, the illustrations invite interpretations of the book as a domestic and transnational space: a space in which national boundaries are created in tandem with their crossing. Through these threshold images, the volume materially anticipates Holmes's porch and house metaphor. It also articulates a spatial understanding of the book that William H. Sherman dates back to the Renaissance, and that is reflected in nineteenth-century printing terms borrowed from architecture (Sherman, 2007: 67, 81).[16] Appearing at the entrance of both volume and series, these paratexts depict their own role as 'thresholds of interpretation', as theorised by Gérard Genette: paratexts are 'a zone without any hard and fast boundary...a zone not only of transition but also of *transaction*' (1997: 2). The BSN paratexts embody both those qualities: they look outwards towards the market, attempting to attract readers, but also manifest the transatlantic currents of that market, mapping them onto the series itself. The liminality of the ocean and the open window emphasise the expansiveness and fluidity of the series over its boundedness, especially as thresholds recur through the illustrations of the first ten BSN. Despite being the work of a different artist and engraver, the vignette for *Caleb Williams* is similar in composition to the frontispiece for *The Pilot*: a woman looks out of a window, with a man seated next to her. The background for the frontispiece for *Caleb Williams* is dominated by an open door. Thus, regardless of the order in which these two volumes had appeared, the series would have begun with images that suggest transitions between spaces. Illustrations for Jane Porter's *Thaddeus of Warsaw* (BSN 4) and *The Scottish Chiefs* (BSN 8), Cooper's *The Last of the Mohicans* (BSN 6), Mary Shelley's *Frankenstein* (BSN 9), and Friedrich

Schiller's *The Ghost Seer* (BSN 10) all feature windows, doors or gates. The repetition of thresholds implies that boundaries are porous: it suggests an ability to move between volumes in the series and make connections across national borders.

The 'Standard Novels' paratexts create transatlantic connections but do not necessitate a sacrifice of American identity. Charles Brockden Brown's *Edgar Huntly* (originally published in America in 1799, and in Britain in 1803), a Gothic novel about the sensational and far-reaching effects triggered by its eponymous narrator's investigation of his best friend's death, was published as the second part of BSN 10 in November 1831. BSN omits Brown's preface, which describes his novel as an attempt at 'calling forth the passions and sympathies of the reader' through 'the perils of the western wilderness' (Brown, 2006: 4). But this omission was probably not an effort to Anglicise the text: the preface was also absent from the first British Minerva Press edition, so Colburn and Bentley may not have known of it, or they may have omitted it because of potentially confusing references to Brown's previous novel *Arthur Mervyn* (1799).

At the same time, the series' own introduction asserts the novel's American identity even whilst situating it in a transatlantic tradition. The BSN introduction, attributed to 'O. C', introduces Brown as 'one of the earliest American novelists, and inferior to none of his countrymen who succeeded him' (Schiller and Brown, 1831: v). However, the writer quickly adds that 'it might truly be said, that in *originality* he has not been surpassed by any inventor of story of whatever age or country': Brown is situated first nationally and then globally (p. v). The introduction then quotes from 'a forgotten journal' (in fact, Volume 1 of the *Attic Miscellany* from 1824), which suggested that Brown 'probably passed his early youth in the house of a settler' (in reality, Brown was born in cosmopolitan Philadelphia, as the introduction itself later notes – p. vi). Leaving its untruth aside, the paratext figures domestic (national) spaces through domestic (household) spaces, an interaction between national and local space that anticipates its mapping of America onto the volume itself: 'we know not where could be found such striking and grand descriptions of American forests, wildernesses, and caverns, and such fearful pictures of savage life and desperate adventure, as occur in the pages before us' (p. xiii). Instead of absorbing Brown into an English tradition, the introduction acts as an advertisement for distinctly American fiction, one that is valuable to a British readership.

However, positioning Brown's novel within the series as a whole reinforces the introduction's simultaneous efforts to situate Brown transatlantically, and ensures that the novel is presented as more than autochthonous curiosity. The quotation from the *Attic Miscellany* also connects Brown to Godwin, suggesting that the two writers formed a 'community of thought', a view shared by modern critics (Schiller and Brown, 1831: vi).[17] The publication of *Edgar Huntly* in the same series as *Caleb Williams* materially reinforced this connection between the writers. Moreover, *Edgar Huntly* was published in the same volume as the second half of Schiller's *The Ghost Seer*, the first half of which had been published in the same volume as *Frankenstein* by Mary Shelley, Godwin's daughter, who was herself influenced by Brown. By placing transatlantic texts not only in the same series but also in the same volume, BSN was responsible for creating transnational relations as much as for fashioning a national canon. Indeed, the word 'national' only appears in the very earliest advertisements for the series, perhaps because the extensive presence of Cooper made it a misnomer.

Presenting American literature within a transatlantic nexus, the series mirrors Brown's own construction of an America shaped by and in dialogue with the Old World. Despite Brown's preface framing *Edgar Huntly* as 'a series of adventures, growing out of the condition of our country', the narrative's complex events reach back to familial, platonic and romantic connections formed in Ireland, and one of its subplots concerns mercantile trade between America and Europe (Brown, 2006: 3). Paradoxically, transatlantic images then begin to enter the novel when its settings and subjects are apparently most indigenous – during Edgar's traumatic stay in the wilderness and his violent encounters with Native Americans. In the untouched American forests, Edgar laments that he 'scarcely knew in what region of the globe I was placed' or whether he is separated from home by 'a river or an ocean' (Schiller and Brown, 1831: 159). Having sleep-walked into a cavern, and then slain a panther and eaten its raw meat, Edgar decides to drink his own sweat after 'remembering the history of certain English prisoners in Bengal, whom their merciless enemy imprisoned in a small room' (p. 147).[18] Comparing himself to an English subject, Edgar seems to require Old World frameworks to understand indigenous American persons and experiences. He nicknames an elderly Native woman 'Queen Mab' as 'there appeared to me some rude analogy between this personage and her whom the poets of old time have delighted to celebrate' (p. 183). Although writing two decades before Cooper, Brown's America similarly emerges through transnational connections: connections that were articulated in *Edgar Huntly*'s publication in BSN.

According to the introduction to *Edgar Huntly*, the publishers intended 'to include in the series some of the other tales of the present writer', but

The material production of American literature

no other works by Brown appeared. Indeed, BSN did not include a wide range of American novelists: Washington Irving and Harriet Beecher Stowe were the only others published within the series. Yet, at times, the series seemed to take on an American identity, via advertisements that acted as another threshold into the series. An advertisement in *John Bull* of 14 March 1831 states that 'a cheap and uniform edition of the entire works of the celebrated author of "*The Pilot*" can only be printed in the present series', and also frames the series as a democratic project, addressing the 'great mass of the public' despite its middle-class pricing (Anon., 1831a: 87). BSN were consistently advertised as an opportunity to collect a full set of Cooper's novels. A puff in the *Morning Chronicle* in April 1832 boasted that 'among the sterling works of fiction, now in course of appearance in the Standard Novels, the productions of Cooper stand pre-eminent' (Anon., 1832a: 1). By September that year, the *Morning Post* was advertising BSN as a 'Cheap and Uniform Edition of Cooper's Novels' (Anon., 1832b: 4). Rather than being uniform with the 'Waverley' series, the advertisement presented BSN as uniform in their own right and centred on Cooper, whose name had become synonymous with American literature: in Britain, his novels were referred to as the 'American Novels' and Cooper as 'the American Scott' or the 'American Novelist'. To sell BSN as an edition of Cooper was to sell the series as American: the American presence in the 'Standard Novels' altered the national character of the whole series. As its first illustration playfully demonstrated, to read the series was to read American books, but that Americanness was manifest in the publisher's framing of the texts as well as in the novels themselves.

* * *

Analysing both the presence and the presentation of American fiction in the 'Standard Novels' reveals the expressive potential of the material forms of the American book in Britain. Attending to the publisher's framing of the texts and series complicates readings of the series itself as a British national canon, and, more broadly, challenges accounts of nineteenth-century British publishers subsuming American literature into a British tradition. Not only did Bentley and Cooper present American literature as culturally valuable to British readers, but the market value of Cooper especially gave a transatlantic identity to the series. Moreover, the fluid form of the publisher's series, emphasised through the 'Standard Novels'' own liminal paratexts, allowed for these shifts in national identity, accommodating both national identities and transatlantic exchanges.

Foregrounding the transatlantic literary exchanges that shaped the 'Standard Novels' reveals an interplay between national and transnational space in the local architecture of both individual numbers and the series itself. These overlapping geographies in and of the book construct American literary spaces in the margins: in the paratexts of books, and through the border-crossings of transatlantic print circulation. However, the 'Standard Novels' is only one example of the multiple material manifestations of American literature in Britain – if an important one, due to the innovation and popularity of Bentley and Colburn's series. More work is required to understand the extent to which the production of American literary texts by British publishers materially constructed American literature as a distinct genre. Examining the various forms of national and transatlantic identity that are impressed upon British editions of American books will allow us to rethink the role of the publisher and the material text in fashioning national and transatlantic cultures both within, and outside of, the nation itself.

Notes

1 Oliver Wendell Holmes to Sampson Low, 26 September 1867: Sampson Low Correspondence, Open University Archives. I am grateful to Mr George Low for permission to use this collection, and to publish this quotation.
2 See, for example, Claybaugh, 2007; Giles, 2001; Tennenhouse, 2007. For an outline of the field, see Manning and Taylor 2007.
3 Nicholas Mason notes that Smith 'actually considered himself a friend to the United States', and that the review of Seybert's *Statistical Annals* is 'generally admiring' (2010: 144–5).
4 James J. Barnes describes Miller's transatlantic career, although he focuses on Miller supplying American publishers Carey & Lea with British books and texts, paying less attention to Miller's dealings in American books (Barnes, 1976).
5 For the law regarding copyrights of American works in Britain, and the efforts of British publishers to police their American copyrights, see: Barnes, 1974: 153–76.
6 In the nineteenth century itself, however, legal but unauthorised reprints were often referred to as piracies: Dickens used the term about legal American reprints of his books.
7 Marie Léger-St-Jean's *Price One Penny: A Database of Cheap Literature, 1837–1860* (2014) can be found online http://priceonepenny.info.
8 Quoted in Gohdes, 1944: 145.
9 Gohdes makes similar arguments about 'the readiness with which American literature was absorbed into the body of English writing' via transatlantic anthologies (1944: 145).

10 Michael Sadleir and Royal Gettmann credit Bentley with the success of the series, although the inclusion of Charles Brockden Brown, whom Colburn published before his partnership with Bentley, might suggest that Colburn had some influence on the venture. I draw upon Sadleir and Gettmann's accounts for my history of the Standard Novels series (Sadleir, 1951: II: 91–5; Gettmann, 1960: 45–54).
11 The Standard Novels edition was textually different from Miller's edition, being printed from Carey & Lea's Philadelphia second edition, and so incorporating authorial revisions. For the textual history of *The Pilot*, see: House, 1986: 435–48.
12 This advertisement can be found in: *The Edinburgh Literary Journal; or, Weekly Register of Literature and Belles Lettres*, 12 February 1831; *The Standard*, 15 February 1831; *Times*, 16 February 1831 (altered by 19 February); *Scotsman*, 19 February 1831.
13 Letters between Cooper and Bentley and Colburn show that Cooper, then residing in Paris, had not received a copy of the book by 7 April, but he began to send corrections on 12 April and the book was published on 2 May.
14 The classic treatment of Cooper's sea fiction is Philbrick, 1961. Philbrick argues that Cooper's romantic vision of the sea attempts to 'give appropriate fictional expression to his doctrine of maritime nationalism' (that a strong navy was central to US nationhood) and is a 'celebration of national independence' (pp. 52, 58).
15 Cooper had negotiated transatlantic publication for two of his previous novels, so would have had such arrangements in mind when writing *The Pilot*.
16 Sherman notes that the word 'frontispiece' is borrowed from architecture, as are mid-nineteenth-century printing coinages like 'sill' and 'gutter' (2007: 72, 79).
17 For Godwin's influence on Brown's politics and aesthetics, see: Apap, 2012: 26.
18 Philip Barnard and Stephen Shapiro read this comparison as part of the novel's criticisms of imperialism, connecting 'two Indian frontiers – one in North America, the other in South Asia', both of which 'belong to the same environment of conflicts between imperial powers mediated through native populations': (2006: xxxi).

References

Altick, Richard D. (1958). 'From Aldine to Everyman: Cheap Reprint Series of English Classics'. *Studies in Bibliography* 11: 3–24.
Anon. (1831a). 'Advert for the Standard Novels'. *John Bull* 14 March: 87.
——— (1831b). 'List of New Books'. *Literary Gazette* 12 February: 108.
——— (1831c). 'Advertisements'. *Literary Gazette* 14 March: 159.

―――― (1831d). 'Prospectus of the Novelist's Miscellany', in *The Pilot*, James Fenimore Cooper. Liverpool: A. C. Baynes.
―――― (1832a). 'Cheap Edition of Cooper's Novels'. *Morning Chronicle* 3 April: 4.
―――― (1832b). 'Cheap and Uniform Edition of Cooper's Novels'. *Morning Post* 24 September: 1.
―――― (1843). 'American Literature'. *Cleave's Penny Gazette of Variety and Entertainment* 20 May: 2.
Apap, Christopher (2012). 'Irresponsible Acts: The Transatlantic Dialogues of William Godwin and Charles Brockden Brown', in *Transatlantic Sensations*, eds. Jennifer Phegley, John Cyril Barton and Kristin N. Huston. Farnham: Ashgate, pp. 23–40.
Barnard, Philip and Stephen Shapiro (2006). 'Introduction', in *Edgar Huntly; Or, Memoirs of a Sleep-Walker*, Charles Brockden Brown. Indianapolis, IN: Hackett, pp. ix–xlii.
Barnes, James J. (1974). *Authors, Publishers and Politicians: The Quest for an Anglo-American Copyright Agreement, 1815–1854*. London: Routledge and Kegan Paul.
―――― (1976). 'John Miller: First Transatlantic Publisher's Agent'. *Studies in Bibliography* 29: 373–9.
Beard, James Franklin (1960). *Letters and Journals of James Fenimore Cooper*, Vol. 2 (6 vols.). Cambridge, MA: Belknapp Press.
Berger, Jason (2008). 'Killing Tom Coffin: Rethinking the Nationalist Narrative in James Fenimore Cooper's *The Pilot*'. *Early American Literature* 43: 643–70.
Blackett, R. J. M. (2002 [1983]). *Building an Antislavery Wall: Black Americans in the Atlantic Abolitionist Movement, 1830–1860*. Baton Rouge: Louisiana State University Press.
Brown, Charles Brockden (2006 [1799]). *Edgar Huntly; Or, Memoirs of a Sleep-Walker*, ed. Philip Barnard and Stephen Shapiro. Indianapolis, IN: Hackett.
Cooper, James Fenimore (1831 [1824]). *The Pilot*. London: Colburn and Bentley.
―――― (1991). *Sea Tales: The Pilot and the Red Rover*. New York: State University of New York Press.
Claybaugh, Amanda (2007). *The Novel of Purpose: Literature and Social Reform in the Anglo-American World*. Ithaca, NY: Cornell University Press.
DeSpain, Jessica (2014). *Nineteenth-Century Transatlantic Reprinting and the Embodied Book*. Farnham: Ashgate.
Genette, Gérard (1997). *Paratexts: Thresholds of Interpretation*, tr. Jane E. Lewin. Cambridge: Cambridge University Press.
Gettmann, Royal A. (1960). *A Victorian Publisher: A Study of the Bentley Papers*. Cambridge: Cambridge University Press.
Giles, Paul (2001). *Transatlantic Insurrections: British Culture and the Formation of American Literature, 1730–1860*. Philadelphia: University of Pennsylvania Press.

Gohdes, Clarence (1944). *American Literature in Nineteenth-Century England*. New York: Columbia University Press.
House, Kay Seymour (1986). 'Textual Commentary', in *The Pilot: A Tale of the Sea*, James Fenimore Cooper, ed. Kay Seymour House. Albany: State University of New York Press, pp. 435–48.
Howsam, Leslie (1992). 'Sustained Literary Ventures: The Series in Victorian Book Publishing'. *Publishing History* 31: 5–26.
Léger-St-Jean, Marie (2014). *Price One Penny: A Database of Cheap Literature, 1837–1860*. (20 October 2014). Faculty of English, Cambridge. Available at: http://priceonepenny.info (accessed 17 December 2014).
Manning, Susan and Andrew Taylor (2007). 'Introduction: What is Transatlantic Literary Studies?', in *Transatlantic Literary Studies: A Reader*, eds. Susan Manning and Andrew Taylor. Edinburgh: Edinburgh University Press, pp. 1–13.
Mason, Nicholas (2010). '*Blackwood's Magazine*, Anti-Americanism, and the Beginnings of Transatlantic Literary Studies'. *Symbiosis: A Journal of Anglo-American Literary Relations* 14(2): 141–58.
McKitterick, David (2008). 'Introduction', in *The Cambridge History of the Book in Britain: Volume VI, 1830–1914*, ed. David McKitterick. Cambridge: Cambridge University Press, pp. 1–74.
Meer, Sarah (2005). *Uncle Tom Mania: Slavery, Minstrelsy, and Transatlantic Culture in the 1850s*. Athens: University of Georgia Press.
Paul, Howard (1853). 'Who Reads An American Book?' *The Lady's Newspaper*, 9 April.
Philbrick, Thomas (1961). *James Fenimore Cooper and the Development of American Sea Fiction*. Cambridge, MA: Harvard University Press.
Rezek, Joseph (2015). *London and the Making of Provincial Literature: Aesthetics and the Transatlantic Book Trade, 1800–1850*. Philadelphia: University of Pennsylvania Press.
——— (2013). 'Furious Booksellers: The 'American Copy' of the *Waverley* Novels and the Language of the Book Trade'. *Early American Studies* 11(3): 557–82.
Sadleir, Michael (1951). *XIX Century Fiction: A Bibliographical Record Based on His Own Collection* Vol. 2 (2 vols). London: Constable & Co.
Schiller, Friedrich and Charles Brockden Brown (1831). *The Ghost Seer and Edgar Huntly*. London: Colburn and Bentley.
Sherman, William H. (2007). 'On the Threshold: Architecture, Paratext, and Early Print Culture', in *Agent of Change: Print Culture Studies After Elizabeth L. Eisenstein*, eds. Sabrina Alcorn Baron, Eric N. Lindquist and Eleanor F. Shevlin. Amherst: University of Massachusetts Press, pp. 67–81.
Smith, Sydney (1820). 'Review of *Statistical Annals of the United States* by Adam Seybert', *Edinburgh Review* 33: 69–80.
Spiers, John (2011). 'Introduction: Wondering about 'the Causes of Causes': The Publisher's Series, Its Cultural Work and Meanings', in *The Culture of the*

Publisher's Series: Volume One: Authors, Publishers and the Shaping of Taste, ed. John Spiers. Basingstoke: Palgrave Macmillan, pp. 1–60.

St Clair, William (2004). *The Reading Nation in the Romantic Period*. Cambridge: Cambridge University Press.

Tennenhouse, Leonard (2007). *The Importance of Feeling English: American Literature and the British Diaspora, 1750–1850*. Princeton, NJ: Princeton University Press.

Williams, Cynthia Schoolar (2014). *Hospitality and the Transatlantic Imagination, 1815–1835*. Basingstoke: Palgrave Macmillan.

Winship, Michael (1999). 'The Transatlantic Book Trade and Anglo-American Literary Culture in the Nineteenth Century', in *Reciprocal Influences: Literary Production, Distribution, and Consumption in America*, eds Steven Fink and Susan Williams. Columbus: Ohio State University Press, pp. 98–122.

8

Gruesome models: European displays of natural history and anatomy and nineteenth-century literature

Laurence Talairach-Vielmas

'We visited the wondrous cave and the little cabinets of natural history'

We passed a considerable period at Oxford, rambling among its environs and endeavouring to identify every spot which might relate to the most animating epoch of English history. Our little voyages of discovery were often prolonged by the successive objects that presented themselves...

We left Oxford with regret and proceeded to Matlock, which was our next place of rest...We visited the wondrous cave and the little cabinets of natural history, where the curiosities are disposed in the same manner as in the collections at Servox and Chamounix. The latter name made me tremble when pronounced by Henry, and I hastened to quit Matlock, with which that terrible scene was thus associated.

Mary Shelley, *Frankenstein* (1986: 430)

Journeys of all sorts punctuate Mary Shelley's *Frankenstein* (1818, revised 1831), from Captain Robert Walton's scientific expedition to the North Pole to Victor Frankenstein's numerous voyages between England and Switzerland, throughout Europe and finally to the North Pole in search of his creature. Frankenstein, in particular, never fails to take the longest route possible in order to discover new regions or places, eager as

Rethinking national contexts and exchanges

he is to take in new sights and acquire new knowledge along the way. During his 'voyages of discovery', moreover, he happens upon various 'objects' or curiosities which feature repeatedly in contemporary accounts of nineteenth-century tourism. This chapter will argue that objects related to natural history and anatomy informed the literature of the long nineteenth century, and underline the importance of material exchanges across cultural borders. Indeed, nineteenth-century novels, just like travel narratives, guidebooks and memoirs, contain many descriptions of visitors' responses to displays of natural history or anatomy. The impact of these displays and objects is a striking feature of late-eighteenth-century and nineteenth-century travelling, and this chapter contends that these transnational exchanges help us rethink how the literature of the nineteenth century was shaped by such relationships. In *Frankenstein*, for instance, the many places seen or visited by the characters shape the novel to some extent as a travel narrative, more especially so as it was published after 1815, when Continental travel was resumed at the end of the Napoleonic Wars (1803–15) (Carroll, 2007: 275). In addition, the novel regularly echoes Mary Shelley's own travels through Europe in 1814 and 1816, recorded in *History of Six Weeks' Tour through a part of France, Switzerland, Germany, and Holland; with Letters Descriptive of a Sail Round the Lake of Geneva and of the Glaciers of Chamouni* (Shelley, 1817). The journal, written by Mary Shelley and Percy Bysshe Shelley, describes two journeys: one through Europe (France, Switzerland, Germany, the Netherlands) in 1814, as the unmarried couple eloped from England with Mary's stepsister, Claire Clairmont, and a second, to Lake Geneva in 1816, which inspired Mary Shelley's story of *Frankenstein*. Four letters and a poem by Percy Shelley were added to the travel narrative. Both *Frankenstein* and the *History of Six Weeks' Tour* were thus written in 1817, and the links between the two narratives invite readers to examine the significance of these texts' shared motifs (see also Colbert, 2005).

The connections between Shelley's travel narrative and her novel are clear from the objects seen, noticed or examined by the characters in both texts; objects which are particularly emblematic of European travel. In each narrative, Shelley mentions cabinets of natural history. The cabinets the Shelleys view at Servoz and Chamonix, which they compare with those in Matlock, Keswick, Clifton and Bethgelert, are mirror images of those which Frankenstein visits in 'Matlock', 'Chamounix' and 'Servox' [sic].[1] Some cabinets of natural history continued to resemble closely the cabinets of curiosities of early modern collectors. Others, however, grouping together several private collections, paved the way for the natural history and medical museums, which opened their doors to the public in the course of the nineteenth century.[2] Whether displaying 'curiosities', the most fantastic forms of nature, or collections of minerals, shells or fossils, they frequently brought under one roof objects from around the world, associating travelling with erudite investigation. In her *History of Six Weeks' Tour*, Mary Shelley relates the purchase of specimens of minerals and plants, such as crystal seals and seeds, which she hopes will 'colonize in [her] garden in England' (Shelley, 1817: 171). This example illustrates how such collections facilitated exchanges of various sorts through the circulation of travellers and their purchases. In their travel narrative, the Shelleys also condemn some of the cabinet-owners, like the proprietor at Chamonix, a 'quack' who 'subsist[s] on the weakness and credulity of travellers as leaches [*sic*] subsist on the sick' (Shelley, 1817: 171); a remark which recalls to some extent Mary Shelley's anatomist, trained by his father not to believe in superstitions. The comparisons between Mary Shelley's travel narrative and *Frankenstein* are telling, for the echoes between the two narratives highlight the traffic between two different literary genres, with Shelley's 'mad scientist', to use an anachronistic term, depicted as a Romantic traveller following in the footsteps of the Shelleys whilst the Romantic couple reveal a taste for scientific inquiry throughout their journey.

Indeed, while the travel narrative is peppered with references to picturesque scenery and ruined castles, the Shelleys also pay attention to minerals and plants, describing for example the horns of the chamois and the bouquetin. In this way, the narrative deals recurrently with the acquisition and dissemination of knowledge.[3] Moving away from Grand Tour narratives, however, Shelley's travel writing constantly merges romantic descriptions with references to natural history. Likewise, Frankenstein's journey is punctuated by sublime descriptions of the Swiss mountains. Moreover, as the example quoted at the beginning of this chapter underlines, the doctor visits cabinets of natural history as well, paying attention to the way in which the objects are displayed. For instance, the arrangement of the natural history cabinet he observes at Matlock revives his memory of the collections at 'Servox' and 'Chamounix', thereby connecting England to mainland Europe. Revealingly, the sudden echo between the collections in Matlock, 'Servox' and 'Chamounix' provokes a sudden surge of horror in Frankenstein, reminding him of his creature. This comes at a significant point in the novel, since Frankenstein is on his way to Scotland to create a mate for the creature, having collected his 'materials' (Shelley, 1986: 428) in London with the intention of touring England and reaching Scotland six months later. Although Frankenstein remains insensitive to his task in the first part of the novel, blind to 'every object the most insupportable to the delicacy of the human feelings' (Shelley, 1986: 312) and unemotionally observes 'the natural decay and corruption of the human body' (Shelley, 1986: 311), the sight of the collection, through a series of associations, shakes him profoundly, thereby drawing attention to the issue of sensitivity that is so central to the novel and to the understanding of Frankenstein's tragic lack of feeling. While the 'curiosities' are not described as such, it is nonetheless significant that the cabinets of natural history mentioned in the novel expose Frankenstein as a flawed Romantic traveller, doomed by his lack of sensibility. As I will show, following such examples of transnational exchanges throughout nineteenth-century literature helps us track aesthetic developments. By recording the way in which visitors looked at displays of natural history and anatomy, for example, or describing the arrangement of some of the objects, as Frankenstein does, nineteenth-century literature followed trends in the representation and exhibition of the body, thus reflecting issues such as that of human – or British – identity.

The gruesome models of a modern Prometheus

The exchanges between the material cultures of natural history and medicine on the one hand, and literature on the other, illuminate how the literature of the period reflected the evolution of scientific knowledge and the role played by museum collections in the construction and dissemination of scientific understanding. But that changing relationship also reflected shifts in the ways visitors were expected to react to these collections. Many of those reactions can be observed in travel narratives, as their authors journeyed through mainland Europe and recorded their impressions. In addition, as suggested earlier, those impressions also later found their way into the literature of the period. To start with, it is important to outline what these 'cabinets of natural history' consisted of at the end of the eighteenth-century. From the second half of the eighteenth century to the end of the nineteenth, cabinets of natural history, just like medical museums, became very popular throughout Europe. Many of the objects exhibited were anatomical specimens, models and preparations, comprising artificial (mainly wax) models, body parts in jars and articulated skeletons. Educating professional medical audiences and thrilling lay audiences,[4] the models circulated widely within Europe. Many were shipped to England, as the scarcity of modellers in England (apart from Joseph Towne [1806–79] who was active at Guy's Hospital in the mid-nineteenth century) compelled anatomists there to import models for their private lessons.[5] Yet, as Mary Shelley's travel narrative highlights, British travellers also visited natural history and anatomical collections abroad. In Italy, the gruesome models of the 'Gabinetto Fisico' became a landmark in European tours at the turn of the nineteenth century, illuminating the impact of anatomical culture in Europe.

As a matter of fact, the 'Gabinetto Fisico', or Specola museum, was one of the most striking collections of human anatomy. This museum of natural history opened in Florence in 1775 and attracted numerous European travellers. Many diaries, travel narratives and guidebooks published throughout the nineteenth century record the vivid impressions of visitors or reviewers. At the end of the eighteenth century, the Marquis de Sade, famous for his erotic novels, recorded his visit to the collections in Florence in 1775 in his *Voyage d'Italie*, just before the opening of the Florentine museum.[6] The morbid wax models he discovered there were those of Gaetano Giulio Zummo (or Zumbo – 1656–1701), then on display in the Medici gallery before being transferred to the cabinet of natural history. The work of the Sicilian modeller, famous for such macabre artworks as *The Plague* or *The Tomb*, featured decomposing corpses likely to distress the senses of the viewer:

> In one of these vitrines is exhibited a sepulchre containing numerous corpses which enable the visitor to observe the various stages of decay, from the one-day-old corpse to the completely worm-eaten cadaver. This bizarre idea is the work of a Sicilian called Zummo. Everything is made of wax and coloured with natural tints. The impression is so intense that the senses seem to mutually warn one another. You naturally and inadvertently apply your hand to your nose when you look at the horrible detail which you can hardly examine without remembering sinister ideas of destruction and, consequently, those, more consoling, of the Creator. Close to this vitrine is another similar one, representing a sepulchre in a church rectory where the same stages of putrefaction may likewise be observed. You can see above all a poor naked man carrying a corpse which he throws over the others and who, suffocated by the smell and spectacle, falls on his back and dies as well. This group is frighteningly truthful. (Sade, 1965)[7]

Interestingly, the scene later appeared in Sade's *Juliette; or Vice Amply Rewarded* (1801), a narrative which accompanied *Justine; or Good Conduct*

Well-Chastized (1791) and was regarded as the prequel of *Juliette*, the female character noticing the very same details:

> We can see a sepulchre full of cadavers, on whom may be observed all the stages of dissolution, from the moment of death to the complete destruction of man. This grim work is made of wax, coloured so naturally that nature cannot be more expressive nor truthful. The impression is so intense, when one looks at this masterpiece, that the senses seem to mutually warn one another: you inadvertently apply your hand to your nose. My cruel imagination delighted in this spectacle. How many creatures have suffered from these horrible stages because of my wickedness?…Not far from there is another sepulchre full of plague victims where the same degrees of putrefaction may be observed: a wretch stark naked may be seen carrying a corpse to throw it with the others and who, suffocated by the stink falls on his back and dies; this group is frighteningly truthful. (Sade, 1963)[8]

As with Mary Shelley, the striking similarities between Sade's travel narrative and his novel indicate the influence of such representations of the body on contemporary culture (see also de Goncourt and de Goncourt, 1894: 140–1). As in *Frankenstein*, moreover, the sight of the wax cadavers spurs a reflection on villainy in the character (which the character here delights in, however). For Ann Williams, the links between the two writers – who were near contemporaries – is not solely to be found in the choice of the name 'Justine' by Mary Shelley for one of the creature's victims. As she argues, Shelley and Sade both 'lived in a period of revolutionary upheaval, and…both deployed Gothic conventions in the service of philosophical romance' (Williams, 2003). Furthermore, she adds that although Sade never appeared on the Shelleys' reading list, Byron was known to own a copy of *Justine* in 1816 before he left England. Whether or not a connection may be traced between Shelley and Sade, the echoes between their travel narratives and novels remain significant, especially as they both revolve around collections exhibited in cabinets of natural history and their impact on late-eighteenth-century travellers. The difference between Shelley's *Frankenstein* and Sade's *Juliette*, however, is that no details are given concerning the 'curiosities' seen by Frankenstein, apart from mentioning their layout in the cabinet. This stress on the arrangement of the collection is typical of the evolution of cabinets of natural history, which aimed increasingly to diffuse knowledge rather than simply striking the beholder with freaks of nature. Indeed, the morbid aesthetics typified by artists such as Zumbo gradually fell out of fashion. Thus when the Florentine museum came to display new objects designed to reveal the secrets and mysteries of the human body to the general public, instead of decay and decomposition, the anatomical models presented in the cabinet of natural history were characterised by the orderly fashion in which they were arranged. French sculptor Charles Dupaty (1775–1825) noted the change in his *Lettres sur l'Italie* (*Letters on Italy* – 1785):

> I would like to describe the cabinet of natural history that the Grand Duke has been enlarging and M. Fontana arranging…It is hard to render the refinement of the apartments, the order, the distribution…the vitrines of this cabinet represent as many boxes in M. Fontana's memory, filled with natural history.[9]

Similarly, the French writer Stendhal, travelling through Italy, visited the Florentine museum on 27 September 1811:

> Museum of Natural History. – How pleasurable it must be for an anatomist to step in this Museum! Nothing is cleaner, more comprehensible nor more instructive. Everything is arranged so as to give intelligible ideas effortlessly. The childbirth room seems to be superior to those in Bologna and Vienna. I remember with delight when I visited the Josephinum in Vienna and saw the childbirth room with lady A.
>
> I behold, with the pleasure of an ignorant, the muscles and the nerves, meticulously represented…I have seen there for the first time a skeleton that looked beautiful. It is easy to feel how beautiful a skeleton can be…It is situated on the left when you enter the rooms with the wax models, in a beautiful glass cage.[10]

Instead of disease and decay, the collection was now characterised by beauty, order and cleanliness. No longer designed for connoisseurs of morbid aesthetics, the models were aimed at 'the anatomist', most likely to appreciate the beauty of the exhibits. Stendhal's comparisons between several collections visited by the European traveller are compelling; showing how collections prompted travellers to develop their own systems of classification – their own natural history of natural history cabinets. This move away from a focus on 'curiosities' as emblems of sixteenth- or seventeenth-century wonder to a more scientific and comprehensive view of the natural world is illustrative of a move away from emotions and passions. Exhibited as it is in a glass case, the skeleton is observed from a distance and the writer's 'feel[ing]' sounds all the more detached. Stendhal's remarks were echoed in England by the board of curators of the Royal College of Surgeons, which noted in July 1813 that 'the utmost order and decorum prevailed' (RCS Board of Curators 2 July 1813, qtd. in Alberti, 2013: 20). For Samuel Alberti, such remarks on order typified new modern ways of displaying and viewing throughout

Europe, especially in the last decades of the century. As he argues, '[i]n the expanding public museum sector in the late Victorian period, the emphasis shifted to transparent, ordered display and clear labelling', so as to set the displayed objects 'within taxonomic schemes' and 'remov[e] them from the realm of the curious' (Alberti, 2007: 381, 390).

As exemplified by Shelley's novel, therefore, nineteenth-century literature charted the gradual changes in natural history and anatomical displays and followed the evolution of museum display on a European scale. In addition, inspired by the impressions of those actually visiting some collections, the literature of the period represented the characters' reactions to the displays, as in the case of Frankenstein. As suggested above, Shelley constructs the scene in which Frankenstein looks at the collection as a pivotal moment in his moral awakening: Frankenstein's clinical detachment when he looks at the collection is followed by a painful memory of the creature. It is tempting to conjecture that Shelley had in mind visitors' responses to such collections. In 1813, Joseph Forsyth mentioned in his travel book the impressive size of the Florentine collection.[11] Forsyth had visited the museum in 1803 and discussed it in an 1813 review which, according to Feldman and Scott-Kilvert, Shelley had not read before April 1819, while she was making preparations for her own journey (Feldman and Scott-Kilvert, 1987: 257). In January 1820, Shelley recorded her visit to the Italian museum in her diary in the following terms: 'The Gabinetto Fisico was a museum of natural history, chiefly celebrated for its collection of wax models of the human anatomy, some of which were extremely gruesome' (Feldman and Scott-Kilvert, 1987: 306, qtd. in Marshall, 1995: 68). If Shelley had not read the Forsyth review when she first wrote *Frankenstein*, it is highly likely that she had heard about the collection, especially as many nineteenth-century writers mentioned it in their own diaries. Moreover, Forsyth's description of the museum focused on the anatomical collection, emphasising the evolution from Zumbo's morbid aesthetics to Fontana's experiments with wax. The following quotation maps out the aesthetic changes in the displays and is worth quoting at length:

> This, being originally an assemblage of several scattered collections in natural history, is rather full than complete. It is richest in fossils, corals, shells, and insects; but celebrated only for the anatomical imitations.
>
> Wax was first used in imitating anatomy by Zumbo, a Sicilian of a melancholy, mysterious cast, some of whose works are preserved here. Three of these bear the gloomy character of the artist, who has exhibited the horrible details of the plague and the charnel-house, including the decomposition of bodies through every stage of putrefaction – the

blackening, the swelling, the bursting of the trunk – the worm, the rat and the tarantula at work – and the mushroom springing fresh in the midst of corruption.

I was struck by the immensity of this collection, which occupies fourteen rooms; yet, considered as a system, anatomists find it both defective and redundant. Sig. Fabbroni told me that many articles should be melted down as useless; that others were inaccurate; that all, from the yielding nature of the wax, wanted frequent retouching; and that, beginning anew, he could make the system more complete in half the compass. But such is ever the course of experiment. Every new step in science is the correction of an old one. Science may be considered as the art of remedies which originate in defect and end in it.

…This museum is under the direction of Felice Fontana…Fontana readily entered into the history of imitative anatomy, 'an art invented by Zumbo, and revived', he said 'by me…I stood alone in a new art, without guide or assistants…Thus obliged to form workmen for myself, I selected some mechanical drudges, who would execute my orders without intruding into my design…'

This active Prometheus is creating a decomposable statue, which will consist of ten thousand separable pieces, and three millions of distinct parts, both visible and tangible. (Forsyth, 1820: 46–9)

Whether Shelley had read the review before 1819 or not, *Frankenstein* appears as an uncanny double of the Florentine modeller, a latter-day Prometheus selecting workers to achieve his art and collect the pieces to create a composite model. As in *Frankenstein*, furthermore, the making of wax anatomical models implied the use of up to a thousand cadavers, as some travellers noted,[12] whilst models which could be disassembled promised to reveal the secret inner workings of the human body. If Feldman and Scott-Kilvert are correct in their assertion that Shelley only read Forsyth's review in 1819, the echoes suggest that recreations of artificial models of the human body from cadavers, especially in Italy (Bologna, Florence) and France, were popularised through many travel narratives which in turn influenced the literary scene of the Romantic period. In the case of *Frankenstein*, the interest lies in the dual nature of Frankenstein's reaction to the 'curiosities' he sees – both in terms of distance and in the emotional reaction generated in him by a series of associations. For Samuel Alberti, the development of literary genres or modes was closely related to the evolution of collections of natural history and anatomy. As he argues,

> The roots of Gothic literature were in the fascination with an imagined and terrible past, and visitors' engagement (with fossils in particular) may reflect this interest. By the late nineteenth century, medicoscientific discourses

contributed to the somatic emphasis of Gothic fiction, which privileged racial degeneration, atavism, deviant sexualities, and monstrosity – examples of which would all be found in anatomical museums. (Alberti, 2007: 390–1)

Alberti refers here to late-Victorian medical Gothic, but the example of *Frankenstein* as a nineteenth-century novel poised between the tradition of the Gothic novel and already foreshadowing the Victorian Gothic is illuminating: the Gothic villain that is Frankenstein experiences contradictory reactions (indifference/horror) when he looks at the objects exhibited in the cabinet of natural history. The oscillation between detachment and empathy mirrors the evolution of aesthetics which marked nineteenth-century representations of human remains and human anatomy more generally. In addition, as Alberti suggests, many of the specimens exhibited played more and more upon tensions between normality and pathology as well as contrasting the wild and the civilised – Britishness and foreign otherness/exotic degeneracy – reaching far beyond European frontiers. Shelley's *Frankenstein*, as an early nineteenth-century example, may, indeed, record how the various forms of nature collected, recreated and exhibited in natural history cabinets impacted contemporary fiction. Frankenstein's creature is compared to a mummy at the opening and the end of the novel: 'A mummy again endued with animation could not be hideous as that wretch' (Shelley, 1986: 319); 'one vast hand was extended, in colour and apparent texture like that of a mummy' (Shelley, 1986: 492). The comparison brings to mind early nineteenth-century Egyptomania and evokes debates around race and national identity. Moreover, the focus on the texture of the skin might even be read as a reference to desiccated specimens, with the mummy subtly constructed as a museum exhibit. This is confirmed by the anatomist's fight against the appearance of death, as manifest in the creature's watery eyes (which signal the onset of putrefaction), the colour of the lips and the texture of the flesh. Frankenstein is a typical anatomist who 'collect[s] [his] materials' (Shelley, 1986: 164), preserves them and exhibits them through his 'monster' – as a living representation of the Latin term *monstrare* (to show), as I have shown elsewhere (Talairach-Vielmas, 2015). In addition, as Stefani Englestein has pointed out, Frankenstein's activities are very close to those of wax modellers: Frankenstein starts with 'bones from the charnel house', and the coloured wax models were 'sometimes constructed on the foundations of real human skeletons' (Englestein, 2008: 183).

Examining *Frankenstein* through its connections with European travel literature or Shelley's own travel narrative therefore enables us to see the links between Frankenstein's creature and the many naturalistic forms that were displayed in museums throughout Europe and/or which tapped into global travelling and its impact upon the construction of British imperial science. Through its creature or through the ways in which Frankenstein reads the displays in the natural history cabinets he visits, the novel also mirrors changing contemporary aesthetics by portraying Frankenstein as the double of artists such as Fontana in Florence. Increasingly associated with a lack of human sympathy or sensitivity, the anatomical collections which appeared in Victorian literature actively influenced forms of characterisation, more especially so, perhaps, when the objects were imported from Europe or the British colonies.

While Shelley's villain responds to the curiosities he sees in the collections he visits, comparing them to those of mainland Europe, later Victorian writers capitalised on the symbolic potential of natural history or anatomical exhibits from overseas. In many Victorian novels, anatomy and natural history collections punctuate the narrative, but they have often been imported into Britain. Represented in the late eighteenth and early nineteenth centuries as the epitome of supremacy, wealth and power, transnational exchanges were now regularly derided by Victorian authors such as Charles Dickens and Wilkie Collins. In *Oliver Twist* (1839), for instance, Dickens points to such emblems of the material culture of medicine as moralising vignettes when Sikes contends that Fagin is 'fit for nothing but keeping as a curiosity of ugliness in a glass bottle' (Dickens, 1839: 76). The 'curiosity' here acts as a metaphor for the character's evil nature (or, it may be surmised, his racial difference). Dickens's trope suggests how the rise of pathological anatomy gradually separated natural history and anatomical displays from the realm of entertainments[13] typically found in old fairs, as illustrated by the following extract from Wordsworth's *The Prelude*:

> The Wax-work, Clock-work, all the marvellous craft
> Of modern Merlins, Wild Beasts, Puppet shows
> All out-o'-the-way, far-fetched, perverted things,
> All freaks of Nature, all Promethean thoughts,
> All jumbled up together to make up
> This Parliament of Monsters.
> (Wordsworth, 1990: 485, l. 680–95)

While medical collections remained a valued teaching aid during the nineteenth century,[14] the Victorian period was especially marked by the opening of many public anatomical museums aimed at professional and lay audiences alike. Highly realistic, heavily moralistic, the collections, which often comprised both natural history and anatomical displays and included 'some very curious specimens of jeux de nature' (Anon,, 1851: 496), revealed the secrets of the body and displayed its pathologies to the lay public. In London, the collections of Antonio Sarti (1839–50), Reimers (1852–53) and Dr Kahn (1851–72) were amongst the most famous, and attracted visitors of both sexes.[15] Some were exclusively reserved for women, such as Madame Caplin's (Bates, 2008: 11). The objects on display were made or prepared in Britain or on the Continent, some of them bearing a typically national flavour, such as the models exhibited at Kahn's showing the progress of sexually-transmitted diseases and which were imported from France: 'The progress of gonorrhoea and syphilis is beautifully exhibited in a series of excellent models, taken from cases in the Hôpital des Vénériens and Val de Grace'(Anon., 1851: 496). However, the 'specific aberrations in Nature's productions' were more and more discredited as 'mere objects of curiosity', more appropriate for entertainment than education and relegated to the world of the travelling fair (Knox, 1836: 131). Indeed, artificial anatomical models, especially after the 1832 Anatomy Act, which allowed the supply of unclaimed corpses to licensed schools, met with an increasingly unenthusiastic reception from medical professionals. Having been particularly associated with women, be they midwives or wax modellers[16] from mainland Europe, by the middle of the nineteenth century, the models were being increasingly dismissed as mere quackery. Anatomical models were therefore regarded more and more in Britain as the teaching tools of those on the fringes of the medical profession and the province of quacks, whilst the use of anatomical preparations, both wet and dry, reflected the skills of bona fide surgeons and anatomists (Bates, 2008: 8).

References to medical collections are found repeatedly in the literature of the Victorian period. Dickens uses a bottled pathological specimen in 'The Lamplighter' (1838), for instance, ironically comparing the reading of the stars with the study of the body. The narrative relates the story of Tom Grig and humorously plays upon the supernatural, prophecies and death by using a large bottle containing a child with three heads which serves as a charm in astrology. The use of the 'curiosity' here is telling: the three-headed child, separated from a medical context, has also been separated from its meaning and is read in a non-scientific way. The distance created by the farce and the jarring irony underlying the narrative thus alludes to the issue of clinical detachment visible in the numerous medical museums, both private and public, where anatomical collections were displayed. Dickens enjoyed denouncing the material culture of medicine and the commodification of the human body, and he was also known for condemning the uses of the bodies of the poor as anatomical material in both his essays published in *Household Words* (Dickens, 1850: 137–9; Dickens, 1858: 361–5) and in his novels, such as *A Tale of Two Cities* (1859), which featured the character of a body-snatcher. But his criticism reached a climax in *Our Mutual Friend* (1864–65), where exotic specimens are brought together and are chaotically exhibited in Mr Venus's shop, the disorderly display of 'human warious' potentially blurring (racial) differences between the exhibits:

> You're casting your eye round the shop, Mr. Wegg. Let me show you a light… Bones, warious. Skulls, warious. Preserved Indian baby. African ditto. Bottled preparations, warious. Everything within reach of your hand, in good preservation. The mouldy ones a-top. What's in those hampers over them again, I don't quite remember. Say, human warious. Cats. Articulated English baby. Dogs. Ducks. Glass eyes, warious. Mummied bird. Dried cuticle, warious. Oh dear me! That's the general panoramic view. (Dickens, 2008: 81)

This museum in reverse illuminates the symbolic potential of the 'objects' that were meant to encapsulate the supremacy of (British) science. The objects on display here, which epitomise transnational exchanges and offer a visual catalogue of various identities, associate British identity (through the articulated English baby) with other human and animal preparations. The panoramic view anticipates Silas Wegg's attempt at buying his own (amputated) leg back so as to complete himself. Indeed, the body parts and specimens from around the world sold at Mr Venus's shop highlight the issue of identity on which the novel hinges. Likewise, Wilkie Collins in *Armadale* (1995 [1866]) uses a private anatomical collection from France (as may be supposed) to construct one of the villains, Dr Downward, as a quack. When Dr Downward reappears in the narrative as Dr Le Doux at the end of the novel, the former abortionist now turned quack psychiatrist has bought his name, diploma and partially completed sanatorium from a French doctor. Tellingly, the decoration of the place includes objects related to the practice of anatomy. The anatomical collection on display in his office, marginal as it may first seem, plays a central part in the characterisation of the villain:

> The doctor's private snuggery was at the back of the house…Horrible objects in brass and leather and glass, twisted and turned as if they were sentient things writhing in agonies of pain, filled up one end of the room.

Rethinking national contexts and exchanges

A great book-case with glass doors extended over the whole of the opposite wall, and exhibited on its shelves long rows of glass jars, in which shapeless dead creatures of a dull white colour floated in yellow liquid. (Collins, 1995: 588)

The contrast between the animated laboratory apparatus able to feel pain and the dehumanised objects exhibited in jars conveys Le Doux's cruelty, debunking the 'gentle treatment' his sanatorium seemingly offers to female patients. As in *Frankenstein*, therefore, the medical collection works in tandem with the issue of sensitivity, underlining Le Doux's lack of feeling and therefore hinting at his villainy. However, Collins also shows how medical collections were increasingly associated with the secrets and mysteries of the human body. Le Doux's medical collection is the second reference made in the novel to exhibited medical specimens. Earlier on in the narrative, a medical practitioner, Dr Hawbury, proposes to explain to Alan Armadale the riddle of his allergy to brandy by showing him his 'collection of curious cases at home' (Collins, 1995: 117). The cases here become interwoven with the secrets of the novel to be elucidated by Dr Hawbury, perhaps with 'the point of his dissecting-knife' (Collins, 1995: 143); secrets on which Le Doux thrives at his sanatorium. Whether it is a matter of Hawbury's cases, which remain unseen (just like Frankenstein's non-described models), or Le Doux's exhibited specimens, imported from France, and which symbolise quackery and villainy, both these Victorian examples of anatomical collections illuminate how anatomical models and specimens from home and abroad informed the literature of the period. Such examples also underline the importance of studying the literature of the long nineteenth century from a more global perspective, and of examining how it absorbed ways of thinking, defining and constructing the (human) body displayed in natural history and medical museums.

Notes

1 'We dined at Servoz, a little village, where there are lead and copper mines, and where we saw a cabinet of natural curiosities, like those of Keswick and Bethgelert', 'There is a cabinet of *Histoire Naturelle* at Chamouni, just as at Keswick, Matlock and Clifton' (Shelley, 1817: 149, 170).
2 Many public anatomical museums that opened in the nineteenth century also closed their doors before the end of the century, such as Dr Kahn's in London.
3 'We saw in this cabinet some chamois' horns, and the horns of an exceedingly rare animal called the bouquetin, which inhabits the desarts [*sic*] of snow to the south of Mont Blanc: it is an animal of the stag kind; its horns weigh at

Gruesome models

least twenty-seven English pounds. It is inconceivable how so small an animal could support so inordinate a weight. The horns are of a very peculiar conformation, being broad, massy, and pointed at the ends, and surrounded with a number of rings, which are supposed to afford an indication of its age: there were seventeen rings on the largest of these horns' (Shelley, 1817: 149–50).

4 The issue of audiences is more complex than may be supposed here and cannot be tackled in the space of this chapter.

5 An early example might be that of the French surgeon Guillaume Desnoues (died 1735), who first worked with the wax modeller Gaetano Giulio Zummo (1656–1701) and rented his anatomical models to British surgeons in the first decades of the eighteenth century. Artificial anatomical models were especially in demand in England because of the shortage of corpses for dissection, which intensified throughout the eighteenth century due to the rise of private medical schools. The 1832 Anatomy Act radically reformed anatomy, granting anatomists the right to use unclaimed pauper bodies from workhouses. As the act allowed the supply of corpses to licensed schools only, artificial models later came to be associated with fringe medicine.

6 'Le prince forme actuellement un cabinet d'histoire naturelle dont toutes les parties de détail m'ont paru bien remplies…On fera de ce cabinet une communication au Palais Pitti. Alors le prince, de là, pourra aller jusqu'à la fameuse galerie' (The Prince is currently setting up a cabinet of natural history whose individual parts seemed to me quite comprehensive. The cabinet will be related to the Pitti Palace. So the Prince will walk from there to the famous gallery) (Sade, 1965: 147–8, qtd. in Lemire, 1990: 40–1). All translations are mine.

7 'Dans une de ces armoires on voit un sépulcre rempli d'une infinité de cadavres, dans chacun desquels on peut observer les différentes gradations de la dissolution, depuis le cadavre du jour jusqu'à celui que les vers ont totalement dévoré. Cette idée bizarre est l'ouvrage d'un Sicilien nommé Zummo. Tout est exécuté en cire et colorié au naturel. L'impression est si forte que les sens paraissent s'avertir mutuellement. On porte naturellement la main au nez sans s'en apercevoir en considérant cet horrible détail, qu'il est difficile d'examiner sans être rappelé aux sinistres idées de la destruction et par conséquent à celle, plus consolante, du Créateur. Près de cette armoire, il en est une dans le même genre, représentant un sépulcre de presbytère, où les mêmes gradations de dissolution s'observent à peu près. On y remarque surtout un malheureux, nu, apportant un cadavre qu'il jette avec les autres, et qui, suffoqué lui-même par l'odeur et le spectacle, tombe à la renverse et meurt comme les autres. Ce groupe est d'une vérité effrayante' (Sade, 1965: 150–3).

8 'On peut y voir un sépulcre empli de cadavres à divers stades de putréfaction, de l'instant de la mort jusqu'à la destruction totale de l'individu. Cette œuvre sombre a été exécutée en cire colorée imitant si bien le naturel que la nature ne saurait être plus expressive ni plus vraie. L'impression est si forte face à ce chef-d'œuvre que les sens semblent se donner l'alarme l'un l'autre: sans le vouloir, on porte sa main à son nez. Mon imagination cruelle s'est délectée

de ce spectacle. A combien d'êtres, ma méchanceté a-t-elle fait éprouver ces degrés épouvantables?...Non loin de là, se trouve un autre sépulcre de pestiférés où l'on observe les mêmes degrés de putréfaction; on y voit surtout un malheureux entièrement nu qui porte un cadavre pour le jeter avec les autres et qui, lui-même suffoqué par la puanteur, tombe à la renverse et meurt; ce groupe est d'une vérité effrayante' (Sade, 1963: 23). A similar passage may also be found in *The 120 Days of Sodom*, written in 1785 where the female character is taken to a wax cabinet (Sade, 1986: 393).

9 'Je voudrais pouvoir décrire le cabinet d'histoire naturelle, que, depuis dix ans, le grand duc s'occupe d'enrichir, et M. Fontana d'arranger...Il est impossible de rendre l'élégance des appartements, l'ordre, la distribution;...Les armoires de ce cabinet représentent les cases de la mémoire de M. Fontana, remplie d'histoire naturelle' (Dupaty, 1843: 63).

10 'Musée d'histoire naturelle. – Quel plaisir doit avoir un anatomiste en entrant dans le Musée! Rien ne m'a paru plus propre, plus net, plus instructif. Ces signes sont disposés de manière à donner sans efforts des idées nettes. La salle des accouchements me semble fort supérieure à celle de Bologne et de Vienne. Je me souviens avec plaisir de la visite que je fis à l'Académie Joséphine et à cette salle with lady A.

Je vois avec le plaisir des yeux d'un ignorant les muscles et les nerfs, qui sont exprimés très nettement...J'ai vu ici le premier squelette qui m'ait paru beau. On sent de quel genre de beauté est susceptible un squelette...Il est à gauche en entrant dans les salles de préparations en cire, dans une belle cage de verre' (Stendhal, 1937: 340–1).

11 In particular, Forsyth noted that the mysteries of the human body on display were not unrelated to sexual reproduction: 'I was struck by the immensity of this collection, which occupies fourteen rooms...This awful region, which should be sacred to men of science, is open to all. Nay, the very apartment where the gravid uterus and its processes lie unveiled, is a favourite lounge of the ladies, who criticise aloud all the mysteries of sex' (Forsyth, 1835: 33–4).

12 This is the case of Charles Dupaty: 'Mais ce qui a arrêté mes regards, c'est l'homme. Une cire savante, et peut-être plus durable que l'airain, en offre, dans ce cabinet, une image complète. Vous voyez tous les pièces les plus secrètes de cette machine si compliquée, d'abord isolées, éparses, ensuite rassemblées, réunies; et toutes prêtes à remplir dans le concert de l'économie générale du corps humain, à leur tour et à leur place, la partie qui les concerne : toutes prêtes à vivre.

Ces détails remplissent une douzaine de chambres; il n'y a, pour ainsi dire, point de cette copie de l'homme qui n'ait exigé le sacrifice d'une exemplaire entier de l'original.

Ce type en cire a consommé mille cadavres. Quel travail! Quelle patience!' (Dupaty, 1843: 63).

13 A key period might be the publication of Saint Hilaire's treatise on teratology (*Traité de Tératologie*, 1832–37).

14 As Bates explains, anatomy teachers were expected to own a museum worth more than £500 in the 1820s to be recognised by the College of Surgeons (Bates, 2008: 5). Bates cites Desmond, 1989: 162–3.
15 Kahn's Museum, first accessible only to men, was opened to women two months later (Bates, 2008: 10).
16 Examples might be Angélique Marguerite Le Boursier du Coudray (1712–98) and Marie-Catherine Biheron (1719–86) in France, or the celebrated Anna Morandi-Manzolini (1714–74) in Bologna.

References

Alberti, Samuel J. M. M. (2007). 'The Museum Affect: Visiting Collections of Anatomy and Natural History', in *Science in the Marketplace: Nineteenth-Century Sites and Experiences*, eds. Aileen Fyfe and Bernard Lightman. Chicago, IL and London: The University of Chicago Press, pp. 371–403.

——— (2013). 'The Organic Museum: The Hunterian and other Collections at the Royal College of Surgeons in England', in *Medical Museums: Past, Present, Future*, eds. Samuel J. M. M. Alberti and Elizabeth Hallam. London: The Royal College of Surgeons, pp. 17–29.

Anon. (1851). 'Dr. Kahn's Anatomical Museum'. *Medical Times: Journal of Medical Science, Literature, Criticism, and News*, new series, vol. 2 (4 January–28 June): 496.

Bates, A. W. (2008). '"Indecent and Demoralising Representations": Public Anatomy Museums in mid-Victorian England'. *Medical History* 52: 1–22.

Carroll, Victoria (2007). 'Natural History on Display: The Collection of Charles Waterton', in *Science in the Marketplace: Nineteenth-Century Sites and Experiences*. eds. Aileen Fyfe and Bernard Lightman. Chicago, IL and London: The University of Chicago Press, pp. 271–300.

Colbert, Benjamin (2005). *Shelley's Eye: Travel Writing and Aesthetic Vision*. London and New York: Routledge.

Collins, Wilkie (1995 [1866]). *Armadale*, ed. John Sutherland. London: Penguin Classics.

de Goncourt, E. and J. de Goncourt (1894). *L'Italie d'hier. Notes de voyages, 1855–1865*. Paris: Charpentier et Fasquelle.

Desmond, Adrian (1989). *The Politics of Evolution: Morphology, Medicine, and Reform in Radical London*. Chicago, IL: University of Chicago Press.

Dickens, Charles (1839). *Oliver Twist; or, the Parish Boy's Progress*. Paris: Baudry's European Library.

——— (1850). 'A Great Day for the Doctors'. *Household Words* 32(2 [9 November]): 137–9.

——— (1858). 'Use and Abuse of the Dead'. *Household Words* 17(3 April): 361–5.

——— (2008 [1865]). *Our Mutual Friend*. Oxford: Oxford University Press.

Dupaty, Charles (1843). 'à Florence'. *Lettres sur l'Italie en 1785*. Lettre XXVI, 2nd edn. Tours: Ad Mame et Cie, p. 63.
Englestein, Stefani (2008). *Anxious Anatomy: The Conception of the Human Form in Literary and Naturalist Discourse*. New York: State University of New York Press.
Feldman, P. R. and D. Scott-Kilvert (1987). Eds., *The Journals of Mary Shelley Vol. 1* (2 vols.) Oxford: Clarendon Press.
Forsyth, Joseph (1820 [1813]). *Remarks On Antiquities, Arts and Letters, During an Excursion in Italy in the Years 1802 and 1803*, 2nd edn. Geneva: Ledouble.
——— (1835 [1813]). *Remarks On Antiquities, Arts and Letters, During an Excursion in Italy in the Years 1802 and 1803*, 4th edn. London: John Murray.
Knox, John Frederick (1836). *The Anatomist's Instructor, and Museum Companion: Being Practical Directions for the Formation and Subsequent Management of Anatomical Museums*. Edinburgh: Black.
Lemire, Michel (1990). *Artistes et Mortels*. Paris: Chabaud.
Marshall, Tim (1995). *Murdering to Dissect: Grave-Robbing, Frankenstein and the Anatomy Literature*. Manchester: Manchester University Press.
Sade, D. A. F. (1963). *Histoire de Juliette ou les prospérités du vice*, in *Oeuvres completes*, Vol. 8. Paris: Cercle du livre précieux.
——— (1965 [1775–76]). *Voyage d'Italie*, in *Oeuvres completes*. Paris: Tchou.
——— (1986). *Les Cent-vingt Journées de Sodome*, in *Oeuvres completes*, Vol. 1. Paris: J. J. Pauvert.
Saint-Hilaire, Isidore Geoffroy (1832–37). *Histoire générale et particulière des anomalies de l'organisation chez l'homme et les animaux...ou Traité de Tératologie*. Paris: J.-B. Baillière.
Shelley, Mary (1986 [1831]). *Frankenstein; or, the Modern Prometheus*, in *Three Gothic Novels*, ed. Peter Fairclough. London: Penguin, pp. 259–505.
Shelley, Percy Bysshe (1817). *History of A Six Weeks' Tour through a part of France, Switzerland, Germany, and Holland: with letters descriptive of a sail round the Lake of Geneva and of the Glaciers of Chamouni*. London: T. Hookham, Jun. & C. and J. Ollier.
Stendhal (1937). *Journal 1810–1811*, Vol. IV. Paris: Le Divan.
Talairach-Vielmas, Laurence (2015). '"I have bottled babes unborn": The Gothic, Medical Collections and Nineteenth-Century Culture'. Special issue on 'Medical Gothic', ed. Sara Wasson. *Gothic Studies* 17(1): 28–42.
Williams, Anne (2003). '"Mummy possest": Sadism and Sensibility in *Frankenstein*'. *Frankenstein's Dream*. *Romantic Circles Praxis Series*. Available at http://www.rc.umd.edu/praxis/frankenstein/williams/williams.html (accessed 28 June 2015).
Wordsworth, William (1990 [1805]). 'Residence in London'. *The Prelude*, in *The Oxford Authors: William Wordsworth*, ed. Stephen Gill. Oxford & New York: Oxford University Press, pp. 375–590.

Part III

Afterlives

9

Adaptive/appropriative reuse in neo-Victorian fiction: having one's cake and eating it too

Marie-Luise Kohlke

The long nineteenth century provides a seemingly illimitable repository for contemporary artists to browse in search of inspiration. Not just for writers, but also for those working in other media – film, comics, graphic novels, drama, poetry, the visual arts, or video/online games – the period functions as a highly adaptable, multi-purpose arena to explore the genealogy and constitution of our own postmodernity. Dianne F. Sadoff and John Kucich aptly refer to the 'postmodern fixation on the nineteenth-century past as the specific site of [Fredric] Jameson's "break," in which the present imagines itself to have been born and history forever changed' (Sadoff and Kucich, 2000: x). This fixation positions the nineteenth century 'as historically central' to late twentieth-century and now twenty-first-century 'postmodern consciousness' (Sadoff and Kucich, 2000: xi) – and *conscience*. The period's obsessive revival in contemporary culture thus plays a crucial part in the latter's self-definition and narrative of origins.[1]

Neo-Victorian fiction participates in this on-going cultural recycling, not just in terms of adaptations of individual period works, but of the nineteenth century more generally, which constitutes the focus of this essay. Hence, rather than 'adaptation' or 'adaptive practice', terms more suitable for re-visionings of specific source-texts, I will employ 'adaptive reuse',[2] borrowing my term from urban planning, conservation and redevelopment. 'Adaptive reuse' refers to the reutilisation of old sites and structures for purposes and functions other than those for which they were originally intended, constructed, and used in the past. It ranges from meticulous restoration, involving preservation orders, listed building status, and the retention of structural and aesthetic features of special significance, to mere facadism, whereby only a building's frontage and perhaps its structural footprint are retained. In the latter case, the building substance as such gives way to creative infilling and replacement with something new and entirely different. This strikes me as an apt analogy for neo-Victorian writing which, on the one hand, preserves and celebrates 'vintage' nineteenth-century narrative features, such as the omniscient narrator and intricate plotting, while on the other, employs the period as a 'front' to conduct postmodern experiments and play elaborate games with reader expectations. Richard Flanagan, for instance, has spoken of employing 'the skeleton' of nineteenth-century events and stories and throwing a kind of 'motley' over them to explore timeless emotions (qtd. in Koval, 2008). Like its architectural counterpart, literary adaptive reuse covers a continuum from partial replication to total re-fabrication.

A. S. Byatt's Booker Prize winning *Possession: A Novel* (1990) offers a striking example of this practice. The novel's numerous plot twists are interspersed with an abundance of lucky coincidences, including the present-day academic Roland Michell's chancing upon a draft letter by the (fictional) Victorian poet Randolph Henry Ash to the (equally fictional) poet Christabel LaMotte; the subsequent discovery of some of LaMotte's hidden epistolary responses when lines from one of her poems are suddenly recognised as strategic clues to the letters' location; and the failed attempted lovemaking of Michell and his fellow academic Maud Bailey, unknowingly occupying the very same hotel room in which Ash and LaMotte (proving far less inhibited than their postmodern counterparts) once consummated their passion. Further fortuitous occurrences relate to the protagonists' foiling of their rival Mortimer Cropper's plot to appropriate later correspondence buried with Ash and the revelation of Bailey's direct descent from both poets, giving her legal claim to the letters. Byatt orchestrates her tangled plot and its (too) ingenious resolutions in Author-God-like fashion according to an overarching teleological plan, as when, almost miraculously, Michell is rewarded for his detective efforts by finally securing a permanent academic post and discovering his 'own' poetic voice – in due course perhaps to become the 'postmodern Ash'. Yet this traditionalist notion of the author's absolute authority over her/his textual creation is juxtaposed with Byatt's excessive use of overdetermined and co-opted intertextuality: nineteenth-century poems and poets' lives, especially those of Coleridge, Browning, Barrett-Browning and Tennyson, are echoed in those of her protagonists, extending even to their personal names, and LaMotte symbolically suffers the fate of the Lady of Shalott in reverse. Like fairy tales, from which the novel also borrows, *Possession* deconstructs the notion of 'the artist as an original, a godlike and inspired creator of unique one-offs, so cherished by our highly individualized culture' (Carter, 2001: x) – but only to simultaneously reconstruct it.

Such self-contradictory tensions pervade the novel. Byatt's narrator urges the reader to recognise Ash's Victorian resistance to narrative open-endedness – '*I cannot bear not to know the end of a tale*' (Byatt, 1991: 176, original italics) – as distinctly passé, since later she warns that '[c]oherence and closure...are presently unfashionable' for all that they may constitute 'deep human desires' (Byatt, 1991: 422). Yet her 'Postscript 1868' scuppers the asserted poststructuralist precept, as it engineers the altered 'final' resolution of Ash's encounter with his illegitimate daughter, whose fate the twentieth-century characters believe him never to have discovered. Functioning like another secret letter, this time directly addressed to her readers, Byatt's postscript reasserts the omniscience of the narrator, generously sharing her superior knowledge. For all its return to 'Victorian' closure Byatt's technique is thus distinctly postmodern, both in its metafictional lead-up and its narrative gameplaying with readers. The last loose end is neatly tied back into the narrative weave at the very moment of the latter's undoing and redoing. Byatt's adaptive reuse retains nineteenth-century aesthetic features and strategies, even as it consumes and spits them out again, repurposing the period to a sounding board to reflect present-day intellectual debates and conveniently facilitate the twentieth-century protagonists' self-discovery and self-actualisation. *Possession*'s adaptation of the nineteenth century both demonstrates and disavows its Janus-faced narrative methodology, that 'superstitious dread in any self-referring, self-reflexive, inturned [*sic*] postmodernist mirror-game', in which 'connections proliferate apparently at random...in response to some ferocious ordering principle, not controlled by conscious intention' (Byatt, 1991: 421). Neo-Victorian fiction likes to have its cake and eat it too.

The 'cakes' neo-Victorianism offers up for consumption resort to a variety of ingredients by way of generic modes, ideological and theoretical approaches, and adopted/adapted voices through which the nineteenth-century past is re-imagined for present-day audiences. To what particular kinds of adaptive reuse, then, does the nineteenth century lend itself?

One might legitimately claim that it becomes all things (or all cakes) to all people:

1. A lumber room of historical curiosities, of the weird and the wonderful to pore over.
2. An echo chamber and spiritualist 'dark circle' in which to stage encounters with individual and collective ghosts.
3. A therapist's office/couch to uncover and work through unresolved historical trauma, guilt, and responsibility (for example in neo-slavery narratives or tales of imperialist and colonial atrocity).
4. A combined theatre-brothel of sexual repression, libidinal liberation, sexploitation and perverse indulgence (including narratives featuring pornography, prostitution, incest, rape and child sex abuse).
5. A classroom offering 'edutainment' lessons in socio-political and cultural history.
6. A fun-house-cum-freak-show of Gothic horrors (including supernatural terrors and monstrous spectacles of deviance, criminality, disability, madness and racial Otherness).
7. A resurrectionist 'reality TV' show, delving the secret lives of historical figures and/or characters from canonical Victorian works, or else providing them with new and entirely different life-stories (for instance with famous writers turned detectives, secret agents or vampire hunters).
8. And a launch pad for marvellous flights of fantasy to alternative nineteenth-century worlds and parallel universes altogether (for example in neo-Victorian steampunk).

So variously repurposed and repackaged, the nineteenth century loses any defining coherent contours. Ann Heilmann and Mark Llewellyn have remarked on 'the ways in which "the Victorian" has become a homogenised identity – even a signifier – in contemporary culture' (Heilmann and Llewellyn, 2010: 2). However I would argue instead that neo-Victorianism involves what might be termed 'heterogenisation'. Rather than blending disparate elements into uniformity, neo-Victorianism produces an accumulation of incongruous elements – according to whichever aspect of the present the past's adaptive reuse is intended to reflect or illuminate. This accounts for the inevitable 'self-analytical drive' that Heilmann and Llewellyn attribute to genuinely neo-Victorian writing (as opposed to just any historical fiction set in the nineteenth century), as well as the 'various ways in which *the present* is negotiated through a range of (re)interpretations of the nineteenth century' (Heilmann and Llewellyn, 2010: 5, 3, added emphasis). Strictly speaking, it is never *the past* per se, or even first and foremost, which is being negotiated. Instead the past is instrumentalised as a means to serve the present's ends. Hence almost inevitably, the period's characteristic features, as represented in neo-Victorian works, are as much (or once again) the national and international concerns of today: political hypocrisy; conflicted gender roles; sexual exploitation and paedophilia; capitalist excess and extreme social inequality; the commoditisation of culture and human relations; the rise of urbanisation and globalisation; crime and violence; dubious medical and scientific ethics; racism and slavery; militarism; oppressive (neo-) imperialism and violent uprisings against it. Julie Sanders aptly stresses that the period proves so 'ripe for appropriation' exactly 'because it throws into sharp relief many of the overriding concerns of the postmodern era' (Sanders, 2006: 129).[3] Or rather, the nineteenth century is (*re-*)*made* to throw them into sharp relief. In any case, it is these topically – or narcissistically – 'present-day' features that supply neo-Victorianism's most prominent 'period' tropes.[4] Artists working in non-literary neo-Victorian media likewise accentuate such historical convergence, as in the case of the BBC's first series of *Ripper Street* (2012–13), created by Richard Warlow. As the lead actor, Matthew Macfadyen, who plays Detective Inspector Edmund Reid, remarks: 'The wonderful thing about the project is that it certainly feels resonant now. Ripper Street deals with subjects like child gangs, child slavery, pornography, striking, protests, and vigilantes. Really there's a lot of stuff which is pretty current and still very relevant today' (qtd. in Rampton, 2012). Indeed, MacFayden's list of correspondences could be expanded to include riots, sexual trafficking, food contamination scares, anti-Semitism, terrorism and government conspiracy. This dense palimpsestic accretion of constructed doublings and mirror-effects produces what might be termed 'reverse temporal echoes'. Yet as Heilmann and Llewellyn point out, such strategic heightening of 'relevancy to the contemporary world' inevitably 'run[s] the risk of hijacking' the nineteenth century and its texts 'in the cause of contemporaneousness', in some cases even resulting in 'an ahistoric sense of the adaptive' (Heilmann and Llewellyn, 2010: 230, 236), instead of enhancing historical consciousness.

Reflecting as they do our own preoccupations and cultural anxieties, any distinctive 'period' features of neo-Victorian texts readily devolve into stereotypical projections that risk over-simplifying and distorting the complexity of the past. It seems no coincidence, for instance, that Isabel

Colegate's novel *The Summer of the Royal Visit* (1991) should centre on the mystery of ritualised child abuse in nineteenth-century Bath (thinly disguised as an unnamed provincial spa town), following the 1980s Satanic abuse panic in the USA and its UK counterparts in the widely publicised 1987 Cleveland and 1989 Nottingham child abuse scandals, both resulting in forced removals of supposedly 'at risk' children from their purportedly Satanist parents. Similarly, Anthony Horowitz's 'new' Sherlock Holmes mystery, *The House of Silk* (2011), centres upon paedophilia committed against Victorian London's rescued street children at a philanthropic institution, a rural residential school for boys. Appearing in the wake of increasing concern about institutional child sex abuse on both sides of the Atlantic, *The House of Silk* seems less concerned with examining a nineteenth-century societal disgrace than responding to, or even capitalising on, present-day offences. These include high profile Catholic Church abuse scandals in the USA and Ireland, the 2008 UK investigation into Haut de la Garenne (the Jersey Home for Boys) in the Channel Island of Jersey, and the investigation into abuse from 1974 to 1990 in North Wales care homes with the subsequent Waterhouse Inquiry report appearing in 2000. In the latter case, allegations continued to emerge during the lead-up to *The House of Silk*'s 2011 publication, forcing the UK government's announcement of a reappraisal of the Waterhouse Inquiry in tandem with a new police inquiry the following year. Roughly the same period also saw the escalation of the Irish Catholic Church abuse scandal,[5] precipitating a pastoral letter of apology from Pope Benedict XVI in March 2010. Had Colegate been writing a decade later like Horowitz, she might have been less inclined to choose a clergyman for her novel's protagonist, who not only discovers the abuse but is killed while helping to save some of the violated slum children from a fire set by the perpetrator. The clergyman's self-sacrifice would have smacked of apologia.

All too often, neo-Victorianism seeks to 'Other' the nineteenth century in self-reflexive/deflective denial of the too meagre 'progress' made since – only to raise the possibility that we are not, in fact, much more socially conscious, morally superior, genuinely egalitarian or even sexually liberated than our nineteenth-century forebears. In doing so, it repeatedly ends up collapsing any essential difference between then and now, in line with Byatt's earlier cited assertion of ineradicable or unchanging 'deep human desires'. Accordingly, the audience is distanced from the period's historical specificity under the very guise of drawing closer to it.

As the nineteenth century recedes beyond literal living memory,[6] this process of adaptive reuse as reification – the confusion of the nineteenth-century 'real' with its fictional recreations – will likely only become more indiscriminate, with fantasy maps of the period increasingly being mistaken for the territory, so to speak. Put differently, the re-imagined simulacrum of the past becomes more 'real' or hyperreal than the referent it effaces and displaces.[7] Yet it must be stressed that this tendency is hardly new. Upon *Possession*'s publication, many readers initially mistook Ash and LaMotte for real-life Victorian poets and Byatt's interpolated pastiche 'Victorian' poems for the genuine nineteenth-century article, puzzled as to why they were not included in reputable verse anthologies. George MacDonald Fraser's Flashman Papers (1969–2005) provide a still more striking, earlier example of the same phenomenon. Fraser's (mock) editorial introduction to *Flashman* (1969), the first in the series, described the text as the personal memoirs of the supposedly real-life Victorian General Sir Harry Flashman, VC, discovered by chance in an auction lot – a literary hoax taken at face value by many at the time. As Fraser's 2008 obituary in *The Telegraph* recalls, '[s]o successfully did Fraser bring off the conceit that some critics, especially in America, believed the memoirs to be authentic. A debate ensued in the *New York Times*, and Flashman's concocted curriculum vitae found its way into works of biographical reference' (Anon., 2008). Indeed, writing in 1969, Alden Whitman noted that of some thirty-four reviews of *Flashman*, which had appeared in the USA, nearly a third 'found the book to be genuine autobiography' (qtd in Fox, 2008). Arguably, Fraser's hoax proved so successful at least in part because his anti-heroic cad protagonist, irrespective of his establishment politics, offered a desecrating exposé of the period in line with the deconstructive tendencies of emergent postmodernism and poststructuralism in the 1960s, as well as the corresponding shift in historiography from the history of the great and the good to social history and 'history from below'. Alternative versions of history such as Flashman's have become the staple of neo-Victorianism, scuppering the age's grand narratives and moral pretensions, chronicling the corrupt machinations of power and empire, and commemorating the victimisation of those once deemed the 'disposables' of the official record.

Understood in its widest possible sense as re-imaginings of the nineteenth century not delimited by specific national contexts, writers' nationalities, generic elements or even temporal settings,[8] neo-Victorianism does more than simply adapt the period's canonical works, iconic figures, its cataclysmic as well as disregarded events, and its aesthetic, cultural and ideological discourses. It irrevocably alters their very character, substance, form, function and condition, while retaining aspects of their superficial features, going well beyond redeploying nineteenth-century traces in new contexts so as to produce new narratives for audiences' combined entertainment and instruction (or 'edutainment'). Hence most critics posit a necessary self-conscious engagement for a text to qualify as neo-Victorian (see Heilmann and Llewellyn, 2010: 4); in Helen Davies's words, it must be *'doing something with* the Victorian era; critically engaging with nineteenth-century fiction, culture and society' (Davies, 2012: 2, original emphasis). Yet I want to propose that critical or self-conscious engagement may just as well be absent from neo-Victorian adaptive reuse, with the audience left to infer or project it if they so choose – or not. Similarly writers may be unconsciously influenced by current events or opt for a topical theme for purely commercial reasons. Original authorial intentions are notoriously difficult to establish in any event, and even the now so common writer interviews about the creative process inevitably offer retrospective reconstructions and/or self-justifications in the service of promoting writers' works. Take the prior example of the neo-Victorian trope of child sex abuse: Colegate and Horowitz's novels may be consumed by many readers simply as 'straightforward' historical mystery/crime fiction (and may have been conceived as such by their authors). Indeed younger readers especially might lack any knowledge of the socio-historical contexts of the novels' productions and instead link the depicted offences anachronistically to more recent sex-abuse scandals, such as the 2011 Jimmy Savile case, the on-going revelations of the subsequent Operation Yewtree investigation, the case of the Rochdale sex-trafficking gang convicted in 2012 or Operation Hydrant's investigation, begun in December 2016, into historical child sex abuse in UK football clubs.

Rather than any attempted recovery of the nineteenth-century world as such, neo-Victorianism involves a potentially (but not essentially) self-conscious *conversion* – both the transformation of our own time into historical guise and of the earlier period into something Other than what it was, namely into what we *want* 'the Victorian' to signify here and now. Neo-Victorianism's Othering of the past is thus always also a self-Othering (or a re-imagining of ourselves and our own world as historical Others). As Nadine Boehm-Schnitker and Susanne Gruss put it, '[t]he process of fashioning the neo-Victorian…crucially entails a self-fashioning', intimately intertwined with 'concerns regarding twentieth- and twenty-first-century identity politics' (Boehm-Schnitker and Gruss,

2014: 1). Instead of 'adaptive reuse', it may thus be more apt to speak of 'appropriative reuse', and it is this latter term that I will adopt for the remainder of this essay.

Implicated in processes and tropes of splitting, doubling and Othering, the neo-Victorian impulse firmly aligns itself with the Gothic that explores the past's pervasive, often insidious influence over the present, whether at personal or collective levels. Accordingly, Christian Gutleben and I have argued that '*neo-Victorianism is by nature quintessentially Gothic*' (Kohlke and Gutleben, 2012: 4, original emphasis). However, Gothic influence never operates unidirectionally: just as the nineteenth-century past shapes the present, so too the present actively reshapes the past. Most writers seem more interested in how the past can be made to speak *for* and *to* the present than in what the past has to say about itself, more in how the period might be re-imagined than in what it actually was. Remarking on the Victorians' own penchant for 'adapting just about everything' and on the proliferation of new post-Victorian media lending themselves to adaptive practice, namely 'not just film, television, radio, and the various electronic media...but also theme parks, historical enactments and virtual reality experiments', Linda Hutcheon argues that '[a]daptation has run amok' (Hutcheon, 2006: xi). This seems especially true of neo-Victorianism's appropriations, which offer writers and artists a carte-blanche for taking liberties with the nineteenth century.

The complexity of appropriative reuse is demonstrated by the multivalence with which current agendas inform re-imaginings of the period, even those based in known fact, as in the case of biofictions that adapt the lives of real historical subjects. Indeed, many of the eight modes of neo-Victorian reuse previously outlined have evident political and/or ideological agendas (most often liberal, feminist, anti-imperialist, and testimonial) or else a clear theoretical bent (most often deconstructive, postmodernist, traumatological, postcolonial, or queer). Hardly mutually exclusive, the two categories frequently overlap, as in Barbara Chase-Riboud's *Hottentot Venus: A Novel* (2003). Chase-Riboud's biofiction has the titular African protagonist, the real-life Sarah (or 'Saartjie') Baartman, recount her traumatic life, initially as a victim-witness of colonial genocide, servitude and rape and later as an exploited freak show exhibit and scientific marvel in early nineteenth-century London and Paris – albeit from the vantage point of her *posthumous* existence as the novel's self-confessed spectral narrator. Chase-Riboud's neo-Victorian-novel-cum-ghost-story evinces a distinct feminist and testimonial ethics: critiquing historical gendered as well as racial, colonial and scientific abuses, commemorating Baartman's historically silenced suffering, and enacting poetic justice for her mistreatment. The novel further incorporates a range of deconstructive, postcolonial and queering strategies. It collapses binaries of civilised self and savage/animalistic Other, as when Baartman reverses the white racist gaze onto the baying audience outside her display cage, or when she portrays Baron Georges Léopold Cuvier as 'a hankering canine' and bestial Ripperesque rapist (Chase-Riboud, 2003: 278). *Hottentot Venus* traces the very basis of patriarchal empiricist science to the oppressive logic of the sexual order, which transforms the Hottentot into both the desired and abjected sign of sexual excess and racial primitivism, in opposition to which heteronormative white masculinity and western civilisation construct themselves while denying their own materiality. Western culture is thus itself pathologised, with its eminent representative, Cuvier, linked to sexual violence, grave-robbing and criminal deception, exposed as driven by monomaniacal self-obsession and racial supremacism, reconstructing human evolution on the basis of fantasy (and sexual fantasy) rather than fact and, when expedient, destroying contradictory evidence. In addition, Chase-Riboud's novel inverts the centre and margins of narrative power, by relegating Baartman's white male 'managers' and cultural authorities, such as Jane Austen and Charles Darwin, to bit parts and replacing derogatory cultural constructions of the 'Hottentot Venus' with empowered self-representations, albeit with strains of victim-feminism. Yet even as it testifies to Baartman's historical victimisation, *Hottentot Venus* also symbolically re-victimises its subject via spectacles of violence and abuse, most resonantly in the postmortem dissection scene in which Cuvier triumphantly excises Baartman's 'Hottentot apron'. Repeatedly, restitution through narrative memorialisation veers into voyeuristic Gothic sensationalism, short-circuiting the novel's liberationist narrative.

On one hand, Chase-Riboud's resort to the trope of dislocated spectrality reflexively references the lack of any self-authored records or autobiographical traces of Baartman's life (and hence her inevitable voicing by others rather than herself), as well as her literal dismembering after death. On the other hand, the narrator's ghostliness underlines the appropriative nature of Chase-Riboud's re-voicing of Baartman by finally affording a dubious consolatory uplift through the historical subject's transcendence of suffering, a move that risks evacuating the full horror of her traumas and undermining the attempted witness-bearing. Such narrative strategies, when employed in non-fictional testimonial literature, have been critiqued by Dominick LaCapra as producing 'fetishized and totalizing narratives' which – however inadvertently – 'deny the trauma that called them into existence by prematurely (re)turning to the pleasure principle, harmonizing events, and often recuperating the past in terms of uplifting messages or optimistic, self-serving scenarios' (LaCapra, 1999: 723). Not least, the Gothic mode attempts a parodic form of restorative justice, by affording Baartman (and Chase-Riboud's readers) the consolation – and satisfaction – of gruesome vengeance on her one-time oppressors (see Chase-Riboud, 2003: 308–9) and of her belated homecoming to Africa. Upon the release of her physical remains by the Musee de l'Homme, Paris, and their 2012 repatriation to post-apartheid South Africa, Baartman's spirit finally finds peace – and her narrative symbolically comes 'to rest'. The hero's welcome she receives, heralded as 'Mama Sarah!' by a 'ten-thousand-voiced chorus of colored women', transform her from 'the dis-human' into 'an icon for all humankind'; as her funeral pyre is lit near the one-time grazing lands of her people, Baartman recounts, 'I was fired back into the embers and clay that made me. My soul combusted, it soared, it rested, it sang, it was free' (Chase-Riboud, 2003: 317). *Hottentot Venus* thus commemorates historical loss and silence/silencing even as it ameliorates the same through the spectral recovery and valorisation of Baartman's voice. At once embodied victim and victimising Spirit-of-Vengeance, Chase-Riboud's Baartman both *succumbs to* and *overcomes* history. Again, neo-Victorian fiction insists on having its cake and eating it too.

Chase-Riboud's highly pejorative portrayal of Cuvier also stresses the extent to which neo-Victorian ethics of re-voicing history's underdogs can prove deeply unethical, with real-life subjects defamatorily repurposed and the past potentially distorted in the service of writers' narrative politics. So too in Richard Flanagan's *Wanting* (2008), which re-imagines Lord John Franklin's term of office as Governor of Tasmania in the aftermath of the genocide of the island's Aboriginal inhabitants, as well as Charles Dickens's later racist defence of the lost Franklin Expedition against imputations of cannibalism, based on the white race's purported superior reason and ability to control unruly primitive desires. Crucially, Flanagan intertwines his critique of Franklin's mismanagement of the colony with a vociferous attack on the private lives of the Governor and his wife, Lady Jane, specifically their adoption – and later abandonment – of the Aboriginal orphan girl Mathinna, whom they rename Leda in line with their self-appointed mission of the child's Anglicisation and salvation. Refiguring the couple's attempted 'experiment' of civilising the savage child 'for science and for God' as a small-scale version of the global British imperialist project (Flanagan, 2010: 69), Flanagan resorts to the well-known trope of the rape of colonised 'virgin' territory – which he literalises through Lord Franklin's eventual quasi-incestuous, paedophilic, and 'cannibalistic' rape of his adopted daughter (Ho Lai-Ming, 2012: 18–21). Shortly thereafter, as they prepare to leave Tasmania, the Franklins callously discard the girl, precipitating her downward spiral to teenage prostitution, drunkenness and vagrancy, with Mathinna ending as a seventeen-year-old murder victim garrotted and drowned in a muddy puddle – which might also be taken to stand for neo-Victorianism's (and Flanagan's) own muddying of the waters. It is one thing to excoriate racist supremacism and imperialist depredations cloaked as paternalistic benevolence. Yet it is something quite different to accuse a once-living person of specific horrendous offences, such as aggravated rape and paedophilia, merely because it serves the text's overarching symbolic pattern, especially when there is no historical evidence to support such claims and no one to speak against such fictional charges.

Flanagan's appropriative reuse makes individual subjects assume the brunt of historical responsibility for a whole system's atrocities. This distances the postmodern/postcolonial reader from implication in the offences portrayed (or in having to dwell on the continuing benefits they themselves might derive from Britain's one-time colonial mission). At the same time, the novel collapses neat distinctions between the Victorians and us through its assertion of all humans' subjection to the vagaries of unchanging universal desires: for love, for belonging, for remembrance, for recognition, for power. While Salhia Ben-Messahel suggests that, in *Wanting*, '[a]ll characters ironically become the puppets of their desires' (Ben-Messahel, 2013: 27), it seems more accurate to say that they become puppets of Flanagan's desires to muse on insidious processes of ethnic Othering and dehumanisation, which extend into the present. Fittingly, his novel of an Aboriginal child cruelly alienated from her own peoples and culture appeared in the same year that the Australian government, under then Prime Minister Kevin Rudd, issued a national apology to Australia's 'Stolen Generations'. Indeed, that apology seems echoed by the novel's close, in the portrayal of the only 'good' white man, Gurney Walch, who once conveyed the child Mathinna to the Governor's residence, and now finds her abject body 'crawling with so many lice it more resembled an insect nest than a human being' (Flanagan, 2010: 250). As he dispassionately rolls the corpse over with his boot tip, Walch 'immediately felt ashamed for treating a fellow human being so' (Flanagan, 2010: 250), modelling the politically correct, racially respectful response expected of present-day readers. Walch's recognition and recall of the vibrant young Mathinna, like his 'carry[ing] the poor child home' for burial (Flanagan, 2010: 252), stages a simultaneous confrontation with and exoneration from white Eurocentric historical guilt.

Flanagan has repeatedly declared that his novel is not intended and should not be read as 'a history', but rather as 'a meditation on desire' (i.e qtd in Ben-Messahel, 2013: 22). Disingenuously, however, this statement also obscures the text's subtle *contemporaneousness*, helping to explain the Victorians' conversion into such hypocritical embodiments of all-consuming western cultural imperialism and dreams of world domination run amok. *Wanting* was written at a time of high profile public debates about the legitimacy and efficacy of the US-led NATO military intervention in Afghanistan combatting what might be termed the 'terrorist desires' of armed non-state organisations such as the Taliban and al-Qaeda to contest western ideology and geopolitical spheres of influence. Indeed, *Wanting* opens with what I take to be a self-reflexive nod to this twenty-first-century context. The narrator comments on the British defeat of the 'once feared Van Diemonian tribes', now reduced to 'a small and wretched bunch' of whom 'it was hard to believe…that they could have defied the might of the Empire for so long, that they could have survived the pitiless extermination, that they could have been the instruments of such fear and terror' (Flanagan, 2010: 1). The statement could equally apply to the NATO allies' Middle Eastern opponents, reflecting the West's consternation at its inability to conclusively win the 'War on Terror' and vanquish the 'terrorist' threat in spite of its own forces' air supremacy, superior weapons technology, relentless bombing campaigns and drone executions of enemy leaders. Thereafter *Wanting*'s narrative briefly merges with the consciousness of the so-called 'Protector' – ironically resonating with the West's self-appointed role as 'Protector' of nascent Middle Eastern democracies – who oversees the Aboriginal survivors on their island reservation, a prison camp in all but name, with the indigenes assuming the role of detainees undergoing an enforced re-education programme. In the chapter's final paragraph, the narrator's voice resurges to fix the exact date of the action: 'It was 1839. The first photograph of a man was taken, Abd al-Qadir declared a jihad against the French, and Charles Dickens was rising to greater fame with a novel called *Oliver Twist*' (Flanagan, 2010: 3). The deliberate inclusion of the emotive terms of terror and jihad, and the ranging of 'civilised' western powers and cultural authorities against indigenous resistance fighters, specifically Abd al-Qadir or Amir Abd al-Qādir al-Jazā'irī (1808–83), constructs uncanny reverse temporal echoes. A descendent of the Prophet Muhammad and an Islamist scholar and poet, al-Qadir became 'the most important leader of the rebellion' when France invaded Algeria in 1830, attaining numerous victories before being 'captured and exiled to France, and later to Damascus', and eventually becoming an inspiration and spiritual forefather of the twentieth-century Algerian independence movement (Anon., 2007). Thus his evocation inevitably conjures up images of twenty-first-century indigenous resistance to western interventions in Arab countries. The fact that al-Qadir plays no further role and is never referenced again in the novel merely underlines the contrivance by which Flanagan establishes his novel's contemporary relevance; again, the *present*'s historical concerns are what is being negotiated. Indeed, Flanagan admits as much when he implicitly compares his appropriative reuse of real-life subjects to that of Shakespeare: 'I don't think Elizabethan audiences went to see *Anthony and Cleopatra* and thought people were getting a bad press from Roman times, they were interested in what it had to say about love and power *now*' (qtd. in Koval, 2008, added emphasis).

Wanting further illustrates neo-Victorianism's frequent double bind of becoming implicated in what it sets out to critique. For *Wanting* could be accused of committing symbolic violence not just against the Franklins but against Mathinna also. Mathinna's story never successfully competes with those of the major white protagonists; nor can it, since her voice and viewpoint are never wholly inhabited by Flanagan,[9] who prefers to observe her through others' eyes, such as those of Lady Franklin: 'what did she know, what did she think, that smiling black enigma?' (Flanagan, 2010: 134). As a result, Mathinna is re-exoticised and re-marginalised by the western gaze, rendered most interesting for her function of catalysing revelations about the Franklins as historical celebrities. Momentary glimpses into her mind cease altogether during moments of trauma – the very points where the narrative might be expected to attempt an act of after-witness by imaginatively filling in a testimonial gap or historical silence. During the rape scene, for instance, as Franklin towers over her in a black swan costume, Mathinna falls literally silent; following her horrified whisper '*Rowra*' upon catching sight of what she presumes to be the indigene God of death, '[t]he child said not a word more' (Flanagan, 2010: 152, original emphasis), with the remainder of the scene mediated solely from Franklin's viewpoint. Similarly, while Franklin's dying thoughts are lingered over, Mathinna's end is narrated from an external third-person narrative point of view. Hence Flanagan's postcolonial re-visioning of history in part implodes, scuppering its commemoration of

Adaptive reuse in neo-Victorian fiction

what is 'wanting', missing, or left out of the historical record. If in some ways, Flanagan's appropriative reuse of the Victorians goes too far, in others it does not go far enough, simply reinscribing subaltern powerlessness – and perhaps readers' own sense of political powerlessness and/or apathy. As Christian Gutleben remarks, 'since it denounces a number of social and historical wrongs, neo-Victorian fiction feels exempt from any other political responsibility – as if the operation of denunciation were a self-sufficient and ground-breaking eye-opener' (Gutleben, 2001: 169). From one point of view, then, *Wanting* is not so much a postcolonial 'rewriting' or 'writing back' as a Gothic 'writing over' and 'writing Other' of Mathinna all over again.

It is the power of the best of literature, of course, to quite literally change our view of the world and reality, but in the case of neo-Victorian fiction that may not always expand historical knowledge or consciousness. It seems likely that few readers, disturbed by Flanagan's haunting novel, will ever think of Mathinna again as *un*-violated by Franklin or apart from her symbolic conflation with Leda and the rape of the Tasmanian Aboriginal homeland she is made to represent. Yet this remains a fantasy conversion of the past akin to Dickens's self-serving staging and partial rewrite of Wilkie Collins's *The Frozen Deep* (1856) featured in Flanagan's novel. Here too, real-life subjects (Franklin, the Arctic explorer) become models for entirely new fabrications to serve current agendas (Dickens's own racism and refutation of charges of cannibalism against Franklin's expedition). Nor is neo-Victorian appropriative reuse of historical subjects, resulting in history's instrumentalised oversimplification, restricted to biofiction. One might think here of Robert Knox (1791–1862), doctor, anatomist and Fellow of the Royal Society of Edinburgh, who serves as the model for the megalomaniac Dr Potter in Matthew Kneale's *English Passengers* (2000) as noted in the authorial 'Epilogue' (see Kneale, 2001: 456). In a sense, Potter's racist ravings and grave robbing of Aboriginal bones are thus pre-programmed, at least for readers familiar with Knox's personal history, that is, his best-selling *The Races of Man* (1850) and his implication in the Burke and Hare body-snatching and murder scandal of 1828. As do other neo-Victorian re-imaginings for stage and screen specifically focused on the Burke and Hare case, Kneale's novel contributes to Knox's reduction to a two-dimensional Gothic villain in the popular imagination, eradicating from cultural memory his numerous 'intellectual attainments', his contributions to medical science, and 'his services…of inestimable value; to the Royal College of Surgeons of Edinburgh and its famous museum (MacLaren,

2000). Similarly, Sarah Waters's self-professed basing of Christopher Lilly, the reclusive pornography bibliophile in *Fingersmith* (2002), on Henry Spencer Ashbee, aka Pisanus Fraxi (1834–1900), contributes to an over-simplification of Ashbee. Admittedly, Waters's novel only contains depictions of symbolic rather than literal paedophilia, with the child Maud forced to entertain her uncle's guests by reading aloud pornography and later to help catalogue Lilly's collection, a form of quasi sexual 'slavery'. Nonetheless the abiding image of Ashbee-as-Lilly is arguably that of a monomaniacal pervert and abuser, effacing all ordinary aspects of the subject's life: Ashbee's solid 'yeomen' origins, his apprenticeship to 'Manchester warehousemen' and later employment by a Hamburg firm of 'merchants and silk mercers' (Fryer, 1970: 2, 3), his extensive travels and travel writings, his equal obsession with the high literature of Cervantes, or his conviviality as a family man, even if his extreme conventionality led to his eventual desertion by his once-loving wife and children. In Peter Fryer's succinct summation of Ashbee, 'he was a human being, not a dry-as-dust bookworm' (Fryer, 1970: 2). Yet Waters's neo-Victorian novel only perpetuates the latter simplistic stereotype of the 'dry-as-dust bookworm' pornographer in popular memory, as a single proclivity of Ashbee's metamorphoses into the be-all and end-all of his cultural remediation. Fantasy conversion substitutes for informed cultural memory.

Neo-Victorian appropriative reuse instantiates a central paradox: neo-Victorian writers and works, but also their readers, are far from sure what they want *from* – and what they want to do *with* – the nineteenth century. Reading both for defilement and redemption, we want to wallow in historical traumas but also be exempted and reassured that we are not culpable (or no longer capable) of the cruelties and indecencies committed. We want to hear the historically silenced speak in their own voices, but preferably in *our* language, idiom, metaphors, and meanings – with the added benefit of the feel-good factor of saving their stories from oblivion, even as we ignore the defacing and forgetting of other stories. We want to be outraged by the past's Gothic excesses, while vicariously partaking and pruriently indulging in all that is now politically incorrect. We want to relive the past, immersing ourselves sensually within it, but we want it safely distanced and contained, a carefully stage-managed haunting by appointment only. We want to confront the past *in natura*, no holds barred to its secrets, but only to discover our own historical moment in the process, encountering our doubled selves in the controlled *in vivo* environment of the text. We want the re-imagined nineteenth century served up on a plate as a virtual delectable, as we relive and consume historical Others' lives as fictions – and fictions as real life. In the end, like neo-Victorian novels and writers, neo-Victorian readers also want to have their cake and eat it too.

Notes

1 Unsurprisingly, the nineteenth century and its Industrial Revolution featured prominently in Britain's self-representation at the opening ceremony of the 2012 Summer Olympics in London.
2 As far as I am aware, only Elizabeth Ho has previously related adaptive reuse to neo-Victorianism, but only in relation to architectural practice, specifically the repurposing of the former colonial Hong Kong Marine Police Headquarters into a combined heritage, hotel, and shopping complex (see Ho, 2015: 331–53).
3 Sanders's list of parallel concerns highlighted by neo-Victorianism differs slightly in emphasis from mine: 'questions of identity; of environmental and genetic conditioning; repressed and oppressed modes of sexuality; criminality and violence; the urban phenomenon; the operations of law and authority; science and religion; the postcolonial legacies of the empire' (Sanders, 2006: 129).
4 In contrast, since increasingly less important in the UK's economy, which is now based primarily on services and information technology, heavy industry and industrialisation play a comparatively minor role in neo-Victorian fictions.
5 The Irish Catholic Church agreed to establish a compensation fund in 2002 and issued the McCullogh Report in 2005. The Irish government commenced the Ferns Inquiry in 2005, and the Irish Child Abuse Commission's 2,600-page report into 250 church-run institutions appeared in 2009.
6 On 16 January, 2015, the *Mirror* reported the death of the 'last Victorian', Ethel Lang, at the age of 114 (Palmer, 2015).
7 Heilmann and Llewellyn suggest something similar in their discussion of Scarlett Thomas' *The End of Mr Y* (2006): 'there is nothing "real" about the Victorian outside our imaginary constructions of them' (Heilmann and Llewellyn, 2010: 201).
8 Neo-Victorian storylines are not just set in the nineteenth century. They may also involve parallel Victorian and present-day time-frames, as in Byatt's *Possession*; a Victorian setting as part of multiple historical time-frames, as in the opening and closing frame of David Mitchell's *Cloud Atlas* (2004); or they may even be set wholly in the present, but intently focused on the nineteenth century and its legacies, as in Brian Moore's *The Great Victorian Collection* (1975). Additionally, neo-Victorian fantasy, science fiction and/or steampunk texts may involve time travel or be set wholly in the future or in nineteenth-century alternative realities.

9 A more positive reading of Flanagan's narrative technique might argue that, as a white and western writer, he was wary of usurping the subaltern's voice in an act of literary neo-colonialism.

References

Anon. (2007). 'Amir 'Abd al-Qadir', *Studies in Comparative Religion*. Available at www.studiesincomparativereligion.com/public/authors/Amir-Abd-al-Qadir. aspx (accessed 18 February 2015).

Anon. (2008). 'George MacDonald Fraser [Obituary], *The Telegraph* [online], 4 January. Available at www.telegraph.co.uk/news/obituaries/1574486/ George-MacDonald-Fraser.html (accessed 20 January 2015).

Ben-Messahel, Salhia (2013) 'Colonial Desire and the Renaming of History in Richard Flanagan's *Wanting*'. *Commonwealth Essays and Studies* 36(1 [Autumn]): 21–32.

Boehm-Schnitker, Nadine and Susanne Gruss (2014). 'Introduction: Fashioning the Neo-Victorian—Neo-Victorian Fashions', in *Neo-Victorian Literature and Culture: Immersions and Revisitations*, eds. Nadine Boehm-Schnitker and Susanne Gruss. New York and London: Routledge, pp. 1–17.

Byatt, A. S. (1991 [1990]). *Possession: A Romance*. London: Vintage.

Carter, Angela (2001 [1990]). 'Introduction', in *The Virago Book of Fairy Tales*, ed. Angela Carter, illus. Corinna Sargood. London: Virago Press, pp. ix–xxii.

Chase-Riboud, Barbara (2003). *Hottentot Venus: A Novel*. New York: Doubleday.

Davies, Helen (2012) *Gender and Ventriloquism in Victorian and Neo-Victorian Fiction: Passionate Puppets*. Basingstoke and New York: Palgrave Macmillan.

Flanagan, Richard (2010 [2008]). *Wanting*. London: Atlantic Books.

Fox, Margalit (2008). 'George MacDonald Fraser, Author of Flashman Novels, Dies at 82', *The New York Times* [online], 3 January. Available at www.nytimes. com/2008/01/03/arts/03fraser.html?_r=0 (accessed 20 January 2015).

Fryer, Peter (1970). 'Editor's Introduction', in *Forbidden Books of the Victorians: Henry Spencer Ashbee's bibliographies of erotica*, ed., abridged and with Introduction and notes Peter Fryer. London: The Odyssey Press, pp. 1–15.

Gutleben, Christian (2001). *Nostalgic Postmodernism: The Victorian Tradition and the Contemporary British Novel*. Amsterdam and New York: Rodopi.

Heilmann, Ann and Mark Llewellyn (2010). *Neo-Victorianism: The Victorians in the Twenty-First Century, 1999–2009*. Basingstoke: Palgrave Macmillan.

Ho, Elizabeth (2015). 'Adaptive Re-Use: Producing Neo-Victorian Space in Hong Kong', in *Neo-Victorian Cities: Reassessing Urban Politics and Poetics*, eds. Marie-Luise Kohlke and Christian Gutleben. Amsterdam and New York: Rodopi/Brill, pp. 331–53.

Ho Lai-Ming, Tammy (2012). 'Cannibalised Girlhood in Richard Flanagan's *Wanting*'. Special issue on 'The Child in Neo-Victorian Arts and Discourse:

Renegotiating 19th Century Concepts of Childhood'. *Neo-Victorian Studies* 5(1): 14–37.

Hutcheon, Linda (2006). *A Theory of Adaptation*. London: Routledge.

Kneale, Matthew (2001 [2000]). *English Passengers*. Harmondsworth: Penguin Books.

Kohlke, Marie-Luise and Christian Gutleben (2010). 'The (Mis)Shapes of Neo-Victorian Gothic', in *Neo-Victorian Gothic: Horror, Violence and Degeneration in the Re-Imagined Nineteenth Century*, eds. Marie-Luise Kohlke and Christian Gutleben. Amsterdam and New York: Rodopi, pp. 1–48.

Koval, Ramona (2008). '*Wanting*: Richard Flanagan', The Book Show. Available at www.abc.net.au/radionational/programs/bookshow/wanting-richard-flanagan/3179486#transcript (accessed 18 February 2015).

LaCapra, Dominick (1999). 'Trauma, Absence, Loss', *Critical Inquiry* 25(4 [Summer]): 696–727.

MacLaren, I. (2000). 'Historical Review: Robert Knox MD, FRCSEd, FRSEd 1791–1862: The first Conservator of the College Museum'. *Journal of the Royal College of Surgeons Edinburgh* 45(6): 392–7.

Palmer, Alun (2015). 'Ethel Lang dead, Britain's oldest person and last Victorian dies aged 114', *Mirror* [online], 16 January. Available at www.mirror.co.uk/news/uk-news/ethel-lang-dead-britains-oldest-4989097 (accessed 20 January 2015).

Rampton, James (2012). 'Matthew Macfadyen: Watching the detective', *The Scotsman*, 30 December. Available at www.scotsman.com/what-s-on/tv-radio/matthew-macfadyen-watching-the-detective-1-2712200 (accessed 15 June 2013).

Sadoff, Dianne F. and John Kucich (2000). 'Introduction: Histories of the Present', in *Victorian Afterlife: Postmodern Culture Rewrites the Nineteenth Century*, eds. John Kucich and Dianne F. Sadoff. Minneapolis, MN and London: University of Minneapolis, pp. ix–xxx.

Sanders, Julie (2006). *Adaptation and Appropriation*. London: Routledge.

10

Populism and ideology: nineteenth-century fiction and the cinema

Richard J. Hand

In considering English culture of the long nineteenth century, we may immediately think of giants of fiction: the witty and delicate satire of Jane Austen; the Gothic achievement of Mary Shelley; the enigmatic Charlotte and Emily Brontë; the social commentary of Charles Dickens; the panoramic narrative of George Eliot; the thrilling narratives of Robert Louis Stevenson; the universal tragic force within the meticulous regionalism of Thomas Hardy; the forging of a national identity in Sir Walter Scott; the proto-Modernist formalism of Henry James and Joseph Conrad. This formidable body of literature has never been out of print, appearing in a variety of popular or scholarly editions and now having a digital presence in frequently downloaded e-book versions. However, another way these works prevail is as adaptations: the film, television and radio industries will turn to these source texts again and again, reworking these narratives in different styles and for different purposes. The sheer number of adaptations has meant that the dramatisations of Charles Dickens or Jane Austen have become subgenres (if not genres) in their own right. Indeed, in this regard it is significant that a critic such as Pamela Demory, in her enlightening study of adaptations of *Pride and Prejudice*, can state:

> A notable absence in my analysis is any discussion of Jane Austen's novel itself. My purpose…is *not* to study the relation between the film and the 'original' novel, but to look at the intertextual relations among various current iterations of *Pride and Prejudice*. (Demory, 2010: 124)[1]

We live in a time of proliferating adaptations whereby the interplay between media versions of nineteenth-century fiction is as rich and revealing as the more 'obvious' relationship between the original source texts and dramatised versions.

Most of the nineteenth-century fiction considered in this essay was written for the bourgeois reader: to entertain or educate further the already enlightened bibliophile of the period. In terms of literary technique, writers such as Shelley, James and Conrad can be seen to have appropriated conventions of popular genres with a calculated literary ambition. Post-nineteenth century, the multifarious adaptations of these works into performance media reveals an ideological dimension. By taking these narratives 'off the page' and onto the screen, the purpose and reception of the work can be seen to have shifted as much as the media. In this way, a new ideological impact becomes apparent: as we shall see, works of the Gothic such as *Frankenstein* (1818, revised 1831) evolve through adaptation to be sensationalist but also provide politically resonant 'warnings' about technological ambition that continues to mould the most contemporary visions of science fiction. Likewise, in its exquisitely poised ambiguity, the literary achievement that is *The Turn of the Screw* (1898) reverberates through contemporary horror film, raising questions about the ideology of the domestic context and adult–child relationships. *Heart of Darkness* (1899) questions imperialism by appropriating conventions of the adventure genre, but subsequent re-imagining has made the story an ideologically charged denunciation of imperialism and militarism. Similarly, Austen's delightful, satirical world of manners creates an adaptive forum for an exploration of the complex ideology of morality and relationships in the late twentieth and early twenty-first centuries.

In assessing adaptive manifestations of nineteenth-century fiction, we find works that continue to talk to the complexities of our own time, albeit in the contexts of popular genre. Inevitably, the original fiction creates interesting ideological ramifications about the politics of its cultural context, but in and through adaptations into our own time, new political significance becomes apparent. In this way, we find compelling examples of 're-thought' culture: prose fiction mutated into performance media in a way that not only radicalises the source text for a spectator rather than reader, but also unlocks relevant ways of questioning the ideology of a new contemporaneity. This dynamic enables us to rethink the neo-Victorian: it demonstrates how it is not simply an aesthetic issue, but has embedded ideological implications. For academics, through the processes of adaptation that transform a nineteenth-century novel into a different medium, the source text becomes an underlying skeleton for redeployed narratives that interrogate the issues of an evolved world. Despite the ubiquitous place of cross-media adaptation in the twenty-first century, the longer story of the adaptation of nineteenth-century fiction is itself a complex one which has as much to do with legality as it does with aesthetics. Certainly, looking back at nineteenth-century English culture and its great pioneers and figureheads of the novel, our perception of the other literary arts of the era can risk being eclipsed. This is particularly the case for drama, the irony of which was not lost on figures of the time: in short, is not English the language of Shakespeare? If so, where is the theatre? Victorian writer Edmund Gosse reveals the burden of Elizabethan culture when he states: 'It haunts us, it oppresses us, it destroys us' (qtd in Steiner, 1961, 150). For George Steiner, this reflects an overbearing 'Shakespearean shadow' (Steiner, 1961, 150) that falls between the knowledge that the theatre was embarrassingly absent from 'Literature' and that English drama desperately needed to be rejuvenated not least through the actual process of writing these new plays. A prominent figure from the Victorian theatre itself, Henry Arthur Jones, describes English drama as 'a "*Slough of Despond*" in the wide well-tilled field of English literature' (Jones, 1891: vii), significantly quoting the prose of John Bunyan rather than the drama of William Shakespeare.

Of course, the English theatre was not only alive – it was thriving. The popular theatres of melodrama and music hall commanded regular and loyal audiences: this was the stage of Sir Henry Irving and Dame Ellen Terry, but also Dan Leno and Marie Lloyd. However, for some, *popularity* did not equate with the *literary*. After all, even the Irving Shakespeare productions were effectively melodramatisations, probably a tendency that prompted Thomas Hardy to assert that Shakespeare 'will cease altogether to be acted some day, & [will] be simply studied' (Hardy, 1982: 313). In lamenting that the English theatre seemed so poor and ailing in contrast to the vivacity of the English novel, Henry Arthur Jones argues that the curse of English drama lies in its antithetical condition:

> It is a hybrid, an unwieldy Siamese Twin, with two bodies, two heads, two minds, two dispositions, all of them, for the present, vitally connected. And one of these two bodies, dramatic art, is lean and pinched and starving, and has to drag about it, wherever it goes, its fat, puffy, unwholesome, dropsical brother, popular amusement. (Jones, 1891: vii)

Nineteenth-century fiction and the cinema

For Jones, William Archer and other prominent figures of the English theatre towards the end of the Victorian era, the hope for the medium lay in creating an 'English Literary Theatre' and they imagined that novelists would play a key role in this by being lured into writing scripts for the stage.

A key genre of nineteenth-century playwriting was *adaptation*. Dramatised fiction was a huge money-spinner in the period. There were countless adaptations of nineteenth-century fiction: it was an inevitable and expected process. In some cases, such as C. H. Hazlewood's phenomenally successful stage adaptation (1863) of Mary Elizabeth Braddon's novel *Lady Audley's Secret* (1862), there were plays that would eventually eclipse the source fiction in popularity. Many novelists attempted the adaptation of their own fiction. In 1838 we find Charles Dickens declaring:

> I propose to dramatize Oliver for the first night of the next season...I am quite satisfied that nobody can have heard what I mean to do with the different characters in the end, inasmuch as at present I don't quite know myself. (Dickens, 1975: 189)

It is interesting that Dickens confesses that he is not aware what will be done with the characters in the end as this implies that a change in genre must also change the plot: an observation that continues to be a fascinating aspect to the processes of adaptation into the twenty-first century. We shall never know what Dickens intended because he did not, after all, adapt *Oliver Twist* (1837). Nevertheless, this did not mean that theatre audiences were deprived of stage versions of the novel: indeed, there were five dramatisations in 1838 alone. The fact that numerous playwrights leaped into Dickens's novel with adaptation in mind reflects the legal situation in regard to stage adaptation. In fact, a central impetus for novelists to adapt their own fiction as swiftly as they could was for reasons of copyright. In the inadequate copyright laws of the time, a novelist did not have any rights over the stage adaptation of their fiction unless they themselves adapted their own *novel* and thus held copyright over their own *script*. If novelists were tardy in making this manoeuvre, they could have a lot to regret. Hence we find a furious Charles Reade complaining about the phenomenal success of 'piratical versions' of his penal reform novel *It is Never too Late to Mend* (1865), 'Saloons rose into theatres by my brains, stolen. Managers made at least seventy thousand pounds out of my brains, stolen: but not one would pay the inventor a shilling' (Reade, 1887: 164–5). It was not until 1911 that an Act was passed through Parliament which amended the laws relating to copyright and protected novelists from, amongst other things, the dramatisation of narrative works.

Until the laws changed, a consequence of the need for a rapid production of a stage adaptation in order to protect copyright led to a somewhat mechanical and cynical process wherein a 'play' based on the author's novel would be cobbled together, a licence for performance paid and a one-off 'production' (essentially little more than an on-stage reading) mounted on a theatre stage in front of a paying audience (which could be as few as a single person, as long as they had paid for their seat). Few of these adaptations exist in print, although Sylvia Starshine's edition of Bram Stoker's *Dracula: Or the Undead – A Play in Prologue and Five Acts* (1897), reveals a 'play' that uses swathes of the novel pasted in to be read aloud, a performance contrived solely to plug the absurd gaps in contemporary copyright law. With this in consideration, it is no surprise that adaptation probably had, for many novelists, a rather dispiriting connotation. Although Henry Arthur Jones and William Archer did successfully tempt several novelists to write for the stage – frequently adapting their own fiction with objectives different to copyright-protecting cynicism – the results were generally disappointing. Novelists who ventured into playwriting such as Thomas Hardy and Joseph Conrad produced a few stage adaptations, which were not without merit but were not successful enough to lure them to the theatre more permanently. In contrast, Henry James was extremely keen to be a playwright and his output of plays was not only prolific – it was disastrous.[2]

Although stage adaptation had a problematic status for some of the writers of the period, the situation changed not just with the 1911 copyright laws; it had already began to change with the arrival of the last great invention of the nineteenth century: cinema. This new technology would not only open up aesthetic and financial opportunities, it would have a voracious appetite for dramatic material and would eventually source this through adaptation. Despite various precursors and other contested beginnings, the Auguste and Louis Lumière film screenings in Paris in 1895 are normally taken as marking the inauguration of the cinema age. In the first years after the invention of the motion picture, the medium was seen as having primarily a 'scientific' use, fulfilling what we would see as a 'documentary' function. Eventually, there were examples of cinema producing short entertainments and playful novelties. However, Eileen Bowser argues that, after 1907, US cinema no longer had a solely scientific or 'novelty' status and there was an increasing

Nineteenth-century fiction and the cinema

demand for more sophisticated narratives and the adaptation of literary works provided one solution (Bowser, 1990: 42–3). In 1908 there was a flurry of Shakespeare adaptations across the film industry after which the Edison Company produced one-reel versions of Goethe's *Faust* in 1909 and Charles Dickens's *A Christmas Carol* and Mary Shelley's *Frankenstein* in 1910. In addition, there was also an element of 'moral panic' at play. The cinema was an irresistible target for those seeking a root cause for the social calamities they saw infecting the newly arrived twentieth century. Interestingly, the 1909 Cinematograph Act in Britain was passed ostensibly to safeguard the physical environment of buildings where (highly inflammable) films were exhibited, but it was also the beginning of film censorship. In the USA, Thomas Edison warned in July 1907 that the success and future of the cinema industry depended upon it establishing a 'good moral tone' (Bowser, 1990: 37). Cinema therefore attempted to protect itself by using 'the prestige of the classics' (Bowser, 1990: 43) through adaptation. Indeed, some film exhibitors at the time would meet with local schools to encourage teachers to use soon-to-be-adapted literary texts on their curricula.

The aforementioned adaptation of *Frankenstein* (J. Searle Dawley, 1910) by the Edison Company is not only a significant example in the first wave of cinematic adaptation: it is also a landmark moment in cinematic genre. Mary Shelley's 1818 novel had been adapted before in numerous melodramatic versions from the 1820s onwards. The central concept was irresistibly dramatic and sensational. It offered the Gothic at some of its most spectacular and – as a precursor to science fiction – speculative. With the invention of cinema, *Frankenstein* brings this spectacle and speculation to the screen.

However, as much as Edison's *Frankenstein* attempted to attain the prestige of the 'good morality' implicit in the adaptation of a literary classic, it would not be unproblematic. This was a pioneering moment, a horror movie before the horror film genre really existed. As Winston Wheeler Dixon reveals: 'Many exhibitors found the film too horrid to show' (Dixon, 2000: 117). This controversy can be explained if we consider the decisions that are taken in the adaptation of the novel. Approximately one quarter of this short one-reel film is devoted to the creation scene: it is not only the most dominant sequence but the focus of the narrative and the set-piece of the film. Yet, of course, in the original novel (and also in many earlier stage adaptations) it is what Mary Shelley chooses to leave in ellipsis, not dissimilar to classical Greek tragedy wherein acts of violence or murder occur strictly offstage. The Edison film decides to fill in the gaps of the novel and add a creation sequence: it wants us to *see* the monster come into being, to the viewer's fascination or mortification. Regardless of reception, in explicitly showing us the birth of the monster, a huge step forward is made for what will become the horror genre. Arguably, 'the creation sequence in the Edison *Frankenstein* creates the horror genre' (Hand, 2007: 12).

As well as the focus on technology, Edison's *Frankenstein* also foregrounds the performer. Charles Ogle as the Creature clearly draws on the stage tradition of *Frankenstein*: he is an image of unkempt 'savagery' with wild hair, long fingers and enormous feet, shambling recklessly in stark contrast to the elegant, melodramatic posturing of Dr Frankenstein (Augustus Phillips). Although Ogle looks the part of a melodramatic monster, recalling images of many Calibans from nineteenth-century stage versions of Shakespeare's *The Tempest*, he is evidently a human beneath the costume and this deep-seated humanity will also define Boris Karloff in his iconic embodiment of the role for Universal in 1931. Things might not have gone this way: David J. Skal reproduces prototype designs for the Universal *Frankenstein* which includes what can only be described as a robot image (Skal, 1993: 133), more of a *Wizard of Oz* Tin Man than a creature of stolen flesh and blood. Moreover, Skal also reveals how a different paradigm might have been established in the late 1920s when Willis O'Brien – the chief technician on *King Kong* (Merian C. Cooper and Ernest B. Schoedsack, 1933) – had planned to produce his own adaptation of *Frankenstein*, 'The O'Brien conception of *Frankenstein* would have involved a stop-motion monster in miniature, thus allowing for superhuman feats impossible for an actor or stuntman to achieve. The film never got past the planning stages' (Skal, 1993: 128). This decision prevented a stop-motion creature but quite possibly, longer term, prevented a costumed Kong. Either way, Frankenstein's monster has continued to follow Ogle and Karloff in remaining emphatically human beneath the scars, disfigurement and once-necrotic flesh.

Another common point between Ogle and Karloff's monsters is their muteness. The Edison *Frankenstein* is a silent film but the creature is given no intertitles: although he seems to speak as he gesticulates to his creator, he is given no actual *words*. In the first Universal version, Karloff can growl but not speak. This casts a long shadow over subsequent screen adaptations of *Frankenstein*. This even extended to radio versions such as *Frankenstein* adaptations on the US show *Suspense* in the 1950s wherein we hear the strength and destruction of the creature but never a voice, despite the fact that radio would seem to be the perfect medium for a *speaking* monster. In fact, the resulting productions use the uncanny potential of the radio medium to the full: the audio plays capture the chilling presence of the abject creature: 'if horror radio proves anything, it is that spoken words are not everything and the shuffling, heaving ferocity of *Suspense*'s monster is terrifying in its sheer speechlessness' (Hand, 2014: 55).

More recent *Frankenstein* adaptations have returned to the source novel to find an articulate rather than mute monster: in *Mary Shelley's Frankenstein* (Kenneth Branagh, 1994) Robert de Niro plays a creature that speaks and this trend has continued. Nick Dear's 2011 stage adaptation of *Frankenstein* for the National Theatre vividly establishes the context of the play into the Industrial Revolution and strikes an exquisite balance between Dr Frankenstein and his creation in speech and argument. In the first series of the television drama series *Penny Dreadful* (2014), Frankenstein's monster is called Caliban (Rory Kinnear) and, though articulate and embittered, finds his *metier* working as a stage technician in the Grand Guignol horror theatre. It is an apt image of the neo-Victorian Gothic re-imagined for twenty-first-century popular horror: an icon of popular horror, Frankenstein's monster, pumps the stage blood and operates the trapdoors to the shrieks and screams (of laughter and terror) of a thrill-seeking audience. Even in the contemporary superhero genre, the shadow of *Frankenstein* continues to be detected. In *Avengers: Age of Ultron* (Joss Whedon, 2015), Tony Stark (Iron Man) and Bruce Banner (The Hulk) discuss mounting an experiment that may just save – or totally destroy – the world, with Stark shrugging off the risks with a fatalistic and fanatical passion: 'We're mad scientists, monsters. You gotta own it'. Stark's statement is deliberately playful but is uttered in the context of a world in peril thus signalling an ideological point: it is possibly the unethical genius of these modern Frankensteins that has pushed humanity to the chasm of doom.

The post-*Frankenstein* can also be detected in other works of dark fantasy that allude to Mary Shelley's novel. For example, 'Be Right Back' (Channel 4, 2013) is an episode of the television drama series *Black Mirror* scripted by Charlie Brooker, which reflects a Frankensteinian theme: in the near future, a recently bereaved woman Martha (Hayley Atwell) can 'talk' to her late husband Ash (Domhnall Gleeson) through an app which collates all of his social media presence and other digital 'memories'. Firstly communicating through texts she upgrades to speak to a reconstructed version of Ash's voice before purchasing a synthetic model of him which will activate and download the accumulated digital material to become a 'living' simulacrum of her dead husband. Although the process helps Martha through the stages of grieving – Ash seems to be as witty, compassionate and physically passionate (in fact, more so) than the original – inevitably the result is a failure: this faultless copy designed-to-please is merely a 'ripple' of the original human's character and his life. This perfectly rendered creation is empty, it is no phoenix rising from (the) Ash(es): it is 'nothing'. The drama works as an ingenious re-imagining of *Frankenstein* for the twenty-first century: instead of physical bits of body, the creation is an assemblage of personal digital presence. Although he ostensibly 'lives', the resurrected Ash (despite learning, adapting and 'improving') cannot be a 'true' human being any more than Frankenstein's Creature can be. Just as Frankenstein's monster flies to the remotest ends of the earth, Ash is ultimately put up into the attic (the remotest realm of the domestic space) alongside boxes of fading photographs, a trace of the departed, a mere *aide-memoire*. 'Be Right Back' raises ideological provocations about the contemporary (over)dependence on ubiquitous social media, compelling the audience to think of the ethical issues surrounding technology nearly two hundred years after Mary Shelley did the same. After all, in both works (and every adaptation in between), the reader/spectator knows full well that this unethical experiment 'cannot end well'.

If *Frankenstein*'s sensationalism and spectacle did not need to rely upon the spoken word on the early screen, the successful adaptation of Jane Austen's fiction had to wait until the invention of sound cinema. The delicate wit and dialogue of Austen needed to be *heard* rather than mutely enacted or read in intertitles. Moreover, it needed to be developed through duration: these could not be one-reel narratives. The first Austen screen adaptation is usually taken to be the early BBC television drama of *Pride and Prejudice*, broadcast live in a fifty-five-minute long version in May 1938. Soon afterwards, Hollywood produced its own version of the 1813 novel, with a full-length film of *Pride and Prejudice* (Robert Z. Leonard, 1940) starring significantly *British* actors Greer Garson and Laurence Olivier. After this successful film, the Austen oeuvre would be steadily – albeit not prolifically – adapted onto cinema and television screens. However, it is the mid-1990s onwards that witnesses the most high profile era for Austen adaptation. Starting with Nick Dear's screenplay of *Persuasion* (Roger Michell, 1995), several screen versions of Austen enjoyed critical and popular acclaim. Since then, the Austen adaptation industry continues, including playful interpretations such as allusive adaptations as *Bridget Jones's Diary* (Sharon Maguire, 2001), based on Helen

Fielding's 1996 novel; the speculative bio-drama *Becoming Jane* (Julian Jarrold, 2007); and the time-travel adventure *Lost in Austen* (ITV, 2008). These postmodernist takes on Austen arguably reach a zenith of mischievous appropriation with the novel *Pride and Prejudice and Zombies: The Classic Regency Romance-now with Ultraviolent Zombie Mayhem!* (2009) by 'Jane Austen and Seth Grahame-Smith', which was filmed in a short version in 2013 with a feature length adaptation released in 2016.

The Jane Austen adaptation boom from the mid-1990s onwards constructs a unique insight into late twentieth- and early twenty-first-century society and culture. Often these Austen adaptations seem to transform these Regency period novels into the broad genre of 'costume drama' and even the contemporary screen genre of 'rom-coms' or 'chick flicks'. Indeed, Lisa Hopkins quotes a newspaper review citing 'Austen's trademark boy-crazy plotting' (Hopkins, 2012: 247), a comment which would startle anyone who knows the novels well. Nevertheless, Pamela Demory argues that even when Austen adaptations can be seen as belonging clearly within the 'chick flick' genre, they nonetheless 'reflect twenty-first-century attitudes about gender and women's roles in society' (Demory, 2010: 124) in an intricate way. Demory also stresses how the complex interplay of Austen adaptations between themselves also 'exemplifies the way texts become transformed and informed by myriad textual and cultural transformations. "Jane Austen" is a complex interweaving of associated texts – literary, filmic, and electronic – as well as less tangible forces of convention, reader reception, and production.' (Demory, 2010: 124).

Despite this plethora of interpretation, there is a particularly keen sense of 'fan' ownership' when it comes to Austen. As Lisa Hopkins writes, films of Austen books are:

> likely to inhabit a secure, unified genre, or to be criticized if they do not, especially if the Austen text at stake has been or is perceived to have been adapted without due sensitivity to the very specific cultural codes and social restrictions within which her characters operate. (Hopkins, 2012: 246)

This has led to expected conventions, reflected when it comes to the casting of 'quality' actors (evident from the beginning with the casting of Olivier and Garson in the 1940s), sets, location and costume. Yet these conventions are only one aspect of the 'real Austen'. As Jeremy Strong writes, '[Aspects] of the social chessboard upon which her marriage plots and moral lessons unfold require significant alterations in adaptation if they are to prove palatable to modern movie audiences'

(Strong, 2008: 209). The wholesale alteration of social structure and mores is also reflected in the radical adaptation of behaviour which is very different to the codified etiquette of the Regency period. As Laurie Kaplan notes, in Austen adaptations 'physical activity and restlessness' can become 'familiarity and intimacy' which would have been 'shocking breaches of the early nineteenth-century codes for decorous behaviour' (cited in Hopkins, 2012: 249).

In this regard, one of the most emblematically radical adaptations of Austen is *Bride and Prejudice* (Gurinder Chadha, 2004). In this film, the popular genre of Austen adaptation is mixed with the popular form of Bollywood. For Sarah Säckel, *Bride and Prejudice* is a consciously global film, 'a Bollywood-Hollywood hybrid, which conveys a utopian message of transnational and cross-cultural understanding on the basis of love and mutual respect' (Säckel, 2010: 249–50). The director Gurinder Chadha herself stated that she wanted to defuse racism and 'diminish the impact of difference' (qtd in Jones, 2012: 178) and the film embraces the vibrant colours and joyous movement of Bollywood dance, centred on the female characters. For Stephanie Jones, 'Chadha's movie can be admired for its anti-imperial statements, or criticized for involving too little history and portraying too much global mobility' (Jones, 2012: 188). Nonetheless, Stephanie Jones goes on to argue that the power of displayed reading and dancing in *Bride and Prejudice* (predominantly female-focused and female-enacted) are 'other movements' that reveal the complexities of textual processes (not least those of adaptation) and 'make available a reading of reading itself' (Jones, 2012: 188). *Bride and Prejudice* is therefore one of the most symbolic examples of Austen adaptation: a work which finds movement and sound a world away from Austen's original novel and many of the film's contemporaneous Austen revisions (although in many ways all contemporary Austen adaptations undertake, by default, the same radical process). It is a powerful emblem of the richness of adaptation: how a nineteenth-century source text can be so thoroughly re-imagined in order to serve a function wherein it takes an ideological stance in attacking racism and actively celebrating the virtues of an increasingly globalised culture. The etiquette and wit of a Regency novel becomes a forum to display – in full song, dance and postmodern textuality – the triumph of interracial relationships and a multiracial world.

At the other end of the nineteenth century, Henry James's *The Turn of the Screw* continues to be acclaimed as a work of perfectly balanced ambiguity and contested truths, a short novel that is an abiding cultural emblem of the tipping point from Victorian certainty into Modern insecurities. It is a work of fiction that consciously plays with genre, deliberately drawing on the popular tradition of the Victorian ghost story and wider Romantic and Gothic traditions but does so with complex narrative style and strategies that obfuscate any unambiguous reading. In contrast, a generation later in the ghost stories of M. R. James, a familiar pattern emerges of a rational and sceptical protagonist who is gradually drawn into an experience of the supernatural: effectively a realisation of the Shakespearean 'There are more things in heaven and earth.../ Than are dreamt of in your philosophy' (*Hamlet* 1.5.167–8). In Henry James, the balance of doubt and contradiction is sustained. As Leonard Orr writes, James uses 'indirection and narrative gaps' with the consequence that, 'The governess rides an emotional roller-coaster of too much certainty and self-confidence followed by too much doubt, of romanticizing and idealizing Bly and the children and then seeing the place as cursed and the children as corrupted and evil' (Orr, 2009: 29).

The argument over whether the ghosts are 'real' or imagined continues to be a central debate (not least in the seminar room), but as T. J. Lustig states, it has become 'tediously predictable' to engage in the question of whether *Turn of the Screw* posits 'reality' against 'reliability' (Lustig, 2011: 5). In other words, to debate whether the ghosts are real or simply imagined by the Governess is an argument which is 'little better than meaningless' (Lustig, 2011: 5). The result of it being impossible to 'prove' the 'truth' of the story beyond subjective opinion means that we should see *The Turn of the Screw* as an exploration of the psyche of the Governess and even the reader. Jana M. Tigchelaar identifies the psychological implications of the narrative when she writes, '(The) governess's efforts to "prove" their ghostly appearances are really her attempts to deny the existence of her desire and passion, knowing as she does that those emotions are forbidden' (Tigchelaar, 2013: 32). Interestingly, although in *The Turn of the Screw* James appropriates Gothic and ghost story conventions in order to blur and confound them, it is a story that has cast a long shadow of influence ever since, especially in cinema. Indeed, the narrative strategies of *The Turn of the Screw* have created a template and subgenre for numerous examples of the cinematic horror genre. However, before looking at James's intertextual influence on popular horror, it is worth exploring examples of the overt adaptation of *The Turn of the Screw* itself.

Henry James has been periodically adapted since the 1930s (as with Austen, it is an oeuvre that relies on sound cinema), with notable successes including *The Heiress* (William Wyler, 1949), based on Ruth and Augustus Goetz's 1947 stage adaptation of James's novel *Washington*

Square (1880). *The Turn of the Screw* was first adapted to the screen in the 1955 television version scripted by Gore Vidal. The first cinema adaptation of *The Turn of the Screw* was *The Innocents* (Jack Clayton, 1961) scripted by John Mortimer, a film which closely interprets the plot of the original novella while successfully using the potential of film form to advantage. *The Innocents* features heavy symbolism and its monochrome cinematography creates a tremendously atmospheric and uncanny effect. The film also introduces aspects with additional layers of intertextuality: the film opens with one of the children singing a 'Willow' song, which alludes to Shakespeare (both *Hamlet* and *Othello*) just as calling Frankenstein's monster 'Caliban' in *Penny Dreadful* does: examples of the adaptation of fiction drawing on the theatre of Shakespeare in the process of dramatisation.

The Innocents effectively uses the language of cinema in what are notable additions to the story. For instance, Anthony Mazzella notes how the Governess starts dressing in black with the consequence that 'she now appears to have taken her dress cues from Miss Jessel' (Mazzella, 2002: 29): in short, the Governess is transforming into the Other, becoming the monster herself. At the same time, Mazzella argues that the film makes a bold assertion presenting to the viewer 'at the penultimate moment, an objective shot beyond all debate: Quint is real' (Mazzella, 2002: 28). If this 'evidence' may seem to diminish the nuance of James's original, this is counterbalanced with the cyclical nature of the film: Mazzella draws attention to how the film opens with an image from the end of the film, with the effect that the film is 'a never-ending nightmare, with the governess forever dissolving into a replay of her early interview with the uncle' (Mazzella, 2002: 29). The effect is powerful and we could argue that it consciously alludes to another classic British horror film *Dead of Night* (Cavaltini et al., 1945), which also uses a 'never-ending nightmare' for its narrative structure. Certainly, by trapping the protagonist in the overarching unreality of a never-ending nightmare *The Innocents* defuses what seems the blatant 'the ghosts are real' acceptance through its structure: Quint may be 'real' but the cyclical structure puts everything in a vicious circle of never-ending doubt. Indeed, a greater ambiguity abides in *The Innocents* than in *The Nightcomers* (Michael Winner, 1971), an erotic and violent prequel that pins down James's delicate ambiguities into explicit events.

The influence of *The Turn of the Screw* and its overt adaptations such as *The Innocents* can be detected elsewhere in cinema in its imagery and its themes. The mournfully dressed Miss Jessel is most blatantly re-seen as numerous ghostly women in black including, in fiction, stage and screen, Susan Hill's *The Woman in Black*. Thematically, one of the all-time classics of horror film *The Exorcist* (William Friedkin, 1973) plays the same game of drawing the viewer into pondering whether the diabolical possession is real or imagined. Even the Catholic Church is sceptical about the need for an exorcism, making the possessed child's mother (Ellen Burstyn) retort to the priest who recommends psychoanalysis: 'She's already seen every fucking psychiatrist in the world and they sent me to you.' More recently, *Dark Skies* (Scott Stewart, 2013), a hybrid of science fiction and horror genres, plays a similar game wherein we speculate whether we are watching an alien visitation and abduction or a deeply dysfunctional family. Similarly, *The Babadook* (Jennifer Kent, 2014) presents a complex and realistically drawn mother and child relationship. Whether the Expressionistic monster that begins to infiltrate the house is summoned by a mysterious pop-up book (or, for that matter, masturbation) it is deeply connected with the psyche of the mother. *The Others* (Alejandro Amenábar, 2001) is a tangential reworking of *The Turn of the Screw*. In this film, the mother (Nicole Kidman) of two children seems to protect them from the haunting spirits in their Gothic mansion until the realisation dawns on us that it is the mother who is the greatest threat. This core to the narrative draws out from *The Turn of the Screw* the subgenre of horror wherein the greatest threat lies in what should protect us: the Governess should protect, not destroy, her charges just as a mother or, in the case of *Hide and Seek* (John Polson, 2005), a father, should protect the children.

A final parallel can be drawn with *Insidious* (James Wan, 2010), which presents another flawed family weighed down by the pressure of a comatose son. The film's key line ('It's not the house that is haunted') is proved emphatically when they move from their appropriately quasi-Gothic house into a smaller, brighter home but the ghosts do not abate. The denouement establishes the chance to exorcise the spirits in an otherworld ('the Further') but what it reveals about the dysfunctionality of the family (and the father above all) echoes the ultimately fatal set-up of the Governess and Miles at the end of *The Turn of the Screw*. In watching *Insidious*, we suspend our disbelief and accept the 'reality' of the Further but even this popular thrill-seeking horror movie draws on a Jamesian study of repression and the malevolent adult guardian. Just as the remake of James's *What Maisie Knew* (Scott McGehee and David Siegel, 2012) worked effectively when contemporised, the appropriation of the author's dysfunctional domesticity in the uncanny *The Turn of the Screw* echoes in some of contemporary horror's most unsettling and ideological provocations.

When it comes to adaptation, Joseph Conrad is a figure as complex and ambiguous as his own fiction. A major figure whose career spans the late Victorian and early twentieth century periods, Conrad's complex literary technique is reminiscent of Henry James's formalism. Despite seeming to disavow theatre, Conrad nursed an interest in becoming a scriptwriter and his experiments with stage writing culminate with him writing for cinema. He researched screen adaptation technique by going to see *Les Misérables* (Frank Lloyd, 1917) and – quite astonishingly – secured a contract as screenwriter with Lasky-Famous Players (later becoming Paramount). This was the twilight phase of Conrad's life and he only managed to complete one screenplay before he died, which has never been filmed. Conrad adapted his own short novel *Gaspar Ruiz* (1906) into the 'film scenario' *Gaspar the Strong Man*. Although the title seems to diminish the story so that it sounds like a melodrama (or even a variety act), the screenplay is a fully realised historical epic of spectacle and dramatic sweep. Conrad's most commercially successful novel *Victory* (1915) was written with a sense of high opera (Conrad was a great opera fan and his tragic tale of Heyst and Lena on their secluded island home resonates with operatic allusion and impetus). The fact that Conrad wrote the novel with a dramatic *modus operandus* was soon to be reflected in adaptation. *Victory* was brought to the London stage with considerable success in 1919 in a production by the acclaimed actor-producer Marie Löhr; and in the same year, Hollywood produced its own screen version of the novel directed by Maurice Tourneur and starring Lon Chaney. *Victory* goes on to be the most frequently adapted Conrad novel: its highly dramatic narrative of troubled lovers confronting a pack of ruthless and violent gangsters on a seemingly idyllic island offers a core story that cinema has continued to adapt with enthusiasm. The philosophical introspection and rich intertextuality in Conrad's novel has been replaced by strong character acting, beautiful location filming and nail-biting sequences of suspense and conflict.

The 1919 *Victory* film was the first Conrad screen adaptation and after this Conrad would be steadily adapted in a wide variety of films including *Sabotage* (Alfred Hitchcock, 1936) and as a tangential influence in the films of Werner Herzog. Although *Victory* is still the most frequently adapted Conrad novel, the most influential and prominent work is undoubtedly *Heart of Darkness*. In this short novel, Conrad creates a modern myth which continues to haunt western culture long after its publication. At the core of the story is the idea of the corruption of Europe: a colonial figure of civilisation, Kurtz, has settled in the Congo and become barbaric and his death revelation of 'the horror, the horror' reveals the 'dark' truth that lies at the heart of European culture. In his essay 'An Image of Africa' (1977), Chinua Achebe denounced *Heart of Darkness* as a racist text and it is an argument that continues to influence the study of Conrad. Despite the difficulty of working with *Heart of Darkness* post-Achebe, the novella continues to abide in adaptation including in the Nicolas Roeg 1993 film version.

However, the real success of *Heart of Darkness* as an adaptive source is revealed in the appropriation of the core narrative in a variety of contexts. Conrad's *Heart of Darkness* is – like Mary Shelley's *Frankenstein* – one of the most convincing examples wherein nineteenth-century English literature has produced works that have become modern myths. In Conrad's case, *Heart of Darkness* with its journey that leads not into religious salvation or humanistic enlightenment but into total horror has become an apt myth for modern and postmodern ideologies. The mythic status of the work is also reflected in the way that the title and the key phrase 'the horror, the horror' continue to be used frequently in a wealth of other contexts including journalism, not least in covering the 1994 genocide in Rwanda to the twenty-first-century crises in the Middle East and Afghanistan. Conrad's exploration of the unjust barbarity of colonial exploitation has become a powerful metaphor for modern war: *Apocalypse Now* (Francis Ford Coppola, 1979) effectively uses the novella as the source for an exploration of the Vietnam War (although, notoriously, Conrad is not cited anywhere in the credits). The 'Conradian journey' also underpins works such as *Windigo* (Robert Morin, 1994) about an indigenous community in Canada striving for independence and *Vinyan: Lost Souls* (Fabrice Du Welz, 2008) about a western couple's search for their missing child after the Indian Ocean Tsunami of December 2004. In these works, we witness the clash of cultures occurring in the most violent and irreconcilable ways. *Windigo* and *Vinyan* would often, like Werner Herzog's films, be classified as 'art films', but the Conradian can be detected in more populist contexts.

Heart of Darkness is clearly an influence on James Dickey's *Deliverance* (1970) and the subsequent John Boorman film (1972), a tale of vacationing middle-class Americans out of their depth in the 'redneck' realm of deepest Georgia. The cruel violence and revenge in the story has, in turn, become an influence on the horror genre: the journey into the 'backwoods/backwards' world of remote America has become a perennial subgenre of the popular horror narrative from the *Texas Chain Saw Massacre* (Tobe Hooper, 1974), *The Hills Have Eyes* (Wes Craven, 1977) and countless other remakes and re-workings of the same core plot. Arguably, in the twenty-first century, the Conradian can even be found in Hollywood blockbusters. In *Iron Man 3* (Shane Black, 2013), what seems to be a Middle East terrorist organisation is ultimately revealed to be a violent conspiracy much closer to home. The revelation of this homegrown threat is a clever dramatic twist, but it is also one which provocatively shows the 'heart of darkness' to be American in its making. In other words, it is an ideological provocation suggesting that post-9/11, the violence of the US-led 'War on Terror' has begot more terrorism than it has extinguished. The Conradesque can even be found in the world of digital gaming. Videogames such as *Far Cry 2* (Ubisoft, 2008) make the player track down an insane arms dealer in the heart of a war-torn African country; while *Spec Ops: The Line* (2K Games, 2012) presents a military mission in a war-ravaged Dubai in search of a missing US Captain John Konrad and is a work that mixes gun-toting action with an increasing sense of moral and ideological complexities.

Nineteenth-century fiction continues to be one of the triumphs of English culture. At the same time, adaptation was never far away: stage adaptations were immensely popular forcing many novelists to hurriedly adapt their own novels to deter unscrupulous playwrights who attempted to steal the story first. After the rise of cinema, the adaptation of fiction offered a way for this new populist medium to strike a highbrow tone, a move contemporaneous with the rectification of inadequate copyright laws. Cinema has continued to have a love affair with nineteenth-century fiction, finding in these prose narratives, stories for cinema that will speak to audiences in diverse ways. In works such as *Frankenstein* and *The Turn of the Screw*, Mary Shelley and Henry James have had an enormous impact on popular genre: their complex fiction resonates in the form and formula of the horror genre and remain central in some of the most ideologically driven examples of horror and science fiction. Jane Austen's fiction has been uncoupled from its specific historical context to speak to the social and sexual mores of our own time, including in visions of our globalised era in a defiant celebration of multiculturalism. Finally, a work like Joseph Conrad's *Heart of Darkness*, despite being problematic to the modern reader, has been widely appropriated to interrogate ideological issues: Conrad's ironic take on the nineteenth-century adventure genre has been used to reflect on military and political tragedies of the modern world from

Vietnam to the present day. At the same time, *Heart of Darkness* has been used – like *Frankenstein* and *The Turn of the Screw* – as a formula for the popular genre of horror, especially in examples that present the clash of irreconcilable cultures. The authors may be long dead but their fiction has never been out of print and is frequently adapted in diverse ways. It is now through adaptation onto the screen that these nineteenth-century texts are most vividly influential and continue to speak to us, amuse us, haunt us and challenge us.

Notes

1 See also Wootton, 2016.
2 As witnessed by the hostile reception accorded to *Guy Domville* on its opening night in 1895.

References

Achebe, Chinua (1977). 'An Image of Africa'. *Massachusetts Review* 17: 782–94.

Bowser, Eileen (1990) *History of the American Cinema: The Transformation of Cinema, 1907–1915*. New York: Charles Scribners.

Demory, Pamela (2010). 'Jane Austen and the Chick Flick in the Twenty-first Century', in *Adaptation Studies: New Approaches*, eds. Christa Albrecht-Crane and Dennis Ray Cutchins. Madison, NJ: Fairleigh Dickinson University Press, pp. 121–49.

Dickens, Charles (1975) Letter March 1838, quoted in *A Bibliography of Dickensian Criticism 1836–1975*, ed. R. C. Churchill. London: Macmillan, p. 189.

Dixon, Winston Wheeler (2000). 'Transferring the Novel's Gothic Sensibilities to the Screen', in *Readings on Frankenstein*, ed. D. Nardo. San Diego, CA: Greenhaven Press, pp. 115–28.

Hand, Richard (2007). 'Paradigms of Metamorphosis and Transmutation: Thomas Edison's *Frankenstein* and John Barrymore's *Jekyll and Hyde*', in *Monstrous Adaptations: Generic and Thematic Transmutations in Horror Film*, eds. Richard J. Hand and Jay McRoy. Manchester: Manchester University Press, pp. 9–19.

――― (2014). *Listen in Terror: British Horror Radio from the Advent of Broadcasting to the Digital Age*. Manchester: Manchester University Press.

Hardy, Thomas (1982). *The Collected Letters of Thomas Hardy*, Vol. 3: 1902–1908, eds. Richard Little Purdy and Michael Millgate. Oxford: Oxford University Press.

Hopkins, Lisa (2012). 'Shakespeare to Austen on Screen', in *A Companion to Literature, Film and Adaptation*, ed. Deborah Cartmell. Oxford: Blackwell, pp. 241–55.

Jones, Henry Arthur (1891). *Saints and Sinners: A New and Original Drama of Modern English Middle-Class Life*. London: Macmillan.

Jones, Stephanie (2012). 'The Ethics of Geography: Women as Readers and Dancers in GC's B+P (2004)', in *Uses of Austen: Jane's Afterlives*, eds. Gillian Dow and Clare Hanson. London: Palgrave, pp. 175–91.

Lustig, T. J. (2011). *Henry James and the Ghostly*. Cambridge: Cambridge University Press.

Mazzella, Anthony J. (2002). '"The Story...Held Us" from Henry James to Jack Clayton', in *Henry James Goes to the Movies*, ed. Susan M. Griffin. Lexington: University Press of Kentucky, pp. 11–34.

Orr, Leonard (2009). *James's The Turn of the Screw*. London: A. & C. Black.

Reade, C. L. and Reade, Rev. C. (1887). Eds., *Charles Reade: A Memoir Volumes I and II*. London: Chapman and Hall, pp. 164–5.

Säckel, Sarah (2010). 'Globalizing Jane Austen: An Analysis of Gurinder Chadha's *Pride and Prejudice* Adaptation *Bride and Prejudice*', in *Locating Transnational Ideals*, eds. Walter Goebel and Saskia Schabio. Routledge, pp. 249–64.

Skal, David J. (1993). *The Horror Show: A Cultural History of Horror*. London: Plexus.

Steiner, George (1961). *The Death of Tragedy*. London: Faber.

Stoker, Bram (1998). *Dracula: Or the Undead – A Play in Prologue and Five Acts*, ed. Sylvia Starshine. Nottingham: Pumpkin Books.

Strong, Jeremy (2008). 'Sweetening Jane: Equivalence through Genre, and the Problem of Class in Austen Adaptations'. *Journal of Adaptation in Film and Performance* 1(3): 205–19.

Tigchelaar, Jana M. (2013). 'Those "Whose Deaths Were Not Remarked": Ghostly Other Women in Henry James's *The Turn of the Screw*, Charlotte Perkins Gilman's *The Yellow Wallpaper*, and Marilynne Robinson's *Housekeeping*', in *The Ghostly and the Ghosted in Literature and Film: Spectral Identities*, eds. Lisa Kroger and Melanie R. Anderson, Lanham, MD: University of Delaware Press, pp. 29–46.

Wootton, Sarah (2016). *The Byronic Hero in Nineteenth-Century Women's Writing and Screen Adaptation*. Basingstoke: Palgrave.

11

True histories of the Elephant Man: storytelling and theatricality in adaptations of the life of Joseph Merrick

Benjamin Poore

Rethinking the Elephant Man

Joseph Carey Merrick, the so-called 'Elephant Man', is a ubiquitous figure in representations of the Gothicised late-Victorian city. Indeed, so suggestive is the imagery associated with Victorian London and its neo-Victorian re-imagining in novels and films, that if Merrick had not existed, it would have been necessary to invent him. Phrases like 'the urban jungle' and the imagery of Margaret Harkness when she describes slum dwellers as 'men lower than beasts' in *In Darkest London* (1889), point ineluctably towards an idea of the Victorian metropolis as having something monstrous and atavistic at its heart (Harkness, 2003: 23). Indeed, Julian Wolfreys sums up writers' views of London as 'a monster, a formless form, constantly reforming and deforming itself' (Wolfreys, 2007: 4). When neo-Victorian works make use of these tropes in their representations of the city, however, Kohlke and Gutleben identify a paradox, that 'while seeking to skew perceptions and jar readers/viewers/consumers out of a complacent and secure self-location within the invented cityscape, neo-Victorian texts also rely on retracing well-trodden paths over and over again in a relentless *recursus ad infinitum*' (Kohlke and Gutleben, 2015: 17). This reliance, Kohkle and Gutleben argue, places these past cities, and their 'prior stylised reimaginings' in a 'cumulative adaptive chain' (2015: 17).

Afterlives

In this chapter, I will argue that this kind of cumulative chain exists with regard to adaptations of Merrick's life story, and that the 'well-trodden paths' of prior adaptations often become mistaken for, or blended with, the historical record. Moreover, the act of retracing this adaptive chain reveals that responses to Merrick and his deformities have not undertaken a straightforward journey from benighted Victorian attitudes to a modern, enlightened outlook. Instead, depictions of the 'Elephant Man' come in waves, in movements and counter-movements. As the chapter will show, Ashley Montagu's book *The Elephant Man: A Study in Human Dignity* (1971) created a particular impression of Merrick based on Montagu's theory of emotional development, while Bernard Pomerance's play (1977) emphasised a political interpretation. David Lynch's film *The Elephant Man* (1980) reacted against this with a melodramatic revision of the story, and Howell and Ford's book *The True History of the Elephant Man* (1980) sought to correct these dramatic versions of Merrick's life with historical research. Nevertheless, Lynch's film has become the culturally dominant manifestation of 'the Elephant Man', and subsequent theatrical adaptations, as I will show, tend to treat Lynch's as the authoritative text, even as they borrow from Pomerance, and from Howell and Ford.

As a complex case study, mixing both history and fiction, and adaptations across media over a forty-year period, the example of the 'Elephant Man' is important because it shows how common it is to rethink the nineteenth century in *reaction to* current representations of and attitudes towards the period. In effect, to paraphrase Lytton Strachey, we all know too much about the nineteenth century – have absorbed too much, from contemporary culture – to ever be able to view it objectively. The examples of stage plays of the 1990s and 2000s that I will be presenting in the second half of this chapter are often raging against an imaginary, Lynchian nineteenth century. The historical record of Merrick's life, consisting mostly of decent people doing their best for Merrick in appalling circumstances, does not contain sufficient melodrama, and Merrick must, therefore, be made to stand for more, to bear the historical resonance of a journey to enlightenment that we repeatedly need to hear.

In the first part of this chapter, I will explain how the circulation of Joseph Merrick's image and myth have lent him such cultural visibility, taking him from a relatively obscure Victorian curiosity to a potent symbol of the outsider. I will also show how the Elephant Man dramas unintentionally helped to kick-start a wave of Oscar-winning representations of disabilities and disorders. I will then compare the Bernard Pomerance play and the David Lynch film, and their treatment of melodrama and the theatre, before exploring a range of Elephant Man plays (and Laurent Petitgirard's 2002 opera) that have been performed since the 1990s.

The Victorian pantheon

I want to begin by suggesting that the treatment of the 'Elephant Man' myth over the last forty years has some elements in common with changes in the representation of two other late-Victorian historical characters, Jack the Ripper and Oscar Wilde.[1] He belongs now, we might say, to a pantheon of posthumous Victorian celebrities: historical figures who are now felt to tell us something about the nineteenth century itself. Usually, as Matthew Sweet has argued, that 'something' is 'the worst excesses and ignorances of our Victorian ancestors' (Sweet, 2001: 140).

The three individuals did, of course, co-exist. As Howell and Ford note, the site of the London Hospital on Whitechapel Road placed it in close proximity to the Ripper murders of 1888–89, and indeed, a waxwork museum on the theme of the Ripper occupied the same site, opposite the hospital, where Tom Norman had exhibited Merrick in 1884 (Howell and Ford, 2006: 8). Kenneth C. Kaleta even suggests that Merrick was an early suspect in the Ripper investigation, though without citing evidence (Kaleta, 1993: 37). Joseph Merrick and Frederick Treves make cameo appearances in several episodes of the second series of the BBC/BBC America series *Ripper Street* (2014), dealing with policing in the Whitechapel area in the immediate aftermath of the Ripper murders.

Both 'Jack the Ripper' and 'The Elephant Man' are also metonyms rather than the names of actual people, and both, because of their many media reiterations, have acquired a set of visual referents. For Jack it is the top hat, cape, and occasionally doctor's bag or knife held aloft, the figure itself almost always in silhouette.[2] For the 'Elephant Man' it is his distinctive yachting cap with the flannel face-covering attached and the eye slit, the stick and the cape. This latter image was made famous by the poster for the David Lynch film *The Elephant Man*, released in 1980, and is reproduced in derivative items such as DVD reissues and the film novelisation by Christine Sparks (1980); it is present in a simplified form on the back cover of the revised edition of Howell and Ford's *The True History of the Elephant Man* (2006). In the case of Jack the Ripper the iconography exists to give form to someone whose actual appearance is a mystery; by contrast, the iconography of Merrick as the Elephant Man is there to denote someone whose actual appearance is widely known as a result of the photographs Treves commissioned on Merrick's first visits to the London Hospital.

Afterlives

The travelling costume thus becomes a way of showing and not-showing Merrick, a way of establishing him as a brand, but also a visual euphemism. The connection with Wilde is less obvious, but perhaps more telling. Wilde, has, of course, been accorded the status of a cultural icon since the 1980s, and strong claims have been made about his formative influence on modern gay identity (see Gardiner, 2002: 206, 213). As with Merrick, the late twentieth century 'rehabilitated' Wilde, finding in him not that which was monstrous but that which was to be celebrated, the Victorians themselves instead being accorded the condemnation for their cruel and inhuman treatment of the two men. Both Wilde and Merrick have a frequently cited incident in their biography which seems to crystallise their outsider status and the cruelty of the Victorian mob: for Wilde, it is the manacled wait at Clapham Junction station after his conviction for 'gross indecency', mocked and baited by the crowds, which he recalls poignantly in *De Profundis* (Wilde, 1973: 183–4), while for Merrick it is the public disturbance caused by his arrival at Liverpool Street Station after being robbed of his life savings by a showman in Brussels (Howell and Ford, 2006: 85). Where both Wilde and Merrick can easily be rendered through fiction into tragic figures or the subjects of sentimental celebration, plays like Neil Bartlett's *In Extremis* and David Hare's *The Judas Kiss*, and Pomerance's *The Elephant Man*, have explored the question of agency, the extent to which Wilde and Merrick actively chose a given path. And, while Wilde's personal and artistic legacy has been explored from such varied points of view as Irish identity, queer identity, feminism, socialism, aestheticism and decadence, Merrick has become a potent symbol of intersectional disadvantage: a poor, barely educated, working-class boy, disabled by a diseased hip and suffering from a rare disorder, whose late mother and sister were also disabled. Merrick's body has become the richly symbolic territory on which ideas of pathology, disability, sociology, psychology, and political economy converge, and which are then overlaid with our own preconceptions about the workhouses, freak shows, and Gothic Victorian London. With Wilde, as John Gardiner observes, 'we find in him what we choose to look for' (Gardiner, 2002: 220). Pomerance makes a very similar point about Merrick in scene 12 of *The Elephant Man*, subtitled 'Who Does he Remind You of?' (Pomerance, 1979: 36–8).

Masterless narrative

The price of membership of such a select group in postmodern culture, of course, is that one's image and imputed characteristics are endlessly reproduced, quoted, pastiched and parodied, in ways that are often (perhaps even deliberately) tonally insensitive to the nuances of the original source materials. If, as Lynn M. Voskuil remarks in a phrase particularly apposite for Merrick, postmodernism is supposed to 'expose the grand narratives by stripping away their cloaks of authenticity' then we have to ask what the 'authentic' story of Merrick is presumed to be (Voskuil, 2004: 7). The 'master narrative' of the London Hospital surgeon Frederick Treves, Merrick's putative saviour and friend, as relayed in Treves's memoir *The Elephant Man and Other Reminiscences* (1923), has been challenged by the pioneering work of Howell and Ford in *The True History of the Elephant Man*, originally published in 1980. But Treves's account had already been accepted in all its particulars by Ashley Montagu in writing his *The Elephant Man: A Study in Human Dignity* (1996 [1971]). Treves's and Montagu's books are named as the source material for both Pomerance's play and Lynch's film.

Howell and Ford uncovered Merrick's family circumstances in Leicester, the account of him given by the showman Tom Norman, and Merrick's own autobiographical pamphlet. These alternative sources reveal Treves's reminiscences, as Graham and Oehlschlaeger suggest, to 'occupy an interesting middle ground between reportage and fiction' (Graham and Oehlschlaeger, 1992: 35). As this narrative has become so fractured and contested, then, we might well ask which 'master narrative' it is that postmodern appropriations are seeking to strip away.

Some of the more unlikely cameos and appropriations of the 'Elephant Man' as a name or an image in recent decades have included: a visual gag in the makeover sequence in *Not Another Teen Movie* (Joel Gullen, 2001); a Jamaican dancehall vocalist; and a minor DC comic-book villain and member of the Brotherhood of Evil (predictably, in this case, a literal man-elephant hybrid). In British comedy, mocking the idea of the 'Elephant Man' seems to have enjoyed a resurgence, many years after the parody musical, *Elephant!*, featured in the film *The Tall Guy* (Richard Curtis, 1989). In fact, *The Elephant Man – The Musical*, a 2001 parody by Jeff Hylton and Tim Werenko featuring a singing Merrick who dreams of being a Broadway star, was staged in London at Camden People's Theatre in 2003. Even more recently, David Schneider's radio comedy *Births, Marriages and Deaths* featured an episode in 2013 called 'The Elephant Malcolm' in which the central character Malcolm keeps accidentally quoting John Hurt in Lynch's *The Elephant Man* after a trip to the dentist and a local anaesthetic. The BBC sitcom *Not Going Out* also included an episode in 2013, 'Rabbit', in which central character Lee

(Lee Mack) has to disguise his identity from an unexpected visitor by putting his head in a pillowcase containing a dead rabbit, and pretending that he is rehearsing an amateur-dramatic play about the Elephant Man. In two Sherlock Holmes-themed comedy productions running simultaneously in December 2014 in London theatres, actors impersonated Merrick, in one case in order to mock an onstage comedy partner, in the other, to present Merrick as a (highly unsuccessful) stand-up comedian and light entertainer.[3]

A rising star

In what follows, I argue that Merrick – or rather, the myth of 'the Elephant Man' – has acquired this status mostly by means of Lynch's film, and it is the film's conventions that are being parodied. In the movie, the trademark travelling outfit is shown extensively, and, famously, audiences have to wait until thirty minutes into the film to see Merrick's face. In the play, by contrast, the actor's face is necessarily exposed, since Pomerance insists in the play's 'Introductory Note' that 'any attempt to reproduce his appearance and his speech naturalistically' would be 'counterproductive' and 'distracting' (Pomerance, 1979: 4). Nevertheless, despite their different forms of representation, the fact that Lynch's film opened while Pomerance's play was enjoying its Broadway run in 1979 undoubtedly helped to deepen the cultural impact of Merrick's story (Graham and Oehlschlaeger, 1992: 135). Moreover, there was clearly something in the air in the 1970s – no doubt assisted by Montagu's book, which reprinted Treves's account – that had created an appetite for performances of Merrick. David Lynch recalls, 'there were other *Elephant Man* scripts floating around. And suddenly it was like, I couldn't turn a corner without hearing something or seeing something about *The Elephant Man*' (Lynch, 2005: 92). Graham and Oehlschlaeger analyse other Elephant Man plays by Thomas Gibbons, William Turner, and Roy Faudree from the 1970s (Graham and Oehlschlaeger, 1992: 119–34), while Holladay and Watt link the play's origins to contemporary British dramatists' interest in 'the racial and sexual dimensions of British imperialism' (Holladay and Watt, 1989: 876. Pomerance was living in the UK at the time, and the play was first produced by his former theatre company, Foco Novo). Thus, there is an element of historical contingency to both play and film: this was the play that happened to be seen by the actor Philip Anglim in London and taken on as a personal project to Broadway; this was the film that happened to get financed because the producer, Mel Brooks, saw and loved

Lynch's *Eraserhead* (Lynch, 2005: 93). Given different circumstances, other Elephant Man plays might have defined Merrick for the late twentieth century.

The simultaneity of the play and film also had an interesting crossover effect that has profoundly shaped our ideas about acting and 'prestige' drama since. His performance as Merrick helped make a major star out of British actor John Hurt, and despite the original casting of the (at the time) lesser-known stage actors David Schofield and Philip Anglim in Pomerance's play, more celebrated figures from music and film have been cast in the role: David Bowie took over from Anglim in the US production in 1980–81, and Bradley Cooper starred in a Broadway and West End revival in 2014–15. As I have suggested elsewhere, the contorted physicality, laboured speech and pathos of Schofield and Anglim's Merrick found their way into David Threlfall's performance as Smike in David Edgar's highly successful adaptation of Dickens's *Nicholas Nickleby* in 1980 (Poore, 2011: 192n.). And more generally, the precise and studied impersonation of persons with distinctive physical or mental disabilities or conditions has become a sure-fire way to professional kudos and Academy Awards success for male actors. Although Hurt was nominated for an Oscar, later Oscar winners in these roles include Dustin Hoffman in *Rain Man* (1988), Daniel Day Lewis as Christy Brown in *My Left Foot* (1989), Tom Hanks for *Forrest Gump* (1994) and Eddie Redmayne as Stephen Hawking in *The Theory of Everything* (2014).

Merrick and melodrama

It could be said that several of the films mentioned above attempt to temper their emotive subject-matter with gestures towards historical or documentary verisimilitude: to balance the melodrama with an unflinching, medically informed portrayal of a disease or condition. By contrast, both the film and play *The Elephant Man* have been characterised as melodramatic, the most developed argument being that of Holladay and Watt (Holladay and Watt, 1989: 870–4). However, I contend that Pomerance's play employs a number of strategies to attempt to short-circuit such a response. The play's focus on Treves in its second half, its 'crossover' structure where Treves becomes as helpless (and without hope) as Merrick once was, its sudden removal of Mrs Kendal from the action, its emphasis on the arbitrary nature of Merrick's life and death instead of the highly orchestrated 'final night' that Lynch shows us, the use of multi-rolling and provocative scene titles, and Merrick's often ironic, sharply perceptive commentary on his situation: all these point to a conscious deployment of theatrical resources to disturb and rupture melodramatic certainties. Although Pomerance himself made light of his debt to Brecht (Rees, 1992: 59), Holladay and Watt are surely correct in asserting that Pomerance in this play 'is quite obviously influenced by Brechtian theory' (Holladay and Watt, 1989: 868). This assertion makes it all the more surprising that the authors should continue to label it a melodrama.

Conversely, it is Lynch's film, and the screenplay he co-wrote with Chris de Vore and Eric Bergren, that takes the decisive step of reshaping the historical narrative so that it resembles the rollercoaster of escape, capture and rescue that structures Dickens's *Oliver Twist* (Graham and Oehlschlaeger, 1992: 141–2), casting Merrick as the orphan Oliver, who represents, according to Dickens, 'the principle of Good surviving through every adverse circumstance, and triumphing at last' (Dickens, 2003: 457). This arrangement casts Bytes and the Night Porter as the villains, Bytes as a wheedling, avaricious Fagin and the Night Porter as a thuggish Bill Sikes. Thus, as well as containing 'deliberate echoes of such compassionate horror films as *The Island of Lost Souls... The Bride of Frankenstein, Freaks* and *The Hunchback of Notre Dame*' as Bruce Kawin has argued (Kawin, 1981: 22), Lynch's *The Elephant Man* and its *chiaroscuro* world seem to owe much, stylistically, to David Lean's *Oliver Twist* (1948), in its emphasis on the shadows and squalor of the Victorian period.

Indeed, unlike Victorian stage melodrama, there is little room for comedy in Lynch's Whitechapel. Michel Chion comments on the 'special kind of humour' in the scenes where Merrick dresses up and acts the part of a gentleman, alone in his room (Chion, 2006: 54). However, the fact that the tenderness of one of these moments is shattered by the appearance of the Night Porter's face at the window, reminding him of the nocturnal visits in which he is once more exploited as a 'freak', means that the mild amusement has only functioned as a prelude to peril, deepening our sense of his helplessness. To laugh at Merrick as he practises genteel conversation would be to be implicated in the Porter's exploitative spectating. The one instance where the film invites us to laugh at slapstick comedy is the rather strained moment when the brutal, burly Night Porter is unconvincingly hit on the head by Mothershead, and falls to the ground.

By contrast, as Nadine Holdsworth has argued, 'multidimensional' Victorian melodrama anticipated the postmodern in its 'juxtaposition of moments of high pathos with comic interludes' (Holdsworth, 1998: 196); or, as Dickens put it in *Oliver Twist*, 'It is the custom on the stage in all good, murderous melodramas, to present the tragic and the comic scenes in as regular alternation as the layers of red and white in a side of streaky well-cured bacon' (Dickens, 2003: 134). Lynch's *The Elephant Man* is so focused in its revulsion for Victorian cruelty, heartlessness and greed that it cannot risk the intrusion of a comedic perspective, or a wink to the audience. As John Hurt recalls of his scenes with Anthony Hopkins (Treves), 'If there was the slightest chance of it being "a bit of a laugh", I would have been sunk' (Interview with John Hurt, 2008). In this way, Lynch's *Elephant Man* is perhaps closer to the film melodramas of the mid-twentieth century, exemplified by the work of Vincente Minnelli and Douglas Sirk, than the multiple perspectives and modes that composed a full Victorian melodrama. The relentless high moral seriousness with which Lynch's film attacks the Victorians explains the attractiveness of the figure of the Elephant Man to modern-day parodists: the comedy must find a release somewhere, even if it is necessarily beyond the confines of the film's own world.

Merrick and the theatre

Furthermore, the Victorian theatre itself plays a key role in conceptions of the public and private self in both the play and in the film, though again with quite different effects. Treves, in his *Reminiscences*, uses a range of modes – Gothic, romantic, parody, science fiction, theatrical – in order to 'plot Merrick into literary narratives', as Andrew Smith suggests (Smith, 2000: 293). Graham and Oehlschlaeger bring out this theatricality in Pomerance and Lynch's source text more explicitly: Treves 'scripts' the actions and reactions of Merrick's lady visitors, creating a 'theatrical illusion', one that Merrick then, to Treves's surprise, comes to believe; he provides Merrick with the 'props' in the 'silver-fitted dressing-bag' to maintain the illusion of his being a 'knockabout Don Juan' (Graham and Oehlschlaeger, 1992: 25–8). Hence, despite their different media and storytelling methods, both Pomerance's play and Lynch's film present the theatre as the quintessential nineteenth-century medium, the art form for a society that was always performing, always pretending to be what it was not.

To this end, both the film and the play, strikingly, invent a personal friendship between Merrick and the actress Madge Kendal, despite the fact that the two probably never met (see Howell and Ford, 2006: 111–12). In both, Merrick and Kendal read from Shakespeare's *Romeo and Juliet*. The narrative of Lynch's film can also be read as following an uplifting journey from the 'wrong' kind of performance – in freak shows – to the 'right' kind of performance, Merrick standing up and receiving applause at a theatrical performance dedicated to him. As Michel Chion points out, on three occasions in the film, Merrick is asked to stand up: at the freak show, as a medical phenomenon at the hospital, and finally in the theatre, although this last occasion is 'the most troubling, for no-one knows exactly why or what they are applauding!' (Chion, 2006: 53). I would add that, even though this standing ovation in the theatre is not recorded as having happened to the historical Merrick,[4] it is seemingly necessary for Lynch's melodrama, where triumph against the odds must be illustrated by public commendation. In the same way, in the mob scene at Liverpool Street Station, it is necessary to the emotional tenor of the film for Merrick to be pursued to the corner of an underground urinal, rather than barred up in a waiting room (Howell and Ford, 2006: 186), in order for him to deliver the film's most famous (and almost always misquoted) lines, '"I am not an elephant! I am a human being. I am a man"'. The lower depths to which his character is brought must be made lower still, in order to provoke the conditions in which Merrick can 'find his voice'.

We might also note that the choice of a urinal – what John Hurt calls a 'ghastly, pompous urinal. Victorian urinal' (Interview with John Hurt, 2008) – underlines, in this scene, the violation of Merrick's private self in public. His '"I am a man"' asserts not only his dignity, but his maleness, his right to be in a gentlemen's lavatory ('"the patient's genitals remain entirely intact and unaffected"', as Treves observes in his presentation to the Pathological Society in the film). Merrick's struggle, then, is to exercise control over his private and public selves, which he is only able to do once the Night Porter has been sacked; he is then able to visit the theatre (to view privately in public), and able to orchestrate his own death. Finally, the journey from fairground to 'legitimate theatre' in Lynch's film perhaps implies that film as an art form is morally and technologically superior to both these other entertainments, since it allows us, as viewers, to 'see' Merrick without him being there at all. We have caused him no moments of anxiety or self-consciousness. The film's choice of black and white photography also seems to be asserting the medium's ability to 'colour' perception. To release a monochrome film in an era of colour implies a number of contradictory claims for the film: it asserts a grainy, gritty, unflinching documentary quality, but also a refusal to satisfy technicolour expectations of Merrick's makeup, yet in so doing it evokes, as Kawin argues, the monster movies of the 1930s; black and white nostalgically evokes films 'like they used to be' but anti-nostalgically damns the

Victorians and the 'good old days' (there are correspondences, here, with the 'gaslight melodramas' documented by Guy Barefoot: monochrome films of the 1940s that revelled in the dark side of Victorian life. See Barefoot, 2001).

The relationship between Pomerance's Merrick and the theatre is rather more complex, since the medium itself is also a stage play. There is no final validation for Merrick at a Victorian theatre in this version, but instead a Victorian actress undresses before him and is promptly banished, by Treves, from the room and from the play. Thus, the journey from Whitechapel 'freak shop' to royal box is not a linear one in Pomerance; Merrick's final moments are heralded by the return of the Belgian freak show's Pinheads in a dream sequence (Pomerance, 1979: 56). However, arguably the play's own existence as a work for the theatre serves to rhetorically elevate the theatre as a means for confronting and understanding the phenomenon of the Elephant Man, in the same way that Lynch's black and white helps to create a rhetoric of film's superiority. We might usefully employ Jon Erikson's distinction between 'dramatic realism, which conceals or effaces the apparatus or representation', and theatrical realism, which is 'self-conscious, ideology-unmasking theatre' that attempts 'to create a self-conscious dialectal relation between the form of representation and the content' (Erickson, 2004: 160). Pomerance's playworld is one which is normatively governed by dramatic-realism rules, but features a character, Merrick, who can seemingly only be represented by theatrical realism.

Merricks for a new century

What I wish to examine in this final part of the chapter is how subsequent adaptations of Merrick's life story have responded to the representational structures put in place by Pomerance and Lynch. In addition to comparing different ways of representing Merrick, I will explore how the Treves master-narrative is challenged by structures that place the surgeon away from the centre of the action, or in competition with Tom Norman over Merrick.

Keiran Gillespie's *The Elephant Man*, first performed at Eden Court Theatre, Inverness in 1995, is immediately distinct from Lynch's all-star cast and Pomerance's small, multi-rolling theatrical cast, in that it uses one professional actor, Joel Strachan, and '26 performers drawn from throughout the Highland Region' (Gillespie, no date: 1). To an extent, the inclusion of a community cast requires the narrative to be reshaped to accommodate set pieces, and so we have a 'Victorian fairground' as the setting of the encounter between Treves and Merrick, instead of a disused shop on the Whitechapel Road, and Merrick's acceptance into high society is presented as a montage of society parties. Other than this, what is remarkable about Gillespie's play is how Lynch's version of events has become a new master-narrative: Tom Norman becomes Bites, a drunken sadist (Bytes in the film); the Night Porter abuses Merrick for profit and allows Bites to abduct Merrick; there is Mrs Kendal, *Romeo and Juliet*, and a triumphant visit to the theatre. Even more surprisingly, the script incorporates situations, devices and even conversations (not quite word-for-word, but they are very similar) drawn from Pomerance, and incorporates them into a structure derived from the film. So, for instance, Strachan evokes Merrick's deformities rather 'via sustained grimace and awkward contortions than layers of laytex' [sic] according to a contemporary review (Villiers, 1995), and Treves's initial conversation with Carr Gomm is very close to Pomerance's. The sacking of the Porter, who behaves as the Night Porter does in the film, is responded to by Merrick as he does to a different Porter's sacking in Scene 8 of Pomerance's play. Nevertheless, the voices that intone at Merrick's death, 'He came from the poorest and most unfortunate background…And he shamed the privileged with his honesty and innocence' indicate that the adaptation, as a whole, sides with Lynchian pathos over Pomerancian detachment (Gillespie, no date: 41).

By contrast, Laurent Petitgirard's opera, *Joseph Merrick, The Elephant Man* (2002) seems to present itself as a post-Howell and Ford opera, in that Tom Norman is given his historical name back, and made into a disconcerting, eccentric character who is nonetheless loyal to Merrick. Merrick initially refuses to go back to the hospital – as in Norman's historical account – (Howell and Ford, 2006: 77), while Treves is peremptory and coldly ambitious in his first appearance, demanding that Merrick return to the London Hospital to be exhibited at an important meeting. However, the opera is not centrally concerned with the rivalry between Norman and Treves as alternative 'showmen'; more significant to Merrick's journey here is an invented figure, an intensely compassionate nurse called Mary who falls in love with Merrick. There is a great deal more that could be said about the design and musical and theatrical language of Petitgirard's opera, but the key observation for this chapter is that, in removing the melodramatic villains of Lynch, de Vore and Bergren's screenplay, we are left with a tale with a heroic Merrick and a slightly less heroic Treves: not a melodrama, but not quite enough for a drama either.

True histories of the Elephant Man

Tuirenn Hurstfield and Gwyndaf Tomos-Evans's *The Elephant Man*, which premiered at the CragRats Theatre, Holmfirth, in 2005, mixes elements from the Pomerance play and film much as Gillespie's play does, albeit in different combinations. Here, as with Eric Nonn's libretto for Petitgirard's opera, the Tom Norman figure has his name restored to him, but his character has again the intemperate rage of Lynch's Bytes (and, in his wheedling visit to attempt to persuade Merrick to be exhibited again, he echoes Ross in Scene 15 of the Pomerance play). Merrick's deformities are indicated by the actor's stance, but also by white masks, with his head and parts of his body masked to illustrate the full extent of his condition (Hurstfield and Tomos-Evans, no date: 15). Hurstfield and Tomos-Evans's play, like the opera, expands the role of the nurse (here called Helen Cole), and, like the Lynch film, features a trip to the theatre and (here, a rather brisk and unlikeable) Madge Kendal. The name Eva Lückes is restored to the hospital's matron (as it is in the opera), although she is placed in the occasionally antagonistic role of Treves's colleague and supporter that was assigned to Mothershead in the film. As in the Pomerance play, we are occasionally transported to a dream world where, in Merrick's nightmare (as opposed to Treves's nightmare in the earlier play) Tom Norman becomes Treves, the Matron becomes Princess Alexandra, and Bishop How prays at the foot of Merrick's bed (Hurstfield and Tomos-Evans, no date: 74).

The play includes an ironic reference to the way that successive works by Treves, Montagu, Pomerance and Lynch misname Merrick as 'John'. Merrick tells Helen, "'I now find it thoroughly entertaining that he should call me John. Everyone else knows my name is Joseph'" (Hurstfield and Tomos-Evans: 31). However, surely the greater irony is the play's own debt to the narrative structures of both prior fictional works – even down to the building of the model of St Philip's Church being 'the action of the play' and its completion signifying his imminent death (Pomerance, 1979: 4). Character names from the historical record are given with one hand, while invented incidents and tropes from fiction are taken with the other. This is not to imply any moral judgement on the adaptation process undertaken here, but simply to suggest that there is a credibility risk in asserting historical authenticity with names, only to then so closely mimic the familiar tropes, stock characters, and structures of previous fictional interpretations. It might look as though the 'authenticity' is, as it were, skin-deep.

Mary Swan and Saul Jaffe's *The Elephant Man*, first performed at Queen Mary's College, Basingstoke in 2007, tries an original approach.

While this play script, too, contains a reference to Joseph being misnamed John, and like Pomerance's play, requires the actor to contort his body to 'morph' into Merrick (Swan and Jaffe, no date: 4), as a one-person show, the results are very different. The first character the audience encounters is Tom Norman, here an amusing and incorrigible scamp rather than a villain. Although the script reproduces the myth of a deep friendship with Madge Kendal ('We would spend the afternoons enacting our favourite works of literature' [p. 14]), one of the interesting notes the script repeatedly strikes is not pathos, so much as awkwardness: encounters that lead to misunderstandings, like Treves's initial proffering of his card, and Kendal's refusal of the Northampton visit (p. 15). More generally, having one body onstage, moving in and out of different physicalities, is a powerful expression of our shared humanity. If Treves, Merrick and Norman share the same body, it is harder for us to see abject villains instead of compromised individuals. Unexpectedly, perhaps, the one-person show seems to be less prone to the dangers of grandstanding than the Pomerance play where, as discussed earlier, the actor playing Merrick is in a different signifying system from the rest of the cast.

Although this section has focused on the scripted and dramaturgical shaping of Merrick's story in a range of adaptations, there is no disputing the fact that the depiction of Merrick himself – the theatrical frame(s) to be used – remains the abiding concern of adapters. That is why, as I have attempted to demonstrate, the shape and sequence of scenes, the deployment of characters, and the presentation of the story-world, are aspects that are easy to miss in our fascinated focus on the 'Elephant Man' himself. Bearing this in mind, it is refreshing to note that the Fourth Monkey play, *Elephant Man*, written by Steven Green, which was first staged at the Edinburgh Festival and which toured the UK in 2014/15, presented itself overtly as 'Inspired by the iconic David Lynch film' (Anon., 2014a: 'Touring'). There is no struggle at the textual level with Pomerance's legacy here. Yet such a statement inevitably led to direct comparisons – for the *Daily Telegraph*'s reviewer Michael Wilkinson – with Pomerance's newly-revived play, the West End transfer of which had recently been announced (Wilkinson, 2015). This is, of course, the point at which this essay began. And, as an added irony, Wilkinson appears to confuse the issue of precedence, saying of the Cooper revival that 'discarding the prosthetics and make-up altogether has allowed him to explore the role in a fresh way', as if the film had come first (the reviewer for *Opera Today* makes a similar mistake in reviewing *Joseph Merrick, the*

Elephant Man, calling the Pomerance play 'a successful stage drama of the 1980s' – Mullins: 2006).

But one last observation is pertinent regarding the Fourth Monkey *Elephant Man*, in this necessarily brief account: Merrick, played by Daniel Chrisostomou, is represented, according to another review, by a 'skeleton of twisted wire' which 'encases his head and other parts of his body to suggest the outline of the deformity, along with fragments that suggest its bulbous nature' (Anon., 2014b). This idea seems to capture very well the 'profoundly doubled experience' of viewing Merrick that Kawin attributed to both the play and the film (Kawin, 1981: 22–3); we are simultaneously viewing a Pomerancian virtuoso acting performance, but also a distorted Lynchian body shape, seeing the play through the framework of the film. Past and present are superimposed on each other. We now see Merrick liminally, even on stage, as both the twisted actor and the prosthetic head.

To conclude. In the last two decades, the Lynch film and the Pomerance play have merged with aspects of the Howell and Ford research to form a new – and sometimes self-contradictory – Elephant Man myth. At the same time, Merrick, or the Merrick costume, has remained a stage and screen comedy staple, not necessarily because of a postmodern lack of affect, but because of a profound cultural need to deflate the seriousness (and, perhaps, the perceived pomposity) of Lynch's film: it is a raspberry directed at the pulpit, after the sermon is over and the church has emptied. The further implication of the Elephant Man's strange journey is that it is easy for modern attitudes to the nineteenth century, transferred to fiction or drama, to ossify into neo-Victorian pieties (Miriam E. Burstein's much-circulated satirical blog post, 'Rules for Writing Neo-Victorian Novels' suggests some of the dangers – Burstein, 2006).

The common assumptions, noted in the last section, that Hurt's is the definitive interpretation of Merrick, and that Pomerance's play is a response to Lynch's film, could, in theory, make Pomerance's *The Elephant Man* seem satirical, even radical, to contemporary audiences when the play is revived. Its dialectical analyses of capitalism, imperialism and medical ethics are not quite what we expect from neo-Victorian fiction and drama today. However, this was not the reception I observed when I saw the revival of *The Elephant Man* at the Theatre Royal, Haymarket, London in June 2015. Rather, this highly anticipated transfer from Broadway, directed by Scott Ellis, featured an Oscar-nominated film actor, Bradley Cooper, seemingly aligning itself with those Hollywood screen depictions of disability mentioned earlier, rather than the stage history of the role. But more strikingly from a storytelling point of view, this version also omits the Pinheads' appearance at Merrick's death, rendering it much more similar to the death sequence in Lynch's film. Other non-naturalistic moments, like the dream sequence where Merrick gives a lecture on Treves, are omitted. And the final stage picture is of Madge Kendal returning and embracing Merrick's body, providing a non-verbal reaffirmation of the significance of their relationship, and thus conforming with conventional rules of character development rather than with Pomerance's episodic, published script, in which she disappears from the play after Scene 14. Hence, with this revival, it could be said that the Pomerance version is itself subjected to a post-Lynchian revision in the cumulative chain of adaptations. It seems we prefer, as a culture, to keep retreading the same brightly lit urban thoroughfares, rather than to explore the dark, disturbing byways of the imagination that Pomerance's original play offers us.

Notes

1 Graham and Oehlschlaeger make a similar point – combining history with a broader sweep of fiction – when they refer to Merrick as belonging to the 'immortal gallery' that includes Jekyll and Hyde, Victor Frankenstein and Jack the Ripper (Graham and Oehlschlaeger, 1992: 1).
2 See, for example, the cover of the Whitechapel Society's (2014) *The Little Book of Jack the Ripper* for a vivid version of this image.
3 The shows were *Potted Sherlock* (Vaudeville Theatre) and *Mrs Hudson's Christmas Corker* (Wilton's Music Hall). The latter also included a singalong comic song about Jack the Ripper.
4 Indeed, great care was taken to 'smuggle' Merrick into the private box behind a screen of nurses on those few occasions when he did visit the theatre, to prevent public disorder if he should be seen by the audience (Howell and Ford, 2006: 121–6).

References

Anon. (2014a) 'Touring.' *Fourth Monkey Theatre Company*. Available at www.fourthmonkey.co.uk/tour-elephant-man-2/ (accessed 26 January 2017).
Anon. (2014b) 'Review of *Elephant Man*'. *The Stage*. 12 November. Available at www.thestage.co.uk/reviews/2014/elephant-man/ (accessed 21 March 2015).
Barefoot, Guy (2001). *Gaslight Melodrama*. London: Continuum.
Burstein, Miriam E. (2006). 'Rules for Writing Neo-Victorian Novels.' *The Little Professor*. Typepad.com. 15 March. Available at http://littleprofessor.typepad.com/the_little_professor/2006/03/rules_for_writi.html (accessed 26 January 2017).

Chion, Michel (2006). *David Lynch*. London: BFI.
Dickens, Charles (2003). *Oliver Twist*. Harmondsworth: Penguin.
Erickson, Jon (2004). 'Defining Political Performance with Foucault and Habermas: Strategic and Communicative Action', *Theatricality*, eds. Thomas Postlewait and Tracy C. Davis. Cambridge: Cambridge University Press, pp. 156–85.
Gardiner, John (2002). *The Victorians: An Age in Retrospect*. London: Hambledon.
Gillespie, Keiran (no date). *The Elephant Man*. Unpublished play script. British Library, London. Manuscript no. 6850.
Graham, Peter W. and Fritz H. Oehlschlaeger (1992). *Articulating the Elephant Man: Joseph Merrick and His Interpreters*. Baltimore, MD: Johns Hopkins University Press.
Harkness, Margaret (2003 [1889]). *In Darkest London*. Cambridge: Black Apollo Press.
Holdsworth, Nadine (1998). 'Haven't I Seen You Somewhere Before?', in *Varieties of Victorianism: The Uses of a Past*, ed. Gary Day. Basingstoke: Macmillan, pp. 191–205.
Holladay, William E. and Stephen Watt (1989). 'Viewing the Elephant Man.' *PMLA* (journal of the Modern Languages Association) 104(5): 868–81.
Howell, Michael and Peter Ford (2006). *The True History of the Elephant Man*. 3rd edn. London: Allison & Busby.
Hurstfield, Tuirenn and Gwyndaf Tomos-Evans (no date). *The Elephant Man*. Unpublished play script. British Library, London. Manuscript no. 11007.
Interview with John Hurt (2008) *The Elephant Man: Special Edition DVD*. Bonus feature. Optimum Releasing.
Kaleta, Kenneth C (1993). *David Lynch*. Twayne's Filmmakers Series. New York: Twayne.
Kawin, Bruce (1981). Review of *The Elephant Man*. *Film Quarterly* 34(4): 21–5.
Kohlke, Marie-Luise and Christian Gutleben (2015). *Neo-Victorian Cities: Reassessing Urban Politics and Poetics*. Leiden and Boston, MA: Brill Rodopi.
Lynch, David (1980). *The Elephant Man* (video). United States: Paramount Home Video.
—— (2005). *Lynch on Lynch*, ed. Chris Rodley, revised edn. New York: Faber.
Montagu, Ashley (1996 [1971]). *The Elephant Man: A Study in Human Dignity*, 3rd edn. Lafayette, LA: Acadian House.
Mullins, Chris (2006). 'Review of *Joseph Merrick, The Elephant Man*'. *Opera Today*. 29 January. Available at www.operatoday.com/content/2006/01/petitgirard_the.php (accessed 20 March 2015).
Pomerance, Bernard (1979 [1977]). *The Elephant Man: A Drama*. New York and London: French.
Poore, Benjamin (2011). *Heritage, Nostalgia and Modern British Theatre: Staging the Victorians*. Basingstoke: Palgrave Macmillan.

Rees, Roland (1992). *Fringe First: Pioneers of Fringe Theatre on Record*. London: Oberon.
Smith, Andrew (2000). 'Pathologising the Gothic: The Elephant Man, the Neurotic and the Doctor'. *Gothic Studies* 2(3): 292–304.
Sparks, Christine (1980). *The Elephant Man*. London: Ballantine.
Swan, Mary and Saul Jaffe (no date). *The Elephant Man*. Unpublished play script. British Library, London. Manuscript no. 11769.
Sweet, Matthew (2001). *Inventing the Victorians*. London: Faber.
Treves, Frederick (1923). *The Elephant Man and Other Reminiscences*. London: Cassell & Co.
Villiers, Sarah (1995). '*The Elephant Man*, Eden Court, Inverness'. *Herald Scotland*. 5 August. Available at www.heraldscotland.com/sport/spl/aberdeen/the-elephant-man-eden-court-inverness-1.668109 (accessed 20 March 2015).
Voskuil, Lynn M (2004). *Acting Naturally: Victorian Theatricality and Authenticity*. Charlottesville: University of Virginia Press.
Whitechapel Society, The (2014). *The Little Book of Jack the Ripper*. London: History Press.
Wilde, Oscar (1973). *De Profundis and Other Writings*. Penguin English Library. Harmondsworth: Penguin.
Wilkinson, Michael (2015). 'The Elephant Man takes to the stage'. *The Telegraph* 19 February. Available at www.telegraph.co.uk/culture/theatre/theatre-features/11422763/The-Elephant-Man-takes-to-the-stage.html (accessed 20 March 2015).
Wolfreys, Julian (2007). *Writing London: Vol. 3: Inventions of the City*. Basingstoke and New York: Palgrave.

Index

Note: an 'n' after a page reference indicates the endnote number

Achebe, Chinua 203
Adorno, Theodor 17, 26–7, 107
Alberti, Samuel 155–6, 157–8
Altick, Richard D. 134
America 129–48
Anand, Mulk Raj 98–9
   Untouchable 99–100, 101
Aphornsuvan, Thanet 105
Appadurai, Arjun 114
Archer, William 192
Armstrong, Isobel 7, 53, 54, 55, 69n.1
Armstrong, Philip 80
Arnold, Matthew 19
   Culture and Anarchy 29–30
Asia, 104–6
   see also China; Korea
Auden, W. H. 16
Aungsan, Suukyi 106
Austen, Jane 188–9, 196, 204
   Pride and Prejudice (film versions) 196–8

Bakunin, Mikhail 27
Bann, Lisa 98
Bannerjee, Sukanya 113
Barefoot, Guy 217
Barnard, Philip 145n.18
Barnes, James J. 132, 144n.4, 144n.5
Barrett Browning, Elizabeth 53, 58–69, 70n.8, 70n.9

   see also Locke, John
Bates, A. W. 160, 165n.14, 165n.15
Baudelaire, Charles 28
Bayly, C. A. 99
Beard, James Franklin 136
Beck, Naomi 43
Beer, Gillian 36, 38
Ben-Messahel, Salhia 180
Benedict, Ruth 112
Benjamin, Walter 6–7, 15, 17, 20, 22, 26
   Arcades Project, The 16, 18, 19–30
Bennett, Arnold 33, 34, 38
   Clayhanger 41–3
   Ghost, The 39
   Human Machine, The 40, 44
   Man From The North, A 40–1
   Old Wives' Tale, The 40
   Price of Love, The 41
   'Rising Storm of Life, The' 7, 44–50
   'Secret of Content, The' 146
Berger, Jason 137
Blackett, R. J. M. 133
Blair, Kirstie 58, 69n.5
Bloom, Harold 53, 54
Boehm-Schnitker, Nadine 176
Bosanquet, Bernard 57–8
Bowser, Eileen 192–3
Bradley, F. H. 68–9
Brantlinger, Patrick 113

225

Index

British Association for the Advancement of Science, The 84–6
see also science
Brown, Charles Brockden 135
Edgar Huntly 130, 141–3
see also Gothic
Bunsen, C. J. 85
Byatt, A. S.
Possession: A Novel 170–1, 175
see also neo-Victorian

Carlyle, Thomas 23, 25, 95
Carroll, Victoria 150
Carter, Angela 171
Chapman, Alison 53–4
Chase-Riboud, Barbara
Hottentot Venus: A Novel 177–9
see also neo-Victorian
Chaudhuri, Amit 102
China 93–8
Chon, Michael 214, 216
Clifford, James 112
Clough, Arthur Hugh 22, 23
Colegate, Isabel
Summer of the Royal Visit, The 174
see also neo-Victorian
Coleridge, Samuel Taylor 57, 58
Collins, Wilkie 183
Armadale 161–2
Connor, Steven 35
Conrad, Joseph 44, 50, 192, 202
Heart of Darkness 189, 202–3
film versions 202–5
Secret Agent, The 26
Victory 202
film version 202
Cooper, James Fenimore 143
Pilot, The 130, 131, 133, 136–40
Crane, Ralph 121, 123, 125
Cunningham, Alexander 115–17

Darwin, Charles 27, 34, 37, 43, 44, 48, 79, 93, 94, 106

see also science; Wallace, Alfred Russel
Davies, Helen 176
Dawson, Gowan 45, 48
degeneration 75–6, 77
Demory, Pamela 188, 197
Derrida, Jacques 15, 16, 18, 26, 81
DeSpain, Jessica 131, 133–4, 135
Dickens, Charles 10, 21, 26, 37, 44, 48, 49, 98, 161, 179, 183, 191
Oliver Twist 159, 191, 214–15
Our Mutual Friend 161
Dickens, David B. 85
Dixon, Thomas 43
Dixon, Winston Wheeler 193
Douglas-Fairhurst, Robert 54
Dowden, Edward 36
Doyle, Sir Arthur Conan
Hound of the Baskervilles, The 74–6
Lost World, The 80
Dupaty, Charles 155, 164n.12

ecology 92–3
Edison, Thomas 47, 193–4
Eighteen-Bisang, Robert 85
Einstein, Albert 24
Eliot, George
Middlemarch 38
Eliot, T. S. 68–9
see also modernism
Englestein, Stefani 158
Erikson, Jon 217
Exorcist, The 201

Feldman, P. R. 156
Felski, Rita 91
Fin de Siècle 49, 72–86, 103
Flanagan, Richard 170
Wanting 179–83
Foldy, Michael 76
Ford, Peter 207, 209, 211, 215, 216, 218, 222n.4
see also Merrick, Joseph
Forsyth, Joseph 156–7, 164n.11

226

Index

Fraser, George MacDonald 175
Freud, Sigmund 93, 94
Friedman, Susan Stanford 91
Fryer, Peter 184
Fu, Yan 94, 95–6

Gandhi 99–100
Gardiner, John 210
Geertz, Clifford 112
Genette, Gérard 140
Gettmann, Royal A. 145n.10
Gibson, Mary Ellis 112
Gide, André 102–3
Giedion, Siegfried 22
Gillespie, Keiran 217–18, 219
  see also Merrick, Joseph
Godwin, William
  Caleb Williams 136, 140, 142
  see also Gothic
Gohdes, Clarence 134, 144n.9
Gooday, Graeme 46
Gopinath, Gayatri 113
Gosse, Edmund 190
Gothic 72–86
Graham, Peter W. 211, 212, 214, 215
  see also Merrick, Joseph
Green, Steven 220–1
  see also Merrick, Joseph
Gruss, Susanne 176
Guha, Ramachandra 99, 102
Gutleben, Christian 10, 177, 183, 207

Hardy, Thomas 190, 192
Harkness, Margaret 207
Hawthorne, Nathaniel
  Scarlet Letter, The 132
Hegel, F. 16, 27–8, 57, 105, 107
Heilmann, Ann 172–3, 176, 185n.7
  see also neo-Victorian
Ho, Elizabeth 185n.2
Ho, Lai-Ming 180
Holdsworth, Nadine 214
Holladay, William E. 212, 213, 214
  see also Merrick, Joseph

Holmes, Oliver Wendell
  Guardian Angel, The 129
Hopkins, Gerard Manley 25
Hopkins, Lisa 197
Horkheimer, Max 107
Horowitz, Anthony
  House of Silk, The 174
  see also neo-Victorian
Howell, Michael 208, 209, 211, 215, 216, 218, 222n.4
  see also Merrick, Joseph
Howsam, Leslie 134
Huang, Max Ko-wu, 95, 96
Huelsenbeck, Richard 23
Hugo, Victor 19
Hurstfield, Tuirenn 219
Hutcheon, Linda 177
  see also Merrick, Joseph
Hwang, Yuh J. 104

Ilaiah, Kancha 101
India 98–102, 111–28

Jaffe, Saul 219
  see also Merrick, Joseph
James, Henry
  Turn of the Screw, The 189, 198–9, 204
  film versions 200–2
  see also Gothic
Johnston, Anna 121, 123, 125
Jones, Henry Arthur 190, 192
Jones, Stephanie 198

Kaleta, Kenneth C. 209
Kant, Immanuel 54, 55, 56–7, 58–9, 60, 105, 107
Kaplan, Laurie 198
Kaufman, Robert 69n.3
Kaviraj, Sudipta 126
Kawin, Bruce 214, 216–17, 221
Kelly, David 104
Khan, Ahmed Hussain 126n.3
Khilnani, Sunil 99, 101

Index

Kierkegard, Soren 17–18
Kilgour, Maggie 76
Kneale, Matthew
  English Passengers 183
  see also neo-Victorian
Knox, John 160
Knowles, James 1, 2, 5
Kochler, Hans 99, 100
Korea 104
Kucich, John 169

LaCapra, Dominick 178–9
Lao, She
  Rickshaw Boy 96–8
Latour, Bruno 94
Lazarus, Neil 104
Lee, Kyun-Young
  Other Side of Dark Remembrance, The 104
Léger-St-Jean, Marie 132–3, 144n.7
Leighton, Angela 67–7, 69n.2, 69n.5
Levine, Caroline 56, 58
Levine, George 36–7
Levinson, Marjorie 54–5, 56, 58
Liu, Lydia 93
Llewellyn, Mark 172–3, 176, 185n.7
  see also neo-Victorian
Locke, John 7, 57–67
Lodge, Sir Oliver 38–9, 40, 47, 48, 50
  see also science
Loesberg, Johnathan 56, 57, 69n.6
Lustig, T. J. 199
Lynch, David 208, 212–22
  see also Merrick, Joseph

Machen, Arthur
  Great God Pan, The 73–4, 79
  see also Gothic
MacLaren, I. 183–4
Malhorta, Anshu 119–20, 125
Marcus, George E. 112
Marinetti, F. T. 18, 24
Marx, Karl 15, 17, 26, 94, 107
Mason, Nicholas 144n.3

Mathus, Thomas 48–9, 94
Mazzella, Anthony 200
Meer, Sarah 133
McGann, Jereome 55
McKitterick, Michael 30
Mellor, Anne K. 53–4
Merrick, Joseph 207–24
Michelet, Jules 17
Mills, J. S. 98, 105, 106
  On Liberty 94–6
Miller, Elizabeth 85
Miller, John 83, 84
Mir, Farina 111, 113, 114, 119–20, 124–5
Mitchell, Robert 46
modernism 68–9
Montagu, Ashely 208, 211, 212
  see also Merrick, Joseph
Motherwell, Robert 15
Müller, Max 85–6
  see also science
Murphy, Anne 126n.3

Naithani, Sadhana 121
Nehru, 100–1
neo-Victorian 10–11, 169–87
New Formalism 56, 57, 58
Nietzsche, Friedrich 18, 21, 23, 24, 26, 27, 94, 107
Nordau, Max
  Degeneration 76–7

Oehlschlaeger, Fritz H. 211, 212, 214, 215, 216n.1
  see also Merrick, Joseph
Orr, Leonard 199
Ottis, Laura 38

Pater, Walter 45
Patwardhan, Dava 121
Paul, Howard, 133
Paxton, Nancy 121
Petitgirard, Laurent 218
  see also Merrick, Joseph

Philbrick, Thomas 145n.14
Poe, Edgar Allan
   'Man of the Crowd, The' 7, 28, 29
   see also Gothic
Pomerance, Bernard 208, 210,
     212–13, 217–22
   see also Merrick, Joseph
Pratt, Mary Louise 112
Proudhon, D. J. 17, 22
Purewal, Navtej K. 118

Rauch, Alan 37
Reade, Charles 191
Rees, Roland 214
Reid, Anthony 104
Renwick, Chris 43
Rezek, Joseph 130, 131
Richter, Virginia 79, 80, 81, 82
Rohman, Carrie 81, 82
Rooney, Ellen 69n.3
Roy, Shampa 123
Ruskin, John 19, 48, 98

Säckel, Sarah 198
Sade, Marquis de 153–4
Sadleir, Michael 136, 145n.10
Sadoff, Diane F. 169
Sanders, Julie 173, 185n.3
Sartre, Jean-Paul
   Nausea 107
Schacker, Jennifer 114
science 33–50, 84–6, 149–66
Scott, Sir Walter 135, 137
Scott-Kilvert, D. 156
Secord, James 37
Shackle, Christopher 125
Shah, Waris
   Hir Andranjha 124, 125
Shapiro, Stephen 145n.8
Shelley, Mary 150, 151, 153
   Frankenstein 10, 149–52, 154, 156,
     157, 158–9, 162, 189, 204
     film versions 193–6
   see also Gothic

Shelley, Percy 150
Sherman, William H. 140, 145n.16
Shih, Shu-Mei 93
Shuttleworth, Sally 37
Skal, David J. 194
Smith, Andrew 215
Smith, Crosbie 37–8
Smith, Sydney 131, 138
Snell, Rupert 125
Southey, Robert 63
Spencer, Herbert 46, 48, 49, 93
   First Principles 43–4, 46–7
   see also science
Spiers, John 134–5
Spivak, Gayatri Chakravorty 118
Spurgeon, C. H. 45
St Clair, William 131, 135
Stead, W. T. 46
Steel, Flora Anne 111, 114,
     117, 120–3
Steiner, George 27, 190
Stendhal 155
Stevenson, Robert Louis
   Strange Case of Dr Jekyll and Mr
     Hyde 82, 87n.9
   see also Gothic
Stoker, Bram
   Dracula 76
   see also Gothic
Stowe, Harriet Beecher
   Uncle Tom's Cabin 133
Strachey, Lytton 1, 2, 6, 12, 208
Strand, David 98
Strong, Jenny 197–9
Sumpter, Caroline 114
Swan, Mary 219–20
   see also Merrick, Joseph
Sweet, Matthew 209

Temple, R. C. 111, 114, 117–20, 121,
     122, 123, 124, 125–6
Tennyson, Lord Alfred 1–2
Thanh, Hoai 103–4
theatre 190–2, 212–22

Index

Tigchelaar, Jana M. 199
Tomos-Evans, Gwyndaff 219
Topham, Jonathan R. 37
Treves, Sir Frederick 211, 215
   see also Merrick, Joseph
Tucker, Herbert 53, 56, 70n.7
Tyndall, John 45

Usborne, C. F. 111, 117, 123–6

vitalism 46
Voskuil, Lynn M. 211

Wallace, Alfred Russel 34, 38, 44, 48, 49
   Wonderful Century, The 33–6, 49
   see also Darwin, Charles; science
Waters, Sarah
   Fingersmith 184
   see also neo-Victorian
Watt, Stephen 212, 213, 214
Watts, Cedric 44
Wells, H. G.
   Island of Doctor Moreau, The 80, 82–3

War of the Worlds, The 81
   see also Gothic
White, Hyden 113
Whitman, Alden 175
   see also Merrick, Joseph
Wilde, Oscar 17, 19, 23, 28, 76, 209, 210
   'Soul of Man under Socialism, The' 102–3, 104
Williams, Ann 154
Williams, Cynthia Schoolar 137
Winship, Michael 130, 131
Wolfreys, Julian 207
Woolf, Virginia 39, 41
   Mrs Dalloway 29
   see also modernism
Wordsworth, William 58, 159

Yang, Haiyan 94

Zhu, Yan 96
Zishu, Mao 96
Zummo, Gaetano Giulio 153, 156–7

EU authorised representative for GPSR:
Easy Access System Europe, Mustamäe tee 50,
10621 Tallinn, Estonia
gpsr.requests@easproject.com